EMBODIED SPIRITUALITY

IN A

SACRED WORLD

SUNY SERIES IN

TRANSPERSONAL AND HUMANISTIC PSYCHOLOGY

RICHARD D. MANN, EDITOR

EMBODIED SPIRITUALITY

IN A

SACRED WORLD

MICHAEL WASHBURN

STATE UNIVERSITY OF NEW YORK PRESS

Cover photograph: "Stormclouds from Washburn Point" by Jeff Nixon is reprinted with permission of the artist.

Published by
STATE UNIVERSITY OF NEW YORK PRESS
ALBANY

For information, contact State University of New York Press, Albany, NY
www.sunypress.edu

Production, Laurie Searl
Marketing, Jennifer Giovani

Library of Congress Cataloging-in-Publication Data

Washburn, Michael, 1943–
    Embodied spirituality in a sacred world / Michael Washburn.
        p. cm.
    Includes bibliographical references and index.
    ISBN 0-7914-5847-4 (alk. paper) — ISBN 0-7914-5848-2 (pbk. : alk. paper)
    1. Transpersonal psychology. 2. Developmental psychology. 3. Psychology, Religious.
I. Title.

BF204.7.W372 2003
150.19'8–dc21   2003052606

10   9   8   7   6   5   4   3   2   1

for

Kirsten, Tracy, and Alison,

with love

CONTENTS

PREFACE

Embodied Spirituality in a Sacred World is the third in a series of books in which I set forth a transpersonal theory of human development. *The Ego and the Dynamic Ground* (SUNY Press, 1988; 2nd edition, 1995) presented the theory in broad outline from an essentially Jungian orientation, stressing the depth-psychological bases and the spiral path of human development. *The Ego and the Dynamic Ground* argued that the ego early in life separates itself from the deep psyche (the Dynamic Ground) and, therefore, must later in life spiral back to the deep psyche if, reunited with the original bases of its being, it is to achieve higher, whole-psyche integration.

Transpersonal Psychology in Psychoanalytic Perspective (SUNY Press, 1994) extended the perspective set forth in *The Ego and the Dynamic Ground* to include the interpersonal as well as the intrapsychic side of development. Using psychoanalytic ego psychology and object relations theory, the book argued that the ego's separation from the Dynamic Ground early in life is at the same time a separation from others and that the ego's spiraling reintegration with the Dynamic Ground later in life is at the same time a spiraling reconnection with others. *Transpersonal Psychology in Psychoanalytic Perspective* also investigated more thoroughly the causes and consequences of the ego-Ground, ego-other separation that occurs early in life and made the case that this separation is at once developmentally necessary (because it facilitates ego development early in life) and developmentally problematic (because it impedes spiritual development later in life).

In finishing *Transpersonal Psychology in Psychoanalytic Perspective*, I realized that the spiral perspective needed to be restated in a way that would more effectively establish two points: (1) that mature spirituality, from the spiral perspective, is a grounded, this-worldly spirituality, an "embodied spirituality in a sacred world"; and (2) that the spiral perspective is free of what Ken Wilber calls "pre-trans fallacies," errors that confuse early (prepersonal) with later (transpersonal) forms of experience. The first of these points was made in the earlier books, but it was not the leading theme, as it is here. The second point, too, was made in the earlier books, but it was not presented as the guiding idea for the formulation of the spiral perspective. Although I had argued generally that the spiral perspective is not based on pre-trans fallacies, I had not set forth the spiral perspective, as I do here, in a way designed to demonstrate, in a stage-by-stage way, that it is free of such errors.

In attempting to establish the two points in question, I have in this book adopted a format that focuses on six important dimensions of development, isolating these dimensions and tracking their unfolding along the spiral path. In thus tracking particular dimensions of development, I have tried to show that the spiral unfolding of these dimensions culminates in a fully embodied, earthly spirituality (the first point) and that the spiral path along which the dimensions unfold is free of pre-trans difficulties (the second point). The dimensions of development selected for consideration reflect the fundamental concerns of depth psychology, ego psychology, and phenomenology. The dimensions are these: (1) the deep psyche or Dynamic Ground, (2) the energy system, (3) the ego system, (4) the perceived other, (5) the experiential body, and (6) the life-world.

Embodied Spirituality in a Sacred World is the product of nearly thirty years of research and reflection. It would be imprudent to say that this book is my last, but as I am approaching my seventh decade, I have written it with this possibility in mind. Whatever the future holds, I believe that *Embodied Spirituality in a Sacred World* presents the spiral perspective in a mature and well-considered way, and I hope the book will be read seriously not only by transpersonal psychologists but also by developmental psychologists more generally and by philosophers, psychologists, and scholars of human spirituality.

I am grateful to Pamela Washburn, who helped me think through many of the ideas presented here from their earliest inception years ago to their current formulation. Pamela also helped me work through countless impasses in writing. My appreciation also goes to C. Michael Smith, who commented on the manuscript as a whole, saving me from mistakes and guiding me in fruitful directions. It is Michael who suggested that I write a glossary for the book—an excellent idea for which I am thankful. My gratitude also goes to Richard Allen and John Lewis, who looked at passages with which I was struggling and gave me helpful feedback.

Another person to whom special thanks are due is Harold G. Coward, Director of the Centre for Studies in Religion and Society at the University of Victoria, British Columbia. Professor Coward is a scholar of the highest rank and a generous mentor. I have benefited in many ways from his constructive criticism of my work.

The readers for the State University of New York Press made many excellent suggestions about how the manuscript could be improved, suggestions that I have tried my best to implement. I would like here to express my appreciation to them for their thoughtful evaluation of my project.

I am grateful to my school, Indiana University South Bend, for having supported this project with a Faculty Research Fellowship (summer 2000). I am grateful as well to *The Humanistic Psychologist* and to Christopher Aanstoos, editor, for permission to use "Embodied Spirituality in a Sacred World" (1999, 27:133–72), which, substantially revised, appears here under different title as chapter 2.

ONE

THE SPIRAL PATH:
HISTORY AND CRITICISM
OF THE IDEA

THIS BOOK PRESENTS an account of human development from a transpersonal, depth-psychological perspective. The perspective is transpersonal because it sees human development as having an ever-present spiritual dimension and in particular as aiming at a spiritual fruition. According to the transpersonal perspective, life can be divided into three groups of stages, the prepersonal (or preegoic), personal (or egoic), and transpersonal (or transegoic) groups.[1] Prepersonal stages extend from birth to about five and a half years of age, the beginning of what psychoanalysis calls the stage of latency. Personal stages extend from the beginning of latency to early or middle adulthood, at least. In turn, transpersonal stages, for those who enter these stages, extend from the time of spiritual awakening—that is, from the time at which spirituality, always at least implicit in life, awakens as the primary dimension of life—to full spiritual maturity. According to the transpersonal perspective, human development can be properly understood only if it is seen as leading beyond the stage of adult ego development to a stage of awakening and ever-deepening spirituality.

The perspective of this book is depth-psychological because it follows the psychoanalytic tradition in acknowledging the reality of hidden psychic depths underlying the ego system, depths including not only a personal unconscious laid down over the course of a person's life but also a deep psychic core (or *deep psyche*), which is inherited and, therefore, universal to the species. Freud, of course, conceived of this psychic core as the id, an exclusively prepersonal (instinctual, prerational) domain. C. G. Jung, in contrast, conceived of the psychic core as the collective unconscious, a source of experience that has both prepersonal (phylogenetic) and transpersonal (telic, spiritual)

1

inherent expressions. In this book the deep psyche—called the *Dynamic Ground*—is conceived in a way that is closer to Jung's understanding, for the deep psyche is here understood to have both prepersonal and transpersonal expressions. This point of agreement with Jung, however, is at the same time a point of disagreement, for the prepersonal and transpersonal expressions of the deep psyche are here understood exclusively in a developmental sense. In this book *prepersonal* and *transpersonal* refer only to stage-specific expressions of the deep psyche, not, as in Jung's understanding, to inherent aspects of the deep psyche.

Views that are both transpersonal and depth-psychological imply that human development follows a spiral course. According to such views, (1) the deep psyche is the seat of essential sources of life; (2) early in life, in the transition from prepersonal to personal stages of development, we close ourselves to the deep psyche, which, to a significant extent, is submerged and quieted; and, therefore, (3) we must reopen ourselves to the deep psyche and allow the sources of life that lie therein to reawaken if, in the transition from personal to transpersonal stages of development, we are to move toward whole-psyche integration. The spiral is evident here in the idea that we must reestablish an open connection with the earliest sources of our existence (the downward loop of the spiral) if we are to move to a higher, transpersonal stage of development (the upward loop of the spiral). The spiral, then, can be formulated as follows: we must spiral back to the deep psyche if we are to spiral up to life lived in its fullness. We must return to sources of life that had expressed themselves in prepersonal ways if, reconnected with those sources, we are to be enlivened and transformed by them in transpersonal ways.

The idea that human development follows a spiral course gives expression to a group of insights found in folk wisdom, mythology, and religion around the world. For example, it gives expression to the fundamental spiritual intuition that life as we normally experience it is missing something essential, something with which we were intimately familiar at an earlier time and must rediscover if we are to be spiritually fulfilled. It gives expression as well to the mythological notion that a treasure is buried deep beneath the ground or deep within us and must be unearthed if we are to enjoy the riches of life. The spiral idea gives expression, too, to the nearly universal insight that young children, despite and perhaps because of their undeveloped state, are special in being uninhibitedly open to instinctual, spiritual, and other dimensions of life from which we feel estranged. Additionally, the spiral idea gives expression to what Mircea Eliade called the "nostalgia for paradise," the longing for a kind of happiness and wholeness that we sense we have tasted before. Finally, and perhaps most profoundly, the spiral idea gives expression to the spiritual theme that life is a path, way, or journey that leads us back ultimately to our original home, now gloriously transformed.

The notion of a spiral path of development has a long history in many spiritual traditions. M. H. Abrams (1971), in his classic *Natural Supernaturalism*, showed that, in Western culture, the notion is rooted in the biblical story of our fall from grace and eventual redemption and that the notion became the principal motif of nineteenth-century romantic literature and philosophy. In its original biblical form, the spiral theme is expressed in the idea that our fall from grace, although a rupture in our relationship with God, was in essential respects a fortunate fall (*felix culpa*).[2] The fall was a fortunate fall not only because it set the stage for eventual redemption but also because, in expelling us from paradise, it forced us to develop ourselves in the world, caused us to experience an appreciation and unquenchable thirst for what was lost, and, therefore, prepared us for a higher redemption. The redemption to which the fall eventually leads is indeed a redemption in the literal sense of being a recovery of something lost: it is a recovery of our original spiritual nature. This redemption, however, is a higher redemption because, in recovering our original nature, we do not revert to our original state. The redemption to which the fall eventually leads is a progressive rather than regressive redemption, a redemption leading forward to transpersonal wholeness rather than backward to a prepersonal Eden.

If the spiral idea has special affinities with the biblical narrative of the Western tradition, it is not for that reason an exclusively Western idea. The spiral idea is found in non-Western traditions as well, particularly in the two principal Asian religions, Hinduism and Buddhism. The spiral idea is implicit in Hinduism in the notion of "liberation in life" (*jīvan-mukti*). Such liberation is conceived as a reyoking (*yoga*) of ourselves to our original spiritual nature (*ātman, purusha*), which we once knew but have somehow forgotten as a consequence of an inexplicable ignorance (*avidyā*). In achieving liberation in life, we overcome this ignorance and rediscover our original nature, which reemerges in spiral fashion as the spiritual basis of a mature "psychophysical vehicle" (*jīva*). The person who is liberated in life, then, is a person who is at once fully awake spiritually and fully developed psychologically, a person who for this reason is able to lead others to liberation in their lives.

A similar view is found in Buddhism, especially Mahayana Buddhism. Mahayana Buddhism extols the Bodhisattva, a fully enlightened being who declines release from the wheel of birth and death to remain within *samsāra* as a loving guide and model of enlightenment for others. The Bodhisattva, in declining a worldless *nirvāna* beyond *samsāra*, integrates *nirvāna* with *samsāra*. The Bodhisattva integrates fully realized enlightenment with fully developed humanness and in this way gives expression to the higher synthesis of spirituality and personhood that is the goal of the spiral path.

The ox-herder of the Zen ox-herding pictures also gives expression to this goal. The ox-herding pictures convey the idea that we are in search of something that unbeknownst to us is an essential part of us, something that, as such, is never truly lost even when missing from view. In searching for the ox, we are searching for our "face before our parents were born," our buddha-nature, the inner dynamic emptiness from which the spontaneities of life spring forth. In finding the ox, we rediscover this inner emptiness *on a higher level.* The ox that we find, having been left on its own for so long, is wild, and for this reason we must be patient and cautious in its presence. We must establish a mutually trusting relationship with the ox before we can mount it and ride it home, thus completing the spiral synthesis. In finding the ox, we rediscover sources of our existence that, having been absent from consciousness, are initially wild in their expression but become progressively more calm as we reconnect with them and ultimately become harmoniously integrated with them.

Like the ox that turns out to be the ox-herder's original nature, the home to which we return at the end of the spiral path turns out to be the very home from which we first set out, now experienced on a higher level. The sacred ground from which the spiral path takes leave and to which it returns is precisely this earth, and our shared, incarnate lives on earth. At the beginning of life we are fully embodied beings participating in a profoundly intimate relationship and living in an enchanted realm. In the beginning our bodies are vehicles of ecstasy, our basic relationship is one of unconditional love, and our world is a garden of delight. This auspicious beginning, however, is only a beginning because we soon face the challenges of the world: the reality principle. In facing these challenges, we develop ourselves as independent persons, we forge worldly identities, and we accomplish worldly goals. We also, however, pay a price according to the spiral view, for in struggling to establish ourselves in the world, we lose touch with fertile, sacred depths, with our original nature. This nature, however, like the ox, remains ever with us, even if out of view. It is, therefore, recoverable when, having completed worldly developmental tasks, we are ready to return to it on the way to psychospiritual awakening and to life lived in its fullness.

Ken Wilber (1980, 1990, 1995, 1998), a leading theorist in the area of transpersonal psychology, is a well-known critic of spiral views.[3] According to Wilber, any view that holds that we must return to sources experienced early in life in order to move toward higher, transpersonal stages of development commits what he calls a "pre-trans fallacy." Specifically, any such view mistakenly assumes that what is earliest in development (i.e., prepersonal or, for short, *pre*) is also what is highest (i.e., transpersonal or, for short, *trans*). Spiral views, Wilber maintains, unavoidably mistake pre for trans levels of experience and, therefore, in effect confuse regression for transcendence. In Wilber's terms, spiral views are really "U-turn" views, views that naively romanticize the infantile or archaic past in thinking that they are opening the way to a superior individual or collective future. All such views Wilber brands with the label "retro-Romanticism."

Wilber's criticism of the spiral perspective presupposes a structural-hierarchical conception of development. According to Wilber, normal human development is a process of sequential emergence of levels of a hierarchy of "basic structures" (Wilber's term). Basic structures, as Wilber conceives them, are abilities, capacities, and powers that are inherent to the psyche and emerge in a level-by-level way, with lower-level basic structures serving as both bases and functional components of higher-level basic structures, for example, as the rudimentary sensorimotor cognition developed in the first two years of life is both a basis and a functional component of higher levels of cognition. Wilber adopts Piaget's account of cognitive development and extends it beyond personal to transpersonal (postformal) levels. He also adopts the findings of a great many other developmental theorists who have tracked particular dimensions of development (e.g., emotions, needs, interpersonal relationships, sense of self), extending their findings, too, beyond personal to transpersonal levels. In his recent work Wilber (2000) has taken pains to explain that different dimensions of development—which he calls developmental "lines" or "waves"—do not always unfold at the same rate. Depending on the person and circumstances, some developmental lines unfold more quickly and others more slowly. Still, Wilber holds, all developmental lines unfold along the same basic path: the hierarchy of basic structural levels.[4]

Because lower-level basic structures are not only bases but also functional components of higher-level basic structures, they are, in normal development, preserved when development moves to a higher level. Normal development, then, according to Wilber, is a process of ever-increasing structural complexity and inclusiveness, a process that, in moving to higher basic structures, does not leave lower, transcended basic structures behind. Wilber acknowledges that development, in moving to higher basic structures, can suppress or repress rather than incorporate lower basic structures, but he holds that this is not the normal pattern. The normal pattern, rather, is one of transcendence *and* preservation of lower basic structures within higher basic structures. In normal development, all basic structures—although not all stage-related or culture-specific expressions of basic structures—are retained as development moves to higher levels. Prepersonal basic structures are preserved within personal basic structures, which in turn are preserved within transpersonal basic structures.

With this conception of development, we can see why Wilber rejects spiral theories. Spiral theories are mistaken, according to Wilber, because (1) nothing essential to the psychic inventory is lost during the course of normal development, and therefore a return to sources as described in spiral views is unnecessary; and (2) if such a return were to occur, it would result only in a descent from higher-level basic structures to lower-level, inherently prepersonal basic structures and, therefore, only in a U-turn of regression rather than a spiral to transcendence. According to Wilber, the nostalgia for a lost paradise of the past that might be rediscovered on a higher level is a lure to regression. It is a misdirected longing that falls prey to pre-trans errors and to retro-Romanticism.

Wilber's criticism of the spiral perspective, although incisive and of heuristic value, is flawed because Wilber, in correcting one pre-trans fallacy, commits a pre-trans fallacy of his own. In exposing the error of equating "earliest" with "highest," Wilber falls prey to the opposite error of equating "earliest" with "lowest." That is, he mistakenly assumes that everything that, in normal development, is *developmentally* pre must therefore also be *inherently* pre. Now of course there *are* inherently pre structures, and many of these, as Wilber explains, are both bases and preserved functional components of later or higher structures. A great deal of research supports this point. An immense amount of evidence supports the structural-developmental perspective generally and Wilber's structural-hierarchical perspective in particular. There is no question that Wilber's structural-hierarchical theory describes important dimensions of human development. There is a question, however, whether it accurately describes *all* of human development, for Wilber's assumption that everything that normally emerges in prepersonal stages of development is inherently—and, therefore, merely—pre is suspect. Indeed, according to spiral theorists, this assumptions is false.

In this book, then, care is taken to distinguish between psychic resources that are inherently pre and psychic resources that, although expressing themselves in a pre way early in life, are not. Among these latter resources are dynamic potentials—here called *nonegoic potentials*—of the deep psyche or Dynamic Ground: energy, instinctual drives, sources of affective response, and the creative imagination or autosymbolic process.[5] Attention is given to these nonegoic potentials because, in the spiral view, they are the original sources of life from which we depart and to which, at a higher level, we return. They are sources of life that (1) express themselves in a pre way early in life, (2) are then quieted to a significant extent in the transition from prepersonal to personal stages of development, and (3) can, if reawakened later in life, begin to express themselves in a trans way. Because nonegoic potentials are inherently neither pre nor trans but can have both pre (early) and trans (later) developmental expressions, they are psychic resources that can be revisited *on a higher level*. They are resources that, having been experienced as pre, can be revisited as trans as part of a spiraling, rather than merely regressive, return to origins.

The reawakening of nonegoic potentials in the course of adult life is, in the spiral view, an essential dimension of the transition from personal to transpersonal stages of development. The nonegoic potentials of the Dynamic Ground, which had been subdued during the course of ego development, begin to reawaken in the fullness of their power; and the ego, which had developed its functions in relative isolation from the Dynamic Ground, begins to be reconnected with the Ground. This reconnection is a return to origins that, to be sure, has a dangerous, regressive aspect in its initial phases, for it is a return to sources of life that had been banished and limited to a pre expression. This reconnection, however, despite its initial regressive aspect, is by no means a merely regressive U-turn. It is rather a spiraling return to nonegoic potentials that, having earlier expressed themselves as pre, are about to begin expressing themselves as trans. It is, then, a return to origins that is the beginning of transpersonal stages of development. To modify an expression coined by psychoanalyst Ernst Kris, this return to origins is a *regression in the service of transcendence*.

Although Wilber's argument against the spiral view does not achieve its aim, it nonetheless has heuristic value because the idea of the pre-trans fallacy presents a needed caution to spiral theorists, alerting them to an error to which many have been prone. Mistaking pre for trans, although not inherent to the spiral perspective, is an error to which many spiral theorists have in fact fallen prey. The prepersonal and the transpersonal, in being alike nonpersonal, are easily confused. If, then, Wilber is incorrect in holding that the spiral perspective is based on a pre-trans fallacy, he is correct in holding that many spiral theorists have mistaken prepersonal levels of experience for transpersonal levels, with most unfortunate, merely regressive consequences. Too many spiral theorists have indeed been retro-Romantics. Too many romantically oriented writers have fallen prey to glorifying young children or "noble savages" for the wrong reasons, as if earlier were necessarily better, when it is not earlier that is better but rather reconnection with earlier, lost psychic resources that is better.

The caution, then, is this: those who espouse spiral views should be extremely careful to avoid pre-trans errors. In particular, they should exercise caution in the following two chief ways: (1) by being careful to distinguish between psychic resources that, like some of Wilber's pre basic structures, are inherently pre and psychic resources that, like the nonegoic potentials discussed in this book, are not; and (2) by being careful to distinguish between pre and trans developmental expressions of resources of the latter type. Lack of care in making either of these distinctions can—indeed, has—led to serious mistakes by spiral theorists. Such mistakes, however, do not detract from the merit of the spiral perspective itself, let alone warrant its dismissal.

The spiral and structural-hierarchical perspectives are not inherently in conflict. Conflict arises only when a proponent of one or the other of the perspectives insists that *only* the spiral or *only* the structural-hierarchical perspective describes *all* of normal development. Such an exclusivist position is self-limiting and traps the proponent in pre-trans fallacies. The person who exclusively endorses the spiral perspective, unmindful that much that is developmentally pre is also inherently pre, falls prey to the kind of pre-trans fallacy that Wilber imputes to the spiral perspective itself. This person does indeed mistake inherently pre structures or potentials for inherently or potentially trans structures or potentials, thus falling prey to the lure of regression. On the other hand, the person who exclusively endorses the structural-hierarchical perspective, unmindful that much that is developmentally pre is not for that reason inherently pre, falls prey to the kind of pre-trans fallacy of which Wilber is guilty. This person mistakes developmentally pre but potentially trans structures or potentials for inherently pre structures or potentials, thus repressively obstructing transcendence.

The implication for transpersonal psychology is clear: an inclusive "both-and" position with respect to the spiral and structural-hierarchical perspectives is needed in order to clear away errors and make progress in mapping human development. Neither the spiral nor the structural-hierarchical perspective is based on a pre-trans fallacy. Wilber commits a pre-trans fallacy only because he holds that all normal development follows a structural-hierarchical course and, therefore, that all that is developmentally pre must also be inherently pre. He commits no fallacy in adopting the structural-hierarchical perspective itself. The challenge for the future, then, will be for transpersonal theorists to explore how the spiral and structural-hierarchical perspectives might be brought into fruitful collaboration on matters of concern to transpersonal inquiry. Initial steps toward such a collaboration were taken in an earlier book, *Transpersonal Psychology in Psychoanalytic Perspective*, and in a recent journal article (Washburn, in press). The focus of this book is primarily on the spiral perspective, and the task is to demonstrate, in concrete and carefully considered fashion, that the spiral perspective can be formulated without committing pre-trans errors. In thus focusing on the spiral perspective, the purpose of this book is to give additional theoretical support to the spiral perspective and to shed light on why it has been compelling to so many people in diverse traditions.

Table 1.1 is a map of the terrain to be explored. The first column, "Stage of Life," presents major stages of development divided into prepersonal, personal, and transpersonal groups. The reader will see that the stages listed in this column are based to a large extent on psychoanalytic and Jungian developmental theories. The prepersonal stages reflect psychoanalytic theory, the transpersonal stages Jungian theory. Psychoanalysis from its beginnings has focused on the first half of life, stressing the ego's differentiation from the deep psyche and its subsequent development in the world in relation to significant others. Jungian analytical psychology, in contrast, has always focused primarily on the second half of life, stressing the ego's response to the call of the deep psyche and to the challenges of spiritual life. The stages listed in the first column of table 1.1 reflect an attempt to tie these developmental accounts together, especially in the middle, personal, stages of life, where the two accounts meet.

The other columns of table 1.1 focus on particular dimensions of development and indicate how these dimensions are expressed at each of the stages of spiral development. The six dimensions selected for consideration reflect fundamental concerns of depth psychology, ego psychology, and phenomenology. The deep core of the psyche and its energy are studied by depth psychology; the ego, of course, is the "subject" of ego psychology; and the perceived other, the experiential body, and the life-world are concerns of phenomenology. The ego is placed in the central column of table 1.1 because it has a Janus character: it faces both the inner world of the psyche and the outer world of social and material reality. Moreover, the ego is given the central column because this book is written from the ego's point of view. Looking inward, we consider the ego's unfolding interaction with the Dynamic Ground and its energy, the power of the Ground; and looking outward, we consider the ego's unfolding experience of others, the body, and the world.

TABLE 1.1

THE SPIRAL PATH

STAGE OF LIFE	DYNAMIC GROUND (psychic core)	ENERGY (power of the Dynamic Ground)	EGO (subject of consciousness)	OTHER (perceived other)	BODY (experiential body)	WORLD (life-world)
Neonatal stage	Primordial source of life	Primordial reservoir	Incipient ego	Caregiver as wholly immanent other	Precosmic universal body	Ouroboric sphere
Early preoedipal stage (approx. 4 to 16 months)	Intrapsychic dimension of Great Mother	Reservoir opens; freely mobile plenipotent energy	Prepersonal body ego	Immanent-transcendent Great Mother	Body of polymorphous sensuality (oral stage)	Garden of delight
Late preoedipal stage (approx. 16 months to 3 years)	Split, nurturant-dangerous Ground	Power of the Ground split into forces of light and darkness	Split body ego	Split Good-Terrible Mother	Splitting of pleasures into good and bad pleasures (anal stage)	Split enchanted-haunted world
Oedipal stage (approx. 3 to 5½ years)	Closing of Ground	From the splitting of the power of the Ground to the repression of the power of the Ground	From a split body ego to a unified mental ego	Oedipal change of object; final steps on the way to object constancy	Initial phases of repressive quieting of body ("phallic" or infantile genital stage)	Transition from potently charged world to natural world

PREPERSONAL

THE SPIRAL PATH (CONTINUED)

STAGE OF LIFE	DYNAMIC GROUND (psychic core)	ENERGY (power of the Dynamic Ground)	EGO (subject of consciousness)	OTHER (perceived other)	BODY (experiential body)	WORLD (life-world)
Latency (approx. 5½ years to puberty)	Ground submerged and quieted at prepersonal level by primal repression: the id	Division of power of the Ground into latent libido (plenipotent, instinctually organized energy of the id) and active psychic energy (nonplenipotent, neutral energy of consciousness)	Fully formed ego system: self-representation, ego ideal, and superego; repressed shadow	Transcendent others; private self and private others	Subdued latency body; recreational body	Natural world I: playground of youth
Puberty and adolescence	Id stirred by awakening sexuality	Libido awakens as intermittently active energy of sexual experience	Latency ego system outgrown and disowned; shadow derepressed	Sexually attractive others; transitional ego ideal figures (idols, mentors)	Sexual awakening of body; presentational body	Natural world II: rehearsal stage for adult life
Early adulthood	Id restabilized on basis of mature genital sexuality	Stable differentiation of awakened libido and psychic energy	Ego system reconstituted on basis of identity project	Partner in life's tasks	Mature genital sexuality; instrumental body	Natural world III: arena of responsible action
Crossroads	Mysterious gravitational attractor	Introversion of psychic energy	Ego "dies to the world"; self-representation deanimated; shadow derepressed	Inauthentic actors	Depersonalized body	Natural world denaturalized: existential desert

PERSONAL

THE SPIRAL PATH (CONTINUED)

STAGE OF LIFE	DYNAMIC GROUND (psychic core)	ENERGY (power of the Dynamic Ground)	EGO (subject of consciousness)	OTHER (perceived other)	BODY (experiential body)	WORLD (life-world)
Awakening	Numinous core of psyche	Awakening of power of the Ground as numinous Spirit	Liminal ego on the threshold of the supernatural	Psychopomps, gurus, guides	Body primed for reawakening	On the threshold of the supernatural
Regression in the service of transcendence	Psychic underworld or sea	Numinous Spirit intermixed with derepressing instincts	Split between "higher" and "lower" selves; archetypal shadow derepressed	Splitting of others into saints and sinners, angels and demons	Derepression of instincts; "resurrection" of the body	Denaturalized world supernaturalized: realm of numinous powers
Regeneration in Spirit	Source of renewing life	Transforming Spirit	Ego harnessed to Spirit; Spirit is ego's counselor, guardian, lover	On the way to higher object constancy	"Reincarnation" of the ego	Supernatural becomes natural: world of transforming Spirit
Ego-Ground integration	Fertile-sacred void	Transparent Spirit	Ego wedded to Spirit; Spirit is ego's higher Self	Siblings in Spirit	"Temple of Spirit"	Native, hallowed ground; "home": world of transparent Spirit

TRANSPERSONAL

Depending on how one reads table 1.1, horizontally or vertically, one gets a different kind of developmental perspective. If the table is read horizontally, proceeding left to right across each row, one gets a *stage* perspective of spiral development, a perspective that shows how the six selected dimensions of development are intertwined at particular stages along the spiral path. If, however, the table is read vertically, proceeding top to bottom down each column, one gets a *dimensional* perspective of spiral development, a perspective that focuses on a single dimension of spiral development, isolating it from other dimensions and tracking its particular course along the spiral path. The stage perspective and the dimensional perspective complement each other. Both are needed for a proper understanding of the spiral view. The stage perspective provides an aerial view, the dimensional perspective a ground-level view. The stage perspective brings into focus the spiral path as a whole; the dimensional perspective brings into focus particular dimensions of human experience as they unfold along the spiral path.

We begin with the stage perspective. Chapter 2 presents an overview of the spiral path, explaining in general terms how the six dimensions of development selected for consideration are intertwined at principal prepersonal, personal, and transpersonal stages. With the context thus set, the ensuing chapters present the dimensional perspective. The Dynamic Ground, the energy system, the ego system, the perceived other, the experiential body, and the life-world—each of these dimensions, in turn, is tracked as it unfolds along the spiral path.

Proceeding in this manner—beginning with the stage perspective and following with the dimensional perspective—has the benefit of providing both overview and depth of detail, as noted. It also has disadvantages, however, two in particular. First, the presentation of the stage perspective in a single chapter is not easily accomplished, for it requires extreme compaction of ideas. Chapter 2 may for this reason be as much of a challenge to read as it was to write. Readers may find chapter 2 too densely packed and may want to skip directly to chapter 3. This temptation should be resisted, however, because chapter 2, in presenting an overview of the spiral path, presents a perspective from which individual dimensions of development can best be seen in their interconnections.

The second disadvantage of our approach is that the dimensional perspective in a sense tries to do the impossible, namely, to isolate dimensions of development that are inherently intertwined. In focusing on one dimension of development, it is not always possible to disregard other dimensions. This means that discussions of dimensions in earlier chapters must frequently anticipate discussions in later chapters, and discussions of dimensions in later chapters must frequently recollect discussions in earlier chapters. Such forward and backward references have been kept to a minimum. Still, they occur more frequently than style guides would recommend.

An extensive glossary of technical terms has been added at the end of the book. The glossary should help the reader unpack ideas presented in overview in chapter 2 and more fully understand forward or backward references made in chapters 3 through 8. The reader is encouraged to consult the glossary often.

TWO

THE SPIRAL PATH:
A STAGE VIEW

IN THIS CHAPTER we set forth a stage view of spiral development, focusing on the stages indicated in the leftmost column of table 1.1. Moving horizontally across each row of table 1.1, we present thumbnail sketches of how, in the spiral view, six major dimensions of development are interrelated during these stages: the Dynamic Ground, the energy system, the ego system, the perceived other, the experiential body, and the life-world. In presenting only thumbnail sketches of complexly intertwined, evolving dimensions of development, we necessarily omit details and documentation. These particulars are provided in ensuing chapters, in which, moving vertically down each column of table 1.1, we devote a chapter to each of the six selected dimensions, providing for each a developmental account from the spiral perspective.

NEONATAL LIFE

We begin life enveloped in the deep psyche, the Dynamic Ground, which at this stage is the primordial source of life, the ego's inner womb. The Dynamic Ground is the seat of *nonegoic potentials:* energy—here called the "power of the Ground"—the instincts, sources of affective response, and the creative, symbol-producing imagination. At the outset of life the power of the Ground is active in its full intensity and is pooled as an inner reservoir. To be sure, when the newborn is alert, the power of the Ground flows out from this reservoir to energize instinctually selected or salient stimuli in the newborn's sensory field. More often, however, when the newborn is drowsy or asleep, the power of the Ground remains pooled as a reservoir. Organized in this most basic way, the power of the Ground is the enveloping "water" of the so-called oceanic experience, the state of blissful suspended animation that precedes ego differentiation.

Although the nascent ego emerges from the Ground during periods of wakeful engagement, it does not yet recognize a world beyond itself. It does not yet divide experience into immanent (self) and transcendent (not-self) domains. The newborn *does* engage experience in discriminating and responsive ways. Indeed, the newborn comes into the world already equipped with a rudimentary "theory of appearances" (Gopnik and Meltzoff 1997), a theory that allows the newborn, for example, to recognize sensory patterns, to match sensory data across modalities, and to track objects as they move. In engaging experience in these ways, however, the newborn does not truly reach out to a world beyond itself, for the newborn does not yet understand that repeated sensory patterns are in many instances reappearances of enduring, independently existing objects (object permanence). So far as the newborn knows, all of existence lies within the realm of the newborn's own experience. The newborn's experience has a center (the incipient ego) but no circumference and is, therefore, an unbounded, all-inclusive sphere.

In being all-inclusive, the newborn's experience contains the newborn's own principal other, the caregiver. The caregiver, although a familiar and powerful sensory pattern with which the newborn interacts, is not yet understood to be an entity that exists when unperceived. This principal other, therefore, is a wholly immanent other, a sensory pattern occurring within rather than an object existing beyond the newborn's experience. The newborn has no understanding of the transcendent nature of the caregiver. Moreover, it has no understanding of the immanent nature of its own bodily self. The newborn does not yet recognize its bodily boundaries as forming an interface between itself and the world, and the newborn consequently experiences its body as having no limit in extension. The newborn's body is for this reason a "precosmic" all-inclusive body, a body from which the differentiated cosmos of immanent self and transcendent world will later be carved. Not only the caregiver, then, but also the world as a whole exists within the newborn's bodily but boundless self. The world as known by the newborn is a completely self-contained realm, an ouroboric sphere.

THE EARLY PREOEDIPAL STAGE

The early preoedipal stage—from four or five to between fifteen and eighteen months of age—is a period during which the ego begins to emerge from the Dynamic Ground, to experience body boundaries as self-boundaries, and to experience objects as enduring things or persons belonging to an independent world. If, however, the ego begins here to distinguish between itself and the world in these ways, it does so only in an initial, incomplete way. The child has only the vaguest understanding of what properly belongs to the transcendent world "out there" and is completely unaware that much of what it perceives as belonging to the world actually derives from within itself and from the Dynamic Ground in particular.

The vibrant, enchanted atmosphere of the early preoedipal world, for instance, is a reflection of the full intensity—the *plenipotency*[1]—of the power of the Ground. When the child is alertly engaged, the reservoir in which the power of the Ground is pooled opens, and the power of the Ground flows out to the newly discovered world, charging it with high-intensity energy. The power of the Ground in this way intensifies and magnifies the world, rendering it superabundantly alive: fascinating, magical, miraculous. Other nonegoic potentials of the Ground, plenipotently charged, play significant roles as well in giving form or power to the world of the early preoedipal child. Instinctual propensities, for example, select and empower instinctual objects, and templates (archetypes) for perceiving instinctual objects bring these objects into focus in biologically preencoded ways.

As nonegoic potentials thus enhance the child's world, they enhance its principal other, the caregiver, in particular. The child, accordingly, experiences the caregiver as a being of awesome magnitude, as the Great Mother. The child experiences the caregiver as a being possessing not only outwardly derived human features but also projectively superimposed magical powers, archetypal guises, and instinctual auras. The caregiver as perceived by the child, then, is a fusion of outer and inner sources. Like everything else in the world of the early preoedipal child, the caregiver is amplified and accentuated by the plenipotent power and other nonegoic potentials of the Dynamic Ground.

The experience of the early preoedipal child is fundamentally positive in tone. The ego is here an orally focused but otherwise polymorphously hedonic body ego. The body boundary is the first dividing line separating first-person experience "in here" from the transcendent world "out there," and the first-person bodily realm is a field of potent and, in the early preoedipal stage, mostly pleasurable sensations. The plenipotent energy that magically amplifies the world "out there" circulates freely within the child's body as well, enlivening it as a vehicle of ecstasy. The early preoedipal child's body is thus an organ of delight. Correspondingly, the world of the early preoedipal child is a garden of delight, a childhood Eden enchanted by the power of the Ground and watched over at all times by a protective and loving Great Mother—or so the child assumes. The child is fundamentally secure and adventures into the world as a fearless sensorimotor explorer (Piaget) or as a "practicing" toddler (Mahler) intoxicated with a sense of power and invulnerability.

THE LATE PREOEDIPAL STAGE

During the early preoedipal stage, the child understands that objects continue to exist when unperceived but assumes that they exist in locations that are easily accessible, either in the locations where they have been seen most frequently or in the locations where they were last seen. This comforting assumption is shattered sometime between fifteen and eighteen months of age, which is the beginning of the late preoedipal stage. The assumption is shattered because the child at this point begins to understand the full independence of objects and, more generally, of the transcendent world "out there." The child begins to understand that objects, and the caregiver in particular, can exist in remote, uncharted regions of space and, therefore, might *not* be accessible when not perceived. This awakening undermines the child's sense of security and riddles it with a fear of being abandoned in a world that has suddenly become vast and dangerous.

Beset with such abandonment anxiety, the child clings to the caregiver and tries to be a "good child," the kind of child the caregiver would never abandon. The child, however, is unable to control its behavior and frequently acts in ways that displease the caregiver. Fearing that these behaviors place it in jeopardy, the child groups them together as behaviors of a separate self, a bad child. The child in this way splits its self-representation; it begins thinking of itself as both an all-good good child and a separate all-bad bad child. This defensive strategy is brilliant because the unacceptable behaviors of the bad child do not detract from the goodness of the separate good child, who, worthy of the love and protection of the caregiver, can always reappear in difficult situations or when abandonment anxiety is especially severe.

The splitting of the child's self-representation is at the same time a splitting of the child's representation of the caregiver. That is, it is a splitting of the Great Mother. This splitting of the child's principal other occurs because the child, now afraid of the world and aware of its need for protection, wants not only to believe that it is a perfectly good child but also to believe that the caregiver is a perfectly good caregiver. The caregiver, however, like the child, is not perfect. In order to sustain its fantasy of an all-good caregiver, therefore, the child groups the caregiver's undesirable aspects together as aspects of a separate person, a bad caregiver. In this way the Great Mother is split into an all-good Good Mother, who is perfectly loving and protective without being smothering, and an all-bad Terrible Mother, who is uncaring, negligent, and hostile when the child misbehaves.

Now because the Great Mother is the caregiver as empowered, colored, and construed by the nonegoic potentials of the Dynamic Ground, this splitting of the Great Mother is not only a splitting of the child's representation of the outer caregiver but also a splitting of the child's experience of the inner Dynamic Ground. The Ground, accordingly, now becomes both a nurturant Ground, a fount from which many of the graces of the Good Mother flow, and a dangerous Ground, an abyss from which many of the dark powers of the Terrible Mother emanate. The child, of course, has no idea that its principal other, the awesome Great Mother, is a fusion of outer caregiver and inner Ground. For the child, the Great Mother is a being belonging entirely to the world "out there." The Great Mother, however, does in fact derive from both outer and inner sources, and the splitting of the Great Mother, therefore, of necessity has both outer and inner dimensions.

Because the child at this age is a concrete body ego, the splitting of its self-representation is perforce also a splitting of its experience of the body and, in particular, a splitting of its experience of bodily pleasures, which are divided into good pleasures and bad. The good child enjoys the good pleasures, the bad child the bad pleasures. The good child enjoys pleasures associated with good behavior, especially those related to successful toilet training; and the bad child enjoys pleasures associated with bad behavior, including those related to violating rules of toilet training and defying prohibitions against exposing or touching private parts. The child, as a concrete body ego, remains a polymorphously hedonic being. Now, however, the child's polymorphous hedonism is a hedonism of split—innocent and perverse—pleasures. The good child is polymorphously innocent; the bad child, to apply Freud's expression to the case it actually fits, is polymorphously perverse.

The splitting characteristic of the late preoedipal stage is reflected in the child's perception of the world in a cleaving of the world into opposed realms of safety, togetherness, and delight on the one hand and danger, abandonment, and dread on the other. The world, which had been a child-centered garden of delight, is now at times terrifyingly transformed, becoming a vast, haunted realm in which the child is alone and exposed to invisible ghosts and monsters. Just as the child now clings to a loving and protecting caregiver who can no longer be taken for granted, so, too, the child now clings to a small, safe world that is slipping away. The child desperately avoids acknowledging that its world is changing; nonetheless, the child senses precisely this, for the world is now subject to the terrifying transformations just described. Such transformations typically occur when the child is punished or put to bed at night, but they can occur at any time, whenever abandonment anxiety surfaces.

THE OEDIPAL STAGE

The oedipal stage—from approximately three to five or six years of age—is a period with its own characteristic triangular conflict. It also, however, is a period during which the conflicts characteristic of the late preoedipal stage are carried over and finally brought to effective resolution, thus preparing the ground for a stage of intrapsychic, interpersonal, and ego-world stability: the stage of latency. Indeed, the conflict characteristic of the oedipal stage is itself the means by which the conflicts of the late preoedipal stage are finally resolved. The oedipal conflict is such a means because the child finally surmounts preoedipal splitting in its many dimensions when it undergoes what psychoanalysis calls the oedipal *change of object*, the process by which the child weans itself from radical intimacy with the preoedipal mother as primary love object and commits itself unconditionally to the oedipal father as primary authority figure.[2]

The child might be able to overcome preoedipal splitting even without oedipal incentives, but the challenge posed by the father accelerates the process and brings it to a close. If the child is to overcome splitting, it must outgrow its symbiotic dependence upon the mother; and the father, in effect, requires the child to do just this. Radical intimacy with the mother and symbiotic dependence on her go hand in hand for the child; therefore, when the father demands that the child forfeit the former, he at the same time, in effect, requires that the child outgrow the latter. The father, then, in forcing the child to choose between the mother and him, forces the child to wean itself from the dependence on which splitting is based.

Because the splitting of the Great Mother is bidirectional in character, being a splitting not only of the outer caregiver but also of the inner Dynamic Ground, the response that brings an end to this splitting is also bidirectional in character. The child's outwardly focused change of object, accordingly, is at the same time an inwardly focused psychodynamic reorganization. When the child draws back from radical intimacy with the mother, it simultaneously shields itself inwardly against energic, instinctual, imaginal, and other spontaneities emanating from the Dynamic Ground. These are not two different responses; rather, they are outer and inner sides of the same response. The preoedipal child's undefended openness to the mother has as its inner correlate an undefended openness to the Dynamic Ground; consequently, the oedipal child's withdrawal from the mother has as its inner correlate a repression of the Dynamic Ground. In putting defensive distance between itself and its primary other, the child at the same time lays down a barrier of repression that separates it from its own inner depths.

The outer dimension of the child's response to preoedipal splitting is here called *primal separation;* and, adopting Freud's expression, the inner dimension is called *primal repression.*[3] Primal separation and primal repression, again, are not two different acts. They are two sides of the same act, which is here called *primal closing.* Primal closing may be necessary as a response to preoedipal splitting whether or not the oedipal father enters the scene. The additional motivations provided by the father, however, bring this two-sided act to decisive completion. The father, in requiring the child to withdraw from the mother as love object and to submit to him instead as authority figure, forces the child to complete a fundamental change not only in the way it relates to its primary other—and, therefore, to others generally—but also in its stance toward its own psychic core. The father forces the child to quit vacillating between splitting-afflicted intimacy and splitting-surmounted independence by paying the necessary price: final commitment to primal closing.

Although primal closing is a negative act that leads eventually to negative consequences, it is nonetheless a developmentally warranted act that, at this juncture, leads to positive—indeed developmentally necessary—consequences. Principal among these positive consequences are (1) the final overcoming of the many dimensions of preoedipal splitting, (2) the quieting of nonegoic potentials (latency), and (3) the differentiation of the ego from the body. A brief account of these consequences of primal closing is given in the next section, on latency. The point here is that these consequences, on balance, are benefits. To be sure, primal closing takes a serious toll. The outer side of this act, primal separation, is responsible for a loss of undefended intimacy, and the inner side, primal repression, is responsible for a loss of plenipotent energy, fully alive corporeality, imaginal creativity, and rootedness in the Ground. These losses acknowledged, the fact remains that in early childhood the positive consequences of primal closing outweigh the negative. Later in life, once ego development is complete, the balance shifts in the opposite direction. In early childhood, however, primal closing plays a positive and necessary developmental role.

The positive consequences of primal closing begin to take shape once the child starts to wean itself from the preoedipal mother. These consequences, then, begin to emerge in the late preoedipal stage, during the subphase of the separation-individuation process that Margaret Mahler (Mahler et al. 1975) called "on the way to object constancy" (twenty-four to thirty-six months). These consequences, however, usually are not firmly established until the child quits vacillating between intimacy with and independence from the mother and makes a decisive, irreversible commitment to the father and, thereby, to primal closing. The favorable consequences of primal closing, then, usually are not firmly established until the end of the oedipal stage.

LATENCY

The oedipal stage comes to an end and the stage of latency begins once primal separation and primal repression are set firmly in place as sides of a psychic structure (five or six years of age). The stage that now begins is properly called the stage of *latency* because primal repression quiets the nonegoic potentials of the Dynamic Ground. According to the view presented here, latency is not exclusively a period of sexual latency, as Freud believed; rather, it is a period of nonegoic latency generally. All nonegoic potentials—not only instinctual drives but also sources of affective response, the autosymbolic imagination, and the power of the Dynamic Ground—are quieted to a significant degree by primal repression.

This quieting of nonegoic potentials, again, is a net advantage for the developing ego. Plenipotently charged nonegoic potentials, in intensifying and otherwise enhancing the child's experience, had magnified both the causes and the effects of splitting and had thereby seriously interfered with the young ego's development. Primal repression, therefore, in quieting nonegoic potentials, frees the young ego from impeding influences and provides it with the calm, clear atmosphere it needs to continue to grow. Primal repression by no means completely deactivates nonegoic potentials; it does, however, quiet these potentials to a significant degree. The Dynamic Ground is submerged and subdued. It is disconnected from consciousness at an early stage of development and in this way becomes the prepersonal id described by classical psychoanalysis.

Chief among the nonegoic potentials reduced to latency by primal repression is the power of the Dynamic Ground. This plenipotent energy is quieted and assumes the form of instinctually organized potential energy: "sleeping" libido, the latent energy of the id.[4] The power of the Ground, in thus being quieted, is not deactivated entirely; it is, though, markedly reduced in intensity, remaining active only in diminished, nonplenipotent form. This diminished form of the power of the Ground is psychic energy, the active, neutral (i.e., noninstinctual) energy of conscious processes. Primal repression, then, not only quiets the power of the Ground; it also divides the power of the Ground into two separate and markedly different energies: latent libido on the one hand and active psychic energy on the other. Latent libido, as the potential energy of the id, and active psychic energy, as the energy of conscious processes, thus emerge as two different organizations of the power of the Ground as a consequence of primal repression.

The interpersonal correlate of latency is *object constancy*, which is an integrated (i.e., no longer split), stable representation of the caregiver. Object constancy is a result of both primal separation and primal repression. It is a result of primal separation because primal separation cuts the child's psychological umbilical cord and thereby brings an end to symbiotic dependence upon the caregiver, which was the weakness responsible for splitting. Object constancy is also a result of primal repression because primal repression, in quieting nonegoic potentials, withdraws these potentials from the caregiver, upon whom they had been projected. The caregiver is in this way divested of plenipotent power and compelling archetypal guises. The caregiver, thus put at a distance by primal separation and defused by primal repression, is markedly reduced in stature and perceived in a new way, no longer as the awesome Good-Terrible Mother and now, simply, as a single human person who, although not perfect, is "good enough."[5] This is object constancy.

As the child begins perceiving the caregiver in this integrated, stable way, it at the same time begins perceiving itself in an integrated, stable way. The child eventually learns that the caregiver loves and protects it even when it has misbehaved, and for this reason it ceases feeling a need to be all good and begins perceiving itself as a child who, although not perfect, is good enough. Much of what had been the all-good side of the preoedipal split self-representation now becomes the ego ideal, a representation of perfect behavior that is no longer a *self*-representation and is, instead, a projected ideal to which the child aspires without being identified. Correspondingly, much of what had been the all-bad side of the preoedipal split self-representation now becomes the repressed and unconscious shadow. Finally, what had been the external voice of oedipal authority now becomes the internal voice of the superego: the child now commands, rewards, and punishes itself to ensure that its behavior is good enough as measured against the newly forged ego ideal. With this reconstitution of the self-representation as a single good enough self-representation governed by both a guiding ego ideal and a disciplining superego, the principal elements of the ego system are fully articulated and unified for the first time.

Primal separation and primal repression also have profound effects upon how the body is experienced. Primal separation has the effect of differentiating the ego from the body, for the child, in withdrawing from radical intimacy with the caregiver, draws back from embodied openness and in doing so discovers the sheltering privacy of psychic space. The child in this way breaks its prior exclusive identification with the body: it ceases *being* the body (a body ego) and becomes an inner ego that *has* a body (a mental ego). This breaking of the prior exclusive identification with the body is not a dissociation from the body. It does not demote the body, in Cartesian fashion, to a mere thing. It does, however, demote the body from being the whole of a bodily self to being an outer extension of an inner self. The child continues to relate to the body as self, and it continues to enjoy the body as a recreational vehicle. Now, however, the child knows that there is a psychic space within the physical space of the body, and, as mental ego, the child now resides in this psychic space as its primary abode.

As primal separation thus differentiates the ego from the body, primal repression changes the body's felt character: it lowers the intensity level of bodily experience, rendering the body a subdued latency body. Primal repression lowers the intensity level of bodily experience because, in quieting nonegoic potentials, it deprives the body of the power of the Ground in its plenipotency. As the power of the Ground is divided into the two forms of latent, plenipotent libido and active, nonplenipotent psychic energy, the body ceases being supercharged with plenipotent energy and is enlivened at a less intense level by psychic energy. The body, in undergoing this decrease in energy, is not deadened; it remains alive and sensitive to pleasure. The child, as just noted, enjoys the latency body as a recreational vehicle, a vehicle of play and intense physical enjoyment. Still, the latency body is subdued in the sense that it is no longer a body of polymorphous *ecstasy*. The quieting of the power of the Ground in its plenipotency is reflected in the body as a loss of ecstatic potential.

The disappearance of the power of the Ground in its plenipotency affects not only the body but also the world; for once primal repression is in place, plenipotent energy ceases flowing from psyche to world, and in consequence the world ceases being an enchanted (or haunted) realm. This depotentiation of the world is not a derealization; the world does not become arid or alien. Although no longer supercharged with the power of the Ground in its plenipotency, the world is animated by psychic energy. Charged with psychic energy, the world of the latency stage is a realm that has both reality and appeal. In particular, it is a playground, a field of pleasurable activity. Although the world of the latency stage is no longer a "supernatural" world saturated with plenipotent power, it is, to introduce a technical expression, a *natural world*, a realm that, animated by nonplenipotent psychic energy, is alive and inviting as a field of activity.

According to psychoanalysis, the beginning of latency marks the consolidation of the tripartite structure of id, ego, and superego. The id and the ego that are established here are based straightforwardly on primal repression and primal separation, respectively. The id is a consequence of primal repression because primal repression submerges and quiets nonegoic potentials while they are still at a prepersonal level of expression, thereby reducing the Dynamic Ground to an invisible realm of instinctual drives, instinctually organized energy (latent libido), and primitive imaginal cognition (the primary process). In similarly straightforward fashion, the ego, as mental ego, is a consequence of primal separation because primal separation is the act by which the child withdraws from radical intimacy with the caregiver and in doing so discovers the inner citadel of psychic space, thus breaking its prior exclusive identification with the body.

As the id and mental ego are brought into being in these ways, the superego is brought into being as the child finalizes its commitment to oedipal authority in the oedipal change of object. The id, mental ego, and superego thus emerge concomitantly as basic psychic structures in the transition from the oedipal stage to the stage of latency. Although the tripartite division of the psyche is a fixture of life as we know it, it is not the original or a necessary organization of the psyche. It is, rather, a product of preoedipal and oedipal vicissitudes, reflecting the child's response to preoedipal splitting within the triangular configuration of the oedipal situation.

Latency is a stage during which the child is free from the overawing influence of nonegoic potentials and from the crippling consequences of preoedipal splitting. Latency is a time of relative quiescence, relief from conflict, and, therefore, stability. It is for these reasons also a time of accelerated ego development.

PUBERTY AND ADOLESCENCE

The quiescence of latency is disturbed by sexual awakening, which kindles hitherto latent libido. Libido, the potential energy of the id, now becomes arousable by means of sexual stimulation. In psychoanalytic parlance, the sexual awakening of puberty is the beginning of a new organization of libido—and, therefore, ultimately of the power of the Ground—known as the genital (as distinguished from "phallic") organization. Libido, which had lain dormant, now awakens in response to sexual stimulation and expresses itself through the sexual system in the form of sexual excitation and, most dramatically, sexual orgasm, a new form of bodily ecstasy. This awakened, genitally channeled expression of libido begins to appear at the onset of puberty and gradually takes form during the years of adolescence. The genital organization of libido is not maturely established until early adulthood.

Adolescence is also a stage during which the ego system begins being reorganized. The adolescent disavows the "childish" self-representation of the latency period and begins testing new identity possibilities by rehearsing roles before audiences of peers. For the adolescent, life is a rehearsal for life. The adolescent takes the rehearsal seriously, indeed all too seriously; nevertheless, the rehearsal is only practice, not the performance itself. The adolescent is not yet ready to make a firm commitment to a new self-representation. The adolescent's self-representation, therefore, is in transition.

The other components of the ego system are in transition as well. Like the latency self-representation, the latency superego and ego ideal are disavowed. The latency superego is disavowed because the adolescent now finds this internalized voice of parental authority oppressive and alien, a voice of a harsh other rather than of a disciplining self. At the same time, the latency ego ideal is disavowed because it is the ideal of a perfect child as defined by parents, and the adolescent no longer wants to be a child. In disavowing the latency superego, the adolescent insists upon self-will, without, however, having yet harnessed the will to a new superego; and in disavowing the latency ego ideal, the adolescent fantasizes about new ideal possibilities as embodied in new ideal role models, without, however, having yet made a commitment to any new long-term ideal goals. Divorced in these ways from the inner moral constraints and ideals of the latency stage, and divorced as well from the "good enough" self-representation of the latency stage, the adolescent is vulnerable to a derepression of the shadow and, thereby, to self-castigation.

Coinciding with these reorganizations of the id and the ego system are marked changes in interpersonal relationships and in the ego's experience of the body and the world. These latter changes, like the reorganizations of the id and the ego system, reflect the instinctually awakened and transitional character of adolescence.

Other people now become possible objects of sexual desire and possible idols to emulate (ego ideal figures). The adolescent's awakening sexuality and need to explore new life possibilities are inherently "object related." They express themselves in fantasies about, trial relationships with, and imitations of people whom the adolescent finds attractive or admirable. In relating to others in these new ways, the adolescent takes initial steps toward establishing independence from parents. The search for a person with whom to satisfy sexual needs is a search for a new love object, for a person who, as primary love object, can replace the parents—and the mother in particular—in that role. The search for idols to emulate also reflects a shift away from parents, for this search is an attempt to find a new ideal role model who can replace the mother (for most girls) or father (for most boys) in that role. So far as relationships are concerned, the adolescent is moving from the microcosm of child-parent relationships to the macrocosm of adult relationships; and in this transition the adolescent searches for new people to fulfill the primary relationship needs previously met by the parents.

The awakening of sexuality is, of course, most conspicuously expressed in the body, in which secondary sexual characteristics appear and new sexual sensitivities and capabilities emerge. The sexually awakening body of the adolescent is a relational body, a body designed for sexually based relationships. The adolescent's body is not yet a sexually mature body; it is an eroticized body in which sexuality is awakening but is not yet stably integrated as a functioning system. The sexual transformation of the body during adolescence is a dramatic physiological marker of developmental change. No other developmental stage is associated with such dramatic changes in the outer appearance of the body, and only one other stage, spiritual awakening, is associated with changes to the inside of the body that are of comparable profundity.

As the body changes from a latency body into a sexually awakening body, the world changes from a playground into a rehearsal stage for adult life. The world remains a natural world in the meaning we have given that expression. That is, it remains a world that, although not charged with "supernatural" (plenipotent) energy, is at least charged with (nonplenipotent) psychic energy and is for that reason alive and inviting as a setting for satisfying activity. In thus continuing to be a natural world, however, the world changes in the kind of setting it provides and the nature of the satisfying activity that takes place in it. The adolescent is no longer interested in child's play and is interested instead in acting out adult possibilities. The world, accordingly, changes from a playground into a rehearsal stage. It becomes the stage on which the adolescent acts out adult relationships, identities, and lifestyles.

EARLY ADULTHOOD

By early adulthood the sexual transformation of the body is more or less complete. Awakened sexuality is by this time a more integral and, therefore, less disruptive dimension of life; the body is fully grown; and the genital organization of libido is maturely established. The id and its libidinal energy are for these reasons stabilized in a new equilibrium. Psychoanalyst Peter Blos (1968) described this new equilibrium as a second latency. To be sure, unlike the first latency of childhood, this second latency is not a stage during which libido is latent. Libido has been awakened and remains awake in the sense of being arousable within the context of mature genital sexuality. The expression of libido as erotic feeling or sexual desire, however, is now less importunate and more situationally contained than it was during adolescence. Libido "calms down," and so, too, does the id more generally. The id returns to quiescence as a repressively submerged, invisible realm.

By early adulthood the mental ego is usually ready to make the long-term commitments that bring the identity and relationship experiments of adolescence to a close. In making a commitment to a form of social participation and, usually, a significant other, the young adult makes a commitment to an *identity project*, which is an endeavor that refashions and reintegrates the components of the ego system. In attempting to be, say, a social worker, Christian, wife, and mother, a woman seeks to earn a socially recognized identity (a new self-representation), and she does so in a way that is motivated both by a self-chosen life ideal (a new ego ideal) and by a sense of obligation to meet the long-term commitments she has made (a new superego). The new self-representation that is forged here is once again, except in pathological cases, a good enough self-representation. It is a self-representation that, although containing negative as well as positive features, is on balance sufficiently more positive than negative when measured against the new ego ideal to allow the young adult a sense of justifying self-worth. Features incompatible with the good enough norm are not acknowledged; they are repressed and become part of a reconstituted shadow.

As the identity project restructures the ego system in these ways, the young adult adopts new stances toward others, the body, and the world. Others now become persons to whom commitments have been made and, therefore, for whom required or expected actions are performed. The body, having finished its growth, now becomes an instrument needing care and maintenance if the young adult is to remain healthy and strong. Correspondingly, the world, as a natural world, now changes from a rehearsal stage to a performance stage: it becomes an arena of goal-directed, responsible action. Adulthood is by no means all work and no play. It is, however, a stage during which play takes a back seat to work. The young adult's primary orientation to life is one of commitment, discipline, and purpose.

The identity project of early adulthood is the final major vehicle of ego development. Once the ego has successfully integrated awakened genital sexuality and has endeavored to establish itself in the world by means of the identity project, there is little more it can do to further its own development. Moreover, the ego by this time—typically in the years of midlife—is usually sufficiently strong and cognitively mature that it no longer needs to be protected from others by primal separation or from the deep psyche by primal repression. The removal of primal separation and primal repression, therefore, becomes a real possibility, a possibility, moreover, that points development in a new direction. Whereas, before, the path of development had led *toward* the ego, it now points *beyond* the ego. There is, of course, no guarantee that development will actually proceed in the new direction it now points. For many if not most people, it seems, the completion of ego development is the completion of development itself. Some people, however, arrive at a crossroads at which their lives change in a fundamental way; they embark upon a path leading beyond the maturely developed ego.

CROSSROADS

In nearing the crossroads in question, many people experience deep dissatisfaction with life. They lose their sense of purpose, either because they have not succeeded in the identity project and ask, "What's the use?" or because they *have* succeeded in the identity project and ask, "Is this all there is?" The passionate ambitions and earnest commitments of early adulthood no longer seem important. People nearing the crossroads are unable to rekindle interest in life and, consequently, begin to withdraw from the arena of action. For many this withdrawal is a psychological depression that is eventually worked through. These people are able to reconstruct the goals of the identity project in a way that rekindles their motivation for engagement in the world. For others, however, the withdrawal cuts sufficiently deep that the identity project is undermined at its foundations. For these people, psychological depression deepens into spiritual despair.

According to psychoanalytic and Jungian theories, severe withdrawal is a consequence of an introversion of psychic energy: energy is withdrawn from the goals of worldly action and from the world itself and flows back to its source in the deep psyche or, as conceived here, the Dynamic Ground. The world is in this way drained of energy, and the Dynamic Ground in turn is invested with energy and, therefore, gravitationally charged. Affected by this introversion, the ego undergoes a withdrawal from the world and finds itself drawn inward toward the Dynamic Ground. The Ground, still organized as the id, is repressed and hidden from view, and so the ego perceives the Ground only as a mysterious "I know not what," a dark center of gravity hidden deep within the psyche. The Dynamic Ground, imbued with gravitational charge, thus becomes an invisible attractor—which in extreme cases can become a psychic black hole—that takes the ego in tow and pulls it ineluctably toward something unknown. Depending on the severity of introversion and the extent to which the ego is subject to the gravity of the Ground, the ego finds it difficult or even impossible to reengage the world and effectively participate in life.

The ego's alienated condition is reflected in its perception of both itself and others. The ego begins to perceive itself, that is to say, its worldly identity, as a lifeless mask. The ego's worldly identity "dies" because the loss of desire to pursue the goals of the identity project carries with it a deanimation of the self-representation based on that project. The ego is no longer inspired by the ego ideal or driven by the superego, and it now sees the very identity that it once was as only a collection of habits and poses, a false façade. The ego thus sees itself as a pretender, as an inauthentic actor wearing a mask. Moreover, in seeing itself in this way, the ego sees others in a similar fashion, with this difference: the ego sees others as actors *who do not know they are acting.* From the perspective of the alienated ego, other people are actors who believe that they are real agents in a real world. Only the alienated ego knows—or, rather, (falsely) believes—that "agency is only acting" and that "no one is to be taken seriously."

The ego's alienated condition is also reflected in its experience of the body. The body, which had been part—even if only an outer extension—of the mental ego's self, is depersonalized when the self-representation is deanimated. The body, that is, is reduced to a mere thing. Correspondingly, the ego is reduced to an *exclusively* mental ego, an ego disconnected not only from the arena of worldly action but also from the instrument of worldly action. The alienated mental ego is a Cartesian "thinking thing," an inner subject for which the body is a complex mechanism to be set in motion by acts of will. Cartesian dualism is problematic in many ways as a metaphysical theory; it does, however, correctly describe the alienated mental ego's experience of the body.

It also describes the alienated mental ego's experience of the world. The world, too, is reduced to a mere thing or, rather, domain of things, for the introversion of energy siphons energy from the world, desiccating and derealizing the world. If we recall, primal repression divests the world of plenipotent energy without thereby derealizing it because the world continues to be animated, as a natural if not "supernatural" world, by psychic energy. Introversion, however, divests the world even of psychic energy and, therefore, leaves the world completely dead and flat, utterly devoid of psychological peaks and valleys, challenges and disappointments, positive and negative values. Introversion denaturalizes the world, reducing it to a lifeless stage, an existential desert or wasteland.

AWAKENING

Introverted psychic energy, accumulating in the Dynamic Ground, sometimes builds in charge to a degree sufficient to awaken the power of Ground in its plenipotency. When this happens, the power of the Ground begins being released from the deep core of the psyche in powerful emanations. The ego, in experiencing these emanations, becomes aware of an immense and irresistible force: the *numinous*. According to Rudolf Otto (1917), the numinous is a *mysterium tremendum et fascinans*, a force that is "wholly other" (transcendent, not-self), unfamiliar (mysterious, ineffable), eclipsing (tremendous, prodigious), compelling (fascinating, captivating), and bivalent (light-dark).[6] The numinous is an overawing bivalent power toward which the ego is strongly ambivalent. Bereft of worldly identity, the ego stands naked before an immense, incomprehensible force, and it experiences "fear and trembling."

The emergence of the numinous—or, as it will be called in this book, *numinous Spirit*—marks the beginning of spiritual awakening. The ego that has just begun to experience numinous Spirit stands on the threshold of the beyond. It is a liminal ego, an ego that has died to the world and to its former identity in the world and is now drawn toward an extraordinary unknown realm.

The person undergoing awakening encounters numinous Spirit not only directly, as an awesome dynamic presence, but also indirectly, through people, or at least through a few special people, namely, those in whom the power of the Ground is active in its plenipotency. To the person undergoing awakening, these people stand out as bivalent—as fascinating but frightening—emissaries from a supernatural realm: psychopomps, seers, hierophants, sages, gurus. The person undergoing awakening is drawn to these numinously charged people, who are at once irresistible and incomprehensible. They have a compelling, captivating effect.

Spiritual awakening is also evident at the bodily level, for the awakening of the power of the Ground in its plenipotency triggers a release of high-intensity energy within the body. This energy, in its initial manifestation, can express itself in a variety of ways, for example, in tingling sensations, twitches, perspiration, shivers, horripilation, heightened sensitivity in erotogenic tissues, and general surplus energy states. Because the power of the Ground that is here awakening is still organized instinctually as libido, some of the initial somatic expressions of its awakening can have a strong erotic coloring. At the outset of the awakening process, the body is primed for a transformation that has not yet fully gotten under way. The body is on the verge of a dramatic "resurrection."

Finally, the awakening of the power of the Ground is evident in the ego's experience of the world. The world, which had been derealized, is now ready to erupt with numinous energy, energy that here manifests itself not only in direct epiphanies and through extraordinary people but also through objects, events, and places of special significance. Such objects (e.g., precious gems and metals, scriptures, relics), events (e.g., ritual actions, unusual natural occurrences), and places (e.g., hallowed or haunted grounds, sacred or eerie openings or enclosures) pulsate with an ineffable, spellbinding power. In face of such manifestations of numinous Spirit, the ego experiences tremors and "goose flesh" and feels as though it is being called forth to a profound but obscure destiny. The ego may entertain the belief that it is on the threshold of sudden enlightenment or salvation. Such a belief, however, would be false, for the ego has only just begun a long journey.

REGRESSION IN THE SERVICE OF TRANSCENDENCE

The journey on which the ego has just set out leads through difficult territory; for the emergence of the numinous signals that primal repression has begun to give way and, therefore, that the submerged Dynamic Ground, still organized as the id, is about to open. Following initial awakening, then, the first phase of the ego's journey into the beyond is a dark odyssey into the unconscious, an odyssey that has been described in many ways, for example, as a descent into the underworld (classical Greece and Rome), as a descent into hell (Christianity, Dante), as a journey into demonic realms (Hinduism, Buddhism), as a struggle with diabolical phenomena (makyō: Zen), as a hero's journey (Jung 1912; Campbell 1949), and as a descent to the Goddess (contemporary feminism). This odyssey—here called *regression in the service of transcendence*—is dark and difficult because the Ground that opens at this point is a Ground that had been organized as the id, and the plenipotent power that awakens is a power that had been instinctually organized as libido, the energy of the id. The opening of the Ground, then, has the character of an opening of a dark, primitive underworld or sea, and the awakening of the power of the Ground, correspondingly, has the character of an unleashing of a dangerous, primitive energy. The ego is understandably put to the test as it is exposed in these ways to the return of the repressed.

The awakening of instinctual life during regression in the service of transcendence does not bring spiritual awakening to an end. On the contrary, the awakening of instinctual life is a natural phase of the continuing awakening of numinous Spirit. These two awakening processes coincide because the instinctual derepression that follows the initial manifestation of numinous Spirit is not only a resurgence of the Ground and the power of the Ground *in* their organizations as id and libido, respectively, but also the beginning of a liberation of the Ground and its power *from* these prepersonal organizations. It is a derepression that dissolves what remains of primal repression and, therefore, that frees the Ground and its power from the primitive, exclusively instinctual limits to which they had been restricted. During regression in the service of transcendence, then, spiritual emergence and instinctual resurgence are dimensions of a single process. During this stage, awakening Spirit is at the same time derepressing libido. As the lotus rises from the swamp, so Spirit rises from the id—or, rather, from what was the id.

Numinous Spirit, again, is a *bivalent* power, a power that in the ego's perception is both light *and* dark, good *and* evil. This bivalence is already evident during initial awakening, and it becomes all the more apparent once regression in the service of transcendence begins. The bivalence of numinous Spirit becomes emphatically evident at this point because the derepression of instinctual life recasts the bivalence of numinous Spirit in instinctual terms, giving the light-good side of this bivalence an immaculately anti-instinctual character and the dark-evil side a primitively instinctual character. In other words, the light-dark bivalence of numinous Spirit here becomes a chaste-obscene bivalence as well. It becomes a bivalence of disembodied purity on the one side and instinctual depravity on the other.

The intermixing of awakening instinctuality with numinous Spirit leads the ego to sense that it is not only caught between light and dark cosmic forces but also torn between corresponding higher (exclusively spiritual) and lower (demonically instinctual) tendencies within itself. In thus perceiving itself as having two such antithetical tendencies, the ego suffers a splitting of the self-representation. This splitting is not a complete cleaving, as occurred in the latter part of the preoedipal period, for the ego here perceives itself as a conflicted but still single self. In particular, it perceives itself as a fledgling, spiritually "reborn" self torn between all-good aspirations and all-bad temptations and, therefore, between corresponding all-good and all-bad *possible* selves rather than as two contrary, all-good and all-bad *actual* selves. Nonetheless, the self-representation is here divided in a problematic way.

The ego, in aspiring to its perceived all-good possible self, projects a new ego ideal of angelic perfection and importunes itself in the voice of a revitalized superego to strive toward this ideal of strictly spiritual purity. At the same time, the ego, tempted by its perceived all-bad possible self, projects an anti-ideal of instinctualized evil (what Jung calls the archetypal shadow) and cajoles or dares itself in the voice of an anti-superego to yield to the enticements of such evil. Divided against itself in this way, the ego is prone to sharply dualistic thinking and to disembodied, gnostic aspirations. It prays for grace from a heavenly spirit so that it might be saved not only from demonic forces but also from itself insofar as it, as an earth-bound instinctual being, is attracted to these forces.

The conflict the ego experiences within itself becomes a lens for its perception of others. In seeing itself as having higher and lower tendencies, the ego sees others as having these tendencies as well. Moreover, it is prone to see some others as complete embodiments of these tendencies, as either angels or devils in human form. The bivalence of numinous Spirit and corresponding division of the ego system render the ego susceptible to borderline idealizations and devaluations of others, especially those who are perceived as spiritual leaders. For this reason it sometimes happens that people previously idealized as spiritual exemplars are later—once their imperfections are exposed—condemned as evil impostors. The splitting of the ego system leads in this way to a corresponding splitting of the ego's perception of others.

It leads as well to a splitting of the ego's perception of the body and the world. It divides the ego's perception of the body because the resurgence of instinctual life enlivens the body with sensations that are at once alluring and alarming. Awakening plenipotent energy, released from its repressed instinctual organization, flows into the body, and the body is thus "resurrected" with new life. It becomes once again what it was in early childhood, a vehicle of polymorphous ecstasy. This new life of the body is a cause of delight, to be sure; but it is also a cause of anxiety, for the instinctual life of the body falls on the dark-evil side of numinous bivalence. People undergoing regression in the service of transcendence are powerfully drawn to the reawakening body as a field of ecstatic pleasures; however, they are at the same time threatened by the reawakening body because they perceive—or at least are prone to perceive—the very pleasures to which they are attracted as temptations to a life of evil.

The splitting characteristic of regression in the service of transcendence divides the ego's perception of the world by shrouding the atmosphere of the world in a way that separates the earth from the sky. The ego sees the world as a dark forest or as an ominous plain overcast with stormy clouds and, therefore, as a realm cut off for the most part from the sky, the radiance of which shines through in only a few places. Numinous Spirit, which had manifested itself in intermittent or local epiphanies, now pervades the world and manifests itself in dramatically opposed ways, either as menacing darkness (derepressing instinctual energy) or as otherworldly light (awakening spiritual energy) shining in forest clearings or breaking through overhanging clouds. The world, which had been derealized or denaturalized as a consequence of the introversion of energy, is here supernaturalized in a starkly bivalent manner. The world now assumes the appearance of a dark realm teeming with dangerous forces penetrated here and there by shafts of celestial light.

REGENERATION IN SPIRIT

The ego is eventually relieved of the sense of being caught in a conflict between good and evil. In time, the ego begins to see that the dark, instinctual side of numinous Spirit is integral rather than antithetical to the overall spiritual process, that the return of the repressed, as St. John of the Cross explained, is the night of Spirit preceding the dawn. In particular, the ego begins to understand that instinctuality is not inherently opposed to Spirit, as at first it seemed, but is in fact an accompanying aspect of Spirit as Spirit breaks free from the prepersonal organization to which it had been restricted by primal repression. As the spiritual process moves beyond the phase of derepression, then, the darkness and instinctual coloring of the process gradually recede and the healing, redemptive character of the process comes increasingly to the fore.

In this way regression in the service of transcendence eventually gives way to regeneration in Spirit. The ego undergoing regeneration is not yet fully adjusted to the plenipotency of the power of Ground and, therefore, continues to experience the power of the Ground as an energy that is overpowering in effect. This "violence" of the power of the Ground, however, is no longer perceived as having a dark, malefic dimension and is seen instead as a salutary violence, a purgative violence of spiritual ecstasy (the ego is infused and transported in ways that are "too much") and agony (the ego is infused and transported in ways that are "too, too much"). The violence characteristic of regeneration in Spirit is, then, a good violence. Moreover, it is a violence that diminishes in degree as the work of purgation is accomplished. Such symptoms of purgative violence as ecstasy and agony, therefore, in time subside and are eventually replaced by more stable states of spiritual infusion as regeneration in Spirit unfolds in the direction of ego-Ground integration.

Given its fundamentally positive character, regeneration in Spirit is a stage during which the Dynamic Ground and the power of the Ground express themselves in fundamentally positive ways. The Dynamic Ground is no longer an ominous underworld or sea and is now a source of renewing life, a fertile soil or wellspring from which emerge regenerating and transforming emanations. Correspondingly, the power of the Ground is no longer a power that is bivalent, instinctually laden, and wholly other and is now a power that is (1) univalent, without a dark side; (2) free of instinctual admixture, for the derepression of the instincts has run its course; and (3) kindred in nature, for the power of the Ground has become an intimate part of the ego's life. The power of the Ground now infuses the ego in ways that, however violent and painful, heal rather than slay and that lead the ego in the direction of integration rather than regression. The transition from regression in the service of transcendence to regeneration in Spirit is the turning point in spiritual life at which the ego begins to feel confident that it will "get to the other side." It is the juncture at which the awakened power of the Ground ceases manifesting itself as bivalent, wholly other numinous Spirit and begins manifesting itself as univalent, kindred *transforming Spirit*, a healing, redemptive power.

Part of the healing that occurs during regeneration in Spirit is a mending of the split in the ego's self-representation. The split between higher and lower possible selves, incurred as a consequence of the ego's relationship with biva-lent numinous Spirit, is mended as the ego begins its relationship with univa-lent transforming Spirit. Spirit no longer has a dark side, and therefore the ego, in its relationship with Spirit, no longer has a corresponding dark lower possible self. If, however, the ego no longer has a lower possible self, this does not mean that it has become the opposite higher possible self, an exclusively spiritual being. The higher possible self was a one-sided self that was posited only as a consequence of splitting and only in correlation with the lower pos-sible self. The disappearance of the lower possible self, therefore, is also a dis-appearance of the higher possible self. Rather than being split between all-bad and all-good possible selves, then, the ego here once again becomes a single good enough actual self. The self-representation is in this way mended and becomes the representation of a person who is keenly aware of falling short of what is spiritually possible for human beings but who nonetheless is accept-ing of herself as someone who is walking the path of Spirit.

The resolution of the split between higher and lower possible selves is at the same time a resolution of the corresponding split between the ego ideal and the archetypal shadow. The ego ideal is humanized, and the archetypal shadow is redeemed. The ego ideal is brought down to earth, becoming the ideal of human rather than angelic spirituality, and at the same time the shad-ow that had been cast over the instincts is lifted. Spirituality thus becomes a spirituality that is at home in the body and in harmony with the instincts, and at the same time the instincts are relieved of the onus of evil and are embraced as completely natural drives. With spiritual life no longer conceived as some-thing that can be pure only apart from instinctual life and with instinctual life no longer perceived as an adversary of spiritual life, the dualism of angelic, heavenly goodness on the one hand and demonic, instinctual evil on the other is finally transcended.

The mending of the ego system in the ways just indicated makes possible a restoration of many of the features of the old "worldly" self, that is, the self-representation of the identity project. Many of these features, deanimated during the ego's withdrawal from the world, are here reanimated and become once again authentic features of self. There is this difference, however: these features are no longer core or primary features of the ego's sense of self, as they were when the ego was pursuing the identity project, and now have a second-ary status as outer or worldly features of an inner spiritual self. The ego has been reborn in Spirit, and it is now the ego's new life in Spirit—and, in par-ticular, its relationship with transforming Spirit—that is the core of the ego's sense of self. The ego's worldly identity is indeed restored to life as a vehicle of authentic self-expression. In being thus restored, however, it shifts from the center to the periphery of the self-system, becoming the outer clothing of an inner spiritual self.

Having shed the appearance of otherness and having become an intimate part of the ego's life, the power of the Ground, as transforming Spirit, becomes a part of the ego system. The ego system in this way becomes an ego-*Spirit* system. The ego is not yet fully integrated with Spirit, and therefore Spirit, although closely akin to the ego, retains some degree of otherness. Spirit is not yet the ego's higher Self, but it is a kindred Spirit, the ego's counselor and guardian, an inner guide and governor of the ego's spiritual transformation. As counselor, Spirit is a power that inspires the ego toward more authentic spirituality and, in doing so, gives direction to the ego as it projects a new (more human, less angelic) ego ideal. At the same time, as guardian, Spirit is a power that impels the ego toward the authentic spirituality to which, as counselor, it points, challenging or purging the ego when it resists growth in Spirit. If, as counselor, transforming Spirit assists the ego as it articulates a new ego ideal, as guardian, it assists the ego as it disciplines itself in the manner of a new superego. In projecting a new ideal goal, the ego at the same time commands itself to persist in striving toward this goal, knowing that if it does less than is good enough, transforming Spirit as guardian will require of it what it should have required of itself.

Transforming Spirit is not only a motivator (i.e., a counselor or guardian) but also a life giver, comforter, and, for some, lover. As lover, transforming Spirit is perceived as an indwelling personal presence with which one experiences a powerfully emotional relationship. This love relationship sometimes assumes a spousal—and sometimes even an erotic—expression. For example, in Roman Catholic Christianity regeneration in Spirit is conceived, among other ways, as a stage of betrothal of the self to Christ. St. Teresa of Avila, who provides the preeminent account of this betrothal, describes in great detail the delectations and devastations she experienced as betrothed lover of Christ. A similarly dramatic account of a love relationship with the divine, this one from India, is provided by Ramakrishna, the nineteenth-century Hindu spiritual genius. Ramakrishna so loved Lord Krishna that he identified strongly with Krishna's lover, Radha, even to the point of dressing in women's clothing.

The ego's experience of others during regeneration in Spirit reflects the healing that occurs during this stage, and in particular it reflects the mending of splitting. Just as the ego no longer splits itself into higher and lower, all-good and all-bad possible selves, neither does it any longer divide others into angels and devils, perfect saints and irredeemable sinners. The overcoming of splitting eliminates unrealistic extremes of good and evil and thus relieves the ego of the tendency to idealize and devalue others. The ego is no longer prone to elevate others to an absolute higher level as beings to be worshiped or to cast them down to an absolute lower level as beings to be condemned. To be sure, the ego still sees some people as spiritually gifted and others as spiritually unawake or wayward. The ego continues to be acutely aware of the distance separating people who strive to give expression to Spirit and people who repress, resist, or defy Spirit. This distance, however, no longer seems unbridgeable, for the ego now sees that even the best among us are imperfect human beings and that even the worst have hearts, however hardened, in which Spirit, even if hidden, is alive. These more realistic perceptions of others indicate that regeneration in Spirit is a stage on the way to higher, transpersonal object constancy.

Regeneration in Spirit is also a stage on the way to higher reembodiment or "reincarnation." The ego overcomes its fear of the body, for by the time regeneration in Spirit begins instinctual derepression has run its course, and the power of the Ground, therefore, is able to express itself in ways that are increasingly free of frightening instinctual admixture. Without being rerepressed, the instincts cease being inflamed, and the body, consequently, is relieved of its prior alluring-alarming bivalence. The body in this way becomes, increasingly, a body of awakened-*integrated* instinctuality and awakened-*liberated* spirituality. The body loses its threatening aspect and assumes a wholly inviting character. The ego, accordingly, having experienced a distressing resurrection of the body, begins to undergo a healing reincarnation in the body. The ego returns—on a higher, transpersonal level—to fully embodied life. The body once again becomes the ego's primary abode.

The world, too, loses its threatening aspect and assumes a wholly inviting character, for the end of instinctual derepression and of numinous bivalence generally clears the atmosphere of the world. The dark forest gives way to open fields, storm clouds disperse, and the sky brightens. The stark extremes of menacing darkness on the one hand and shafts of otherworldly light on the other vanish as the sky opens to light from above and as this light, no longer filtered through a forest canopy or a covering of clouds, becomes light of this world rather than light from another world. The earth and the heavens are in this way progressively integrated as a single realm with open vistas and a sparkling sky. The supernatural becomes natural (Abrams 1971) or, rather, is on the way to becoming natural. The spiritual wayfarer is not yet home, but the wayfarer is no longer lost in darkness and is now on familiar, sacred ground.

INTEGRATION OF THE EGO AND THE DYNAMIC GROUND

The integration of the ego and the Dynamic Ground is the sacred marriage, the *hieros gamos*. In arriving at integration, the ego is harmoniously rooted in the Ground and completely at home in a sacred world. The Ground at this point is no longer an id, a dark gravitational attractor, an ominous, irresistible underworld or sea, or even a source of renewing life and is now instead a fertile, sacred void. It is an ever-present though invisible source of enlivening, creative, and spiritual spontaneities. Similarly, the power of the Ground at this point is no longer numinous Spirit or transforming Spirit and is now instead *transparent Spirit*, a power that is the ego's higher spiritual Self. Whereas numinous Spirit is wholly other and whereas transforming Spirit, as counselor, guardian, and lover, is kindred but still other rather than self, transparent Spirit is wholly self or, rather, Self. Accordingly, the ego system here becomes a completely integrated ego-Spirit system, a self-Self system. The ego is a lesser self in relation to Spirit, which is a superior Self.

In becoming the ego's higher Self, Spirit sheds all vestiges of otherness, even the otherness implicit in being the ego's counselor, guardian, and lover. Spirit ceases being the ego's counselor and becomes the ego's own spiritual wisdom. Spirit ceases being the ego's guardian and becomes the ego's own higher will. Spirit ceases being the ego's lover and becomes the ego's own love of others. The ego does not arrogate these powers of Spirit; rather, the ego is now so wedded to Spirit that these powers belong to the ego as permanent gifts of Spirit. Because, in the spiritual marriage, the ego gives itself completely to Spirit, Spirit in turn gives itself completely to the ego.

The higher object constancy that begins to emerge during regeneration in Spirit leads to a fundamentally new vision of others. Initially, as we have seen, it leads to a disappearance of idealizations and devaluations of others. The person undergoing regeneration in Spirit ceases seeing others in split fashion as either saints or sinners and begins to see others as people who are at once "human, all too human" and inherently spiritual in nature, no matter how awake or asleep, devoted to or defiant of Spirit they might be. This overcoming of the tendency to idealize and devalue others is a disillusioning process that leads to increasing clarity of vision. In particular, it leads to a growing appreciation of others as people who, like oneself, are travelers on the spiritual path. It becomes increasingly evident to the person who is approaching integration that we are all on the spiritual path together, even if some people are ahead of others and even if some seem for the time being to be headed in the wrong direction. This improved clarity of vision leads eventually, once regeneration in Spirit culminates in integration, to a perception of others as "siblings in Spirit," as brothers or sisters in a common spiritual life. In perceiving others as siblings in Spirit, the integrated person cares for the spiritual welfare of others, all others, not only those who are consciously living the life of Spirit but also those who have knowingly or unknowingly set themselves against Spirit. The integrated person is at home with others as members of a spiritual family, a family in which no one is master and from which no one is excluded.

The integrated person is also at home in the body and the world. The integrated person is at home in the body because the ego is now fully "reincarnated" in the body, which itself is fully "resurrected," that is, reawakened in both instinct and Spirit. The power of the Ground, expressed in its highest form as transparent Spirit, is now the enlivening power of the body, which for this reason is not only the integrated person's primary abode but also the "temple of Spirit." The body is thus the fleshly home in which the reincarnated ego and reawakened Spirit live together harmoniously in a sacred marriage. Similarly, the world is a larger homeland in which the integrated person and Spirit live together in an intimate union. The world of the integrated person, in addition to being a realm with open vistas and a sparkling sky, is also, as Martin Heidegger (1954) explained, a dwelling place with hallowed and utterly native ground. The spiral journey has at last led the ego back to the original bases of its being. Here, as at the outset of life, instincts and Spirit, self and other, and earth and heaven coexist in complete harmony in a life lived in the fullness of the present moment.

CONCLUDING OBSERVATIONS

The beginning and end of the spiral path share the same deep foundations. The ego, in reaching the end of the spiral path, is once again rooted in the Ground, enlivened and graced by the power of the Ground in its plenipotency, intimately joined with others, fully embodied, and at home in a hallowedly resplendent world. In sharing these deep foundations, however, the beginning and end of the spiral path are otherwise maximally different; for the ego at the beginning of the spiral path is only starting to emerge from the Ground, whereas the ego at the end of the path is mature and established in the world. The beginning and end of the spiral path are alike in being points at which consciousness is at one with the fullness of life. They differ by the widest possible margin, however, in the extent to which this unity of consciousness and life is developmentally unfolded. At the beginning of the spiral path the unity of consciousness and life is only a primitive prepersonal unity; at the end, in contrast, this unity is a completely actualized transpersonal unity, a higher integration of a fully developed ego with a plenipotently active Dynamic Ground.

In this chapter we have presented a stage view of the spiral path by following selected dimensions of experience as they are intertwined at prepersonal, personal, and transpersonal stages of development. The task ahead is to isolate the selected dimensions from each other and, shifting from an overview to a ground-level perspective, to follow their particular courses along the spiral path. The ensuing chapters, then, track the Dynamic Ground, the energy system, the ego system, the perceived other, the experiential body, and the life-world as they are organized or experienced at principal stages of spiral development.

THREE

THE DYNAMIC GROUND

SWITCHING NOW FROM the stage view to the dimensional view, the task of this chapter is to plot the developmental course of the Dynamic Ground, the deep core of the psyche. The task, more precisely, is to describe the basic organization and primary expressions of the Dynamic Ground at each of the principal stages of the spiral path. The Dynamic Ground, as we shall see, is the seat of the deepest level of the unconscious, the inherited or collective unconscious. For this reason the ensuing developmental account of the Dynamic Ground is at the same time a developmental account of the unconscious.

TABLE 3.1

DEVELOPMENTAL ORGANIZATIONS OF THE
DYNAMIC GROUND (DEEP UNCONSCIOUS)

STAGE OF LIFE	DYNAMIC GROUND
Neonatal stage	Primordial source of life
Early preoedipal stage	Intrapsychic dimension of Great Mother
Late preoedipal stage	Split, nurturant-dangerous Ground
Oedipal stage	Closing of the Ground
Latency	Ground submerged and quieted by primal repression at prepersonal level: the id
Puberty and adolescence	Id stirred by awakening sexuality
Early adulthood	Id restabilized on basis of mature genital sexuality
Crossroads	Mysterious gravitational attractor
Awakening	Numinous core of psyche

37

DEVELOPMENTAL ORGANIZATIONS OF THE DYNAMIC
GROUND (DEEP UNCONSCIOUS) *(CONTINUED)*

STAGE OF LIFE	DYNAMIC GROUND
Regression in the service of transcendence	Psychic underworld or sea
Regeneration in Spirit	Source of renewing life
Ego-Ground integration	Fertile-sacred void

THE PSYCHOID UNCONSCIOUS

Before tracking the developmental unfolding of the Dynamic Ground, it is first necessary to say something about the underlying nature of the Ground itself. In this section, then, developmental considerations are postponed so that we can give a brief account of features of the Ground that, present in all of its expressions, are inherent to the Ground.

As the deep core of the psyche, the Dynamic Ground lies beneath the ego system and is the seat of nonegoic psychic potentials. Principal among these nonegoic potentials of the Ground are energy, biologically governed instincts, the sources of affective response, and the autosymbolic imagination. Lying beneath the ego system, nonegoic potentials are not under the ego's direct control. The ego can influence (e.g., elicit, channel, modulate, resist) the expression of nonegoic potentials; it cannot, however, as it does with its own ego functions, take direct command of them. Nonegoic potentials are always to some extent independent of the ego and spontaneous in expression.

As an underlying source of experience, the Dynamic Ground is inherently unconscious in the sense that its roots extend into neurological structures lying beneath the limits of possible experience. To use a term introduced by C. G. Jung, the Dynamic Ground is for this reason a *psychoid unconscious*, an underlying depth that reaches beneath the limits of the psyche into nonpsychic, physical strata. The Dynamic Ground is a bridge between psyche and soma rather than something lying wholly on the psychic side of this divide. The energies, instinctual impulses, emotive currents, and images that issue from the Ground are indeed psychic in nature; they manifest themselves *within* the psyche and, therefore, within the limits of possible experience. The nonegoic potentials of the Ground that give rise to these phenomena, however, lie *beneath* the psyche and, therefore, are not open to conscious view. As the psychoid basis of life, the Dynamic Ground is inherently unfathomable.

The Dynamic Ground is not only the psychoid unconscious but also, to use another Jungian term, the *collective unconscious*. It is accurately described in this way because it is a source of experience that is inherited and common to all members of the species rather than a psychic formation created as a consequence of the experience of a single person. The adoption of the term *collective unconscious* does not imply acceptance of the particulars of Jung's account of the collective unconscious. The term is used here only as a way of making the general distinction between inherited and biographical, universal and personal levels of the unconscious.

If the Dynamic Ground is inherently the psychoid unconscious, it is also the deepest level of the repressed unconscious; for early in life primal repression submerges the Dynamic Ground, significantly weakening the expression of the nonegoic potentials of the Ground. Once a final commitment is made to primal repression, the Dynamic Ground is effectively lost to consciousness, thus becoming not only an unfathomable psychoid depth but also a source of experience that has been repressively sealed and greatly reduced in activity. Because primal repression is laid down early in life, the reorganization of the Dynamic Ground effected by primal repression is one that arrests the Ground at a prepersonal level of expression. It is a reorganization, therefore, that reduces the Dynamic Ground to the id as described by classical psychoanalysis (see figure 3.1).

FIGURE 3.1

DYNAMIC GROUND BEFORE AND AFTER PRIMAL REPRESSION

	Before Primal Repression	After Primal Repression
Psychic Space, Consciousness	Nonegoic potentials express themselves within consciousness unfettered and with full, plenipotent intensity.	Psychic expressions of nonegoic potentials are greatly weakened. **Primal Repression**
Dynamic Ground	*Psychoid Unconscious* (inherited, collective): Dynamic Ground, the seat of nonegoic potentials, is a source of life that, although unfathomably deep, is not disconnected from consciousness.	*Id:* Dynamic Ground, submerged and quieted by primal repression, is arrested at prepersonal level of expression, thus becoming the id as described by psychoanalysis. Organized as the id, the Dynamic Ground is not only a psychoid unconscious, an unfathomable depth, but also the deepest level of the repressed unconscious.

The Dynamic Ground, although inherently unconscious as a psychoid source, is not inherently either prepersonal or transpersonal in nature. This view departs from Jung. Jung inferred from the premise that the collective unconscious is both a product of phylogenesis and the basis of spirituality that it has both prepersonal and transpersonal inherent aspects. Jung's inference, however, is invalid, for the truth of the premise does not require the truth of the conclusion. Moreover, according to the view presented here, the conclusion is false. Although the Dynamic Ground has both phylogenetic roots and spiritual expressions, it is not itself inherently either prepersonal or transpersonal in nature. Accordingly, the terms *prepersonal* and *transpersonal*—or *pre* and *trans*, for short—are here used to designate only developmental expressions and not inherent sides or dimensions of the Dynamic Ground.

The distinction between developmental and constitutional perspectives helps resolve some of the conflicts among major conceptions of the unconscious, for example, the conceptions of Arthur Schopenhauer and Sigmund Freud, according to whom the unconscious is an exclusively prepersonal (i.e., instinctual, irrational) Will or id; C. G. Jung, according to whom, again, the unconscious has both prepersonal and transpersonal inherent aspects; Roberto Assagioli (1971) and Ken Wilber (1990, 1995), according to whom there is not a single unconscious but rather two, a lower prepersonal unconscious and a higher transpersonal unconscious; and Taoism and Mahayana Buddhism, according to which the unconscious is an inherently transpersonal fertile or sacred void. These conceptions of the unconscious are discrepant and mutually exclusive as they stand. If, however, they are interpreted developmentally rather than constitutionally, they can be fitted together coherently as frames of a developmental sequence revealing how the unconscious unfolds from pre to trans. This sequence, summarized in table 3.1, is set forth in the ensuing discussion.

THE PRIMORDIAL SOURCE OF LIFE

Of the two basic poles of the psyche, the ego and the Dynamic Ground, it is primarily the Ground that is active at the outset of life. This is not to say that the newborn is without an ego. The preponderance of informed opinion is to the contrary, as we shall see in chapter 5. If, however, the ego is not completely absent at the outset of life, neither is it fully formed. The ego of the newborn is only an incipient ego, an ego just beginning to emerge from the Dynamic Ground. The Dynamic Ground is the older system phylogenetically and for this reason is the system that is first active ontogenetically. At birth the Dynamic Ground is active across a wide range of nonegoic potentials; in contrast, the ego is active in only a minimal way. As the active inner source of the newborn's experience, the Dynamic Ground is the primordial source of life.

The following nonegoic potentials are active at birth or soon thereafter: (1) *the power of the Ground,* which affects the newborn either as an inwardly pooled oceanic reservoir (in which the newborn gestates during sleep) or as an outwardly flowing, object-directed stream (which amplifies intentional states when the newborn is awake and engaged); (2) *biological instincts,* which generate impulses in response to target stimuli, prompting corresponding object-related behaviors; (3) *emotive potentials,* which give rise to powerful body-based feelings; and (4) *the autosymbolic imagination,* which projects preencoded images upon genetically selected stimuli as they appear within the field of perception. At the outset of life we are radically open and, consequently, receptive not only to a wide range of external stimuli but also to a wide range of energies, impulses, feelings, and images arising from the Dynamic Ground within.

Not all nonegoic potentials are active at birth, for some (e.g., sexuality as it emerges during puberty) are governed by a biological timetable and become active only at later stages of development. Among nonegoic potentials that *are* active at or near the beginning of life, the autosymbolic imagination may be the last to emerge. Freud (1911a) and Melanie Klein (see Isaacs 1943; Segal 1964, 1991) believed that the imagination is active in newborns as a source of images serving as substitutes for instinctually required objects. Piagetians, however, have called this view into question, arguing that images serving as substitutes for objects cannot emerge until children are able to form representations of objects and that children are not able to form such representations until they understand that objects continue to exist when not perceived (object permanence). Piagetians, that is, have argued that children do not use images to represent absent objects until after they understand that there are such things as absent objects. They have argued as well that newborns have no such understanding.

It is unclear just when children begin to understand object permanence. Piaget dated the first major step in this direction at about eight or nine months of age because this is the age at which children begin looking for objects they have seen being hidden from view. Adopting Piaget's conclusions, psychoanalyst Selma Fraiberg (1969) dated the emergence of images at eight or nine months of age. More recent research (Mandler 1990), however, has shown that Piaget's dating unnecessarily presupposes motor ability: eight or nine months is the age when children begin to locomote toward objects they have seen being hidden from view. More sophisticated studies focusing on eye movements and the surprise response (see Baillargeon 1987) show that children operate with an assumption of object permanence long before they are able to use their bodies to search for hidden objects, perhaps as early as three and a half months of age. More recent research, then, suggests that images serving as representations of objects may emerge during infancy, before the child is able to crawl. If they do, they no doubt are short-lived, extremely primitive formations fusing not only visual data but also data from other sense modalities.[1]

We cannot know for sure just when the imagination becomes active. Suffice it to say that if it is not active at birth, it likely comes into play in a rudimentary way in the first months or at least the first year of life. Many other nonegoic potentials, in contrast, are active at birth, and many are likely active *in utero*. Whereas the ego at the outset of life exists as a seat of functions that are active only minimally (e.g., synthesis, stimulus discrimination, object tracking) or that are not yet active at all (e.g., operational cognition, impulse control, self-reflection), the Dynamic Ground exists as a seat of potentials most of which are powerfully in play.

THE INTRAPSYCHIC DIMENSION OF THE GREAT MOTHER

The infant's unqualified openness to the caregiver is at the same time an unqualified openness to the Dynamic Ground. These outer and inner dimensions of the infant's experience are intimately interconnected, so intimately interconnected indeed that the infant experiences them as one. For this reason the infant, when it begins to bring the caregiver into focus, experiences the caregiver as a person empowered, construed, and colored by the plenipotent nonegoic potentials of the Dynamic Ground. That is to say, it experiences the caregiver as the awesome and compelling Great Mother. We introduced the notion of the Great Mother in the last chapter, and we discuss it at greater length in chapter 6. In this chapter we need consider only the following essential point: In experiencing the Ground and the caregiver as one, the infant experiences each in terms of the other and, therefore, not only experiences the caregiver as enhanced by the nonegoic potentials of the Ground but also experiences the Ground as imbued with the qualities of the caregiver.

Because the infant experiences the Ground as imbued with the qualities of the caregiver and because, in the vast stretches of the human past, the caregiver has been female, it follows that the Ground has been imbued with female qualities. This linking of the Ground with femaleness is an historical rather than a necessary connection. The division of labor between the sexes could have evolved differently, as it has in a few species, giving the role of primary caregiver of the young to males. The fact is, however, that females have performed this role throughout human evolution and, therefore, that the Ground has been imbued with female qualities. Since the beginning of our species, the Ground has been experienced as part of the Great Mother system, and in consequence the Ground has been apprehended in cultural symbols and myths as having a fundamentally female character.

As the intrapsychic dimension of the Great Mother, the Ground is experienced as it expresses itself in the child's interaction with the caregiver. We cannot, of course, know exactly how the Ground expresses itself in this interaction, for we are not able to bracket completely our adult perspective or to access fully the child's. Nevertheless, we can reasonably conjecture that it expresses itself in the following principal ways: (1) as a female-associated *inner source*, a reservoir of energy or a psychic womb from which the child (as ego) emerges and in which, in yielding to the caregiver's embrace, the child dissolves in oceanic bliss; (2) as female-associated *nourishing feelings*, feelings of fullness and satisfaction that well up within the child when the caregiver feeds or otherwise cares for the child; (3) as female-associated *enlivening energy*, energy that quickens the child's alertness when the caregiver attends to the child in ways that draw the child into focused activity; (4) as female-associated *ecstatic energy*, energy that causes the child to burst with delight when the caregiver engages the child in intense play; and (5) as female-associated *images of reassuring or pleasing sorts*, images of the caregiver and of comforting or pleasing objects that arise spontaneously when the child feels in need of protection or stimulation.

The Dynamic Ground is likely associated with femaleness not only in these but also in other ways. The child, in experiencing the Ground as inner source, as nourishing feelings, as enlivening or ecstatic energy, or as reassuring or pleasing images, does so primarily in response to focusing upon or being the focus of the caregiver. The influences of the Ground and those of the caregiver are thus constituent dimensions of a larger, "compound" phenomenon: the Great Mother. Moreover, to the child they are constituent dimensions that are in no way distinguished from each other. They are seamlessly unified aspects of the Great Mother.

THE SPLITTING OF THE DYNAMIC GROUND

The child's experience of the Great Mother changes dramatically near the middle of the second year, for at this point the child splits the Great Mother in two. Beginning about the middle of the second year—which, in Margaret Mahler's terms, marks the transition from the practicing to the rapprochement subphase of the separation-individuation process—the child splits the Great Mother into both a good object and a bad object or, in the Jungian terminology used here, into both a Good Mother and a Terrible Mother. This splitting of the Great Mother is a defense mechanism mobilized in response to the child's awakening to the vastness and dangerousness of the world and, therefore, to its own vulnerability in the world. In sensing its vulnerability, the child desperately needs to believe that the caregiver is a perfect being who will provide for the child without condition and without fail. This need for a perfect provider leads the child to idealize the caregiver as an all-good Good Mother and, consequently, to assume that the actions of the caregiver that are less than perfect are the actions of a separate all-bad Terrible Mother. The causes and consequences of this splitting of the Great Mother are discussed in greater detail in chapter 6. The focus here is on the Dynamic Ground, and the relevant consideration is this: Because the Great Mother is not only the outer caregiver but also the inner Ground, this splitting of the Great Mother is a splitting not only of the child's representation of the caregiver but also a splitting of the Ground.

The ways in which the Ground expresses itself in the child's interaction with the caregiver, then, are now split into contrary opposites. The Ground still expresses itself as an inner source, as nourishing feelings, as enlivening and ecstatic energy, and as reassuring and pleasing images. These expressions of the Ground, however, are now exaggerated in their goodness, becoming dimensions of an all-good Good Mother, and are opposed by equally exaggerated negative expressions, which emerge as dimensions of an all-bad Terrible Mother. Split in this way, the exaggerated positive expressions of the Ground make up what can be called the "nurturant Ground," and the opposed negative expressions make up what can be called the "dangerous Ground." The nurturant Ground consists of the positive inner experiences that arise within the child when it interacts with the Good Mother; and the dangerous Ground consists of the negative inner experiences that arise within the child when it interacts with the Terrible Mother.

The nurturant Ground and the dangerous Ground can, then, be contrasted in the following principal ways: (1) whereas the nurturant Ground is an inner womb in which the child is blissfully dissolved when embraced by the Good Mother, the dangerous Ground is an inner abyss in which the child is dreadfully dissolved when engulfed by the Terrible Mother; (2) whereas the nurturant Ground is a source of nourishing feelings (fullness, contentment) that the child experiences when its needs are met by the Good Mother, the dangerous Ground is a source of toxic feelings (emptiness, anxiety) that the child experiences when its needs are left unmet by the Terrible Mother; (3) whereas the nurturant Ground is a source of enlivening energy that heightens the child's awareness when the child is engaged interactively by the Good Mother, the dangerous Ground is a source of enervating energy that depresses the child's spirits when the child is neglected by the Terrible Mother; (4) whereas the nurturant Ground is a source of ecstatic energy that enraptures the child when the child is played with by the Good Mother, the dangerous Ground is a source of wounding, rupturing energy that devastates the child when the child is punished by the Terrible Mother; and (5) whereas the nurturant Ground is a source of reassuring and pleasing images (e.g., of the Good Mother as kind maiden or goddess), the dangerous Ground is a source of frightening and repugnant images (e.g., of the Terrible Mother as cruel witch or gorgon).

The child of course has no experience of these split manifestations of the Ground apart from their presence in the larger Great Mother system. Nevertheless, these manifestations indicate that the Ground itself is decisively cleaved. They indicate that the deep core of the psyche now has sharply contrasting light and dark, nurturant and dangerous modes of expression.

PRIMAL REPRESSION AND THE CLOSING OF THE DYNAMIC GROUND

Preoedipal splitting is a necessary expedient for dealing with the insecurities that arise near the end of the second year of life. It is not, however, a tenable response in the long term, for in dividing the child's world in two, it seriously interferes with ego development. Splitting, then, soon outlives its usefulness and itself becomes a problem—indeed, the principal problem—that must be solved. The child for this reason must eventually do whatever is necessary to bring splitting to an end. In chapter 6 we shall learn that the child has only one option: to sever remaining ties of internal connection with the Great Mother. If the child is to overcome splitting, it must wean itself from this powerful being.

Now because the Great Mother is not only an interpersonal but also an intrapsychic reality, not only the outer caregiver but also the inner Dynamic Ground, the act by which the child disjoins itself from the Great Mother has both interpersonal and intrapsychic dimensions: it is an act both of withdrawal and of repression. It is an act both of withdrawal from symbiotic intimacy with the caregiver (who is put at a safe distance) and of repression of the Dynamic Ground (which is quieted and thereby rendered safe). In thus separating itself from both the outer and inner dimensions of the Great Mother, the child, it should be noted, does more than just protect itself from the Great Mother: *it actually brings an end to the Great Mother.* The Great Mother disappears because the child, in withdrawing from the caregiver, depersonalizes the Ground and, in repressing the Ground, disempowers the caregiver. The Ground, disconnected from the caregiver, is no longer able to express itself through the Great Mother system and is thus reduced to a merely intrapsychic Ground; and the caregiver, disconnected from the Ground, is shorn of projected plenipotent energies and archetypal images and is thus reduced to a "merely" natural, rather than supernatural, being. The child, then, overcomes splitting by protecting itself from the Great Mother in a way that not only shields the child from the Great Mother but that also, in doing so, dismantles the Great Mother system. Although the Great Mother is an immense, awesome being, the child in effect does away with the Great Mother simply by protectively separating itself from the Great Mother.

In the last chapter we introduced the expression *primal separation* to describe the child's withdrawal from the caregiver and used Freud's expression *primal repression* to describe the corresponding repression of the Dynamic Ground. We noted that primal separation and primal repression are not two different acts but are rather two dimensions of the same act: *primal closing.* The Great Mother is a fusion of outer and inner sources; accordingly, the act by which the child separates itself from the Great Mother has two targets. It is focused at once on the caregiver and the Dynamic Ground. It is an act that is at once a defensive withdrawal from the outer caregiver and a repressive quieting of the inner Dynamic Ground.

It is the inner dimension of primal closing, primal repression, that is relevant to the topic of this chapter, for primal repression reorganizes the Dynamic Ground. Primal repression, in submerging and quieting the Dynamic Ground, transforms the Ground from an underlying source that is fully active within consciousness to a source that, although by no means completely dormant, is markedly reduced in activity and to a significant extent lost to consciousness. Whereas, before primal repression, the

Dynamic Ground is unconscious only in the sense of being unfathomably deep, after primal repression it becomes unconscious also in the sense of being buried beneath consciousness. The Dynamic Ground, in being repressed, is covered over and subdued and, therefore, ceases for the most part expressing itself within consciousness. After primal repression, then, the Dynamic Ground becomes not only the psychoid unconscious but also the deepest level of the repressed unconscious.

We should clarify an important point: primal repression is not a hydraulic (or pneumatic) repression. Freud's hydraulic model of repression has seriously misleading implications, as many critics have noted. The hydraulic model is correct in seeing primal repression as a powerful mobilization of energy, a countercathexis, that pushes down on the underlying Ground. The hydraulic model, however, is misleading in suggesting that the Ground, in being repressed, exerts a continuing counterpressure against the pressure applied by primal repression. The hydraulic model, that is, overlooks the fact that the Ground, in being repressed, is not only submerged but also quieted. The nonegoic potentials of the Ground, although not completely deactivated, are markedly weakened in activity. In effect they are put to sleep and allowed to awaken only when the ego itself goes to sleep, at which time they express themselves in the play of dreams. In this way the ego and the Dynamic Ground take turns expressing themselves. Rather than hydraulically pushing against each other, they alternate between "on" and "off" modes.

The hydraulic model describes suppression, not repression. Both suppression and repression are countercathexes, mobilizations of energy by the ego aimed at excluding psychic materials from consciousness. The difference between the two is that, whereas suppression is a countercathexis focused on materials that continue actively to assert themselves, repression is a countercathexis that succeeds in reducing the targeted materials from an active to an inactive, or at least to a greatly weakened, state. Such deactivated or weakened materials are like seeds that are kept alive but cannot sprout because a covering deprives them of sufficient light or like smoldering wood that cannot burst into flame because a covering deprives it of sufficient oxygen. In somewhat this way, primal repression quiets nonegoic potentials. It does not extinguish them completely, but it subdues them to such a degree that a high-pressure hydraulic system is not required to contain them.

An analogy that can help us understand how primal repression quiets the Ground is that of the genie in the lamp. Once the person who owns the lamp (the ego) puts the cap (primal repression) on the lamp, the genie (the power and other nonegoic potentials of the Dynamic Ground) goes to sleep. A relatively unproblematic situation thus arises of a genie who, asleep, lies hidden and does not interfere with the actions of the owner of the lamp. Similarly, the repressed Ground, submerged and quieted, lies hidden and does not interfere with the actions of the ego. The ego for this reason does not have to exert itself to contain the Ground and in fact does not even know that the Ground exists.

THE ID

The consolidation of primal repression quiets the nonegoic potentials of the Dynamic Ground and thus marks the beginning of the stage of latency. Because primal repression closes the Ground very early in life—latency begins at approximately five years of age—the nonegoic potentials of the Ground are disconnected from consciousness before they have had a chance to be cultivated by developed ego functions. Concrete operational cognition emerges only after the beginning of latency, and formal operational cognition emerges only in adolescence or early adulthood. Nonegoic potentials, then, are disconnected from consciousness before the development of operational cognition of any sort and, therefore, before the development of the many volitional, interpersonal, moral, and other competencies that are based on operational cognition. Because they are disconnected from consciousness without having been cultivated by developed ego functions, nonegoic potentials are submerged at a prepersonal level of expression. They are arrested in development and reduced to the "primitive" potentials making up the id as described by classical psychoanalysis.

Primal repression, in quieting the Ground, does not deactivate nonegoic potentials completely. Nonegoic potentials are essential to life and must remain active to some degree. The Ground, then, is active during the latency years. It is so, however, primarily in diminished and undetected ways, as the source of psychic energy, covert impulses, and unconscious projections. Latency is a stage during which the Ground, like the genie hidden in the lamp, coexists with the ego unbeknownst to the ego. The power of the Ground, no longer active in plenipotent form, expresses itself within consciousness only in the abated and usually invisible form of psychic energy; and instinctual drives are subdued. Latency is for this reason a stage during which the ego is able to develop its autonomous functions without having to struggle against the power and other potentials of the Dynamic Ground. It is, therefore, a stage during which ego development proceeds at an accelerated pace.

After years of quiescence, the Dynamic Ground becomes active once again with the onset of puberty. This reactivation occurs because the sexual drive that awakens at this point is a nonegoic potential belonging to the Ground. Moreover, it is a nonegoic potential that, in awakening, stirs other nonegoic potentials, giving rise not only to sexual impulses but also to powerful emotions and related fantasy elaborations. Adolescence is for this reason a stage during which nonegoic life in general is quickened and during which, consequently, experience in general is intensified. Anna Freud (1946, 1958) explained long ago that this intensification of experience can be frightening to the adolescent and may provoke defensive reactions, especially forms of exaggerated self-control. The awakening of sexuality and consequent stirring of the id that occur during adolescence pose a serious challenge to the ego and its repressive foundations. The id-ego-superego structure that served so well during the latency period is not adequate to this challenge and must be reorganized if psychic stability is to be restored.

The reorganization of the id-ego-superego structure in the transition from adolescence to early adulthood is a complex process. In chapter 5 we discuss how this process reconstitutes the ego system. The germane point here is that this process restabilizes the Ground by controlling the arousal of sexuality. The Ground, which had been kept astir by the burgeoning sexuality of adolescence, "goes back to sleep" once awakened sexuality is functionally integrated within adult life. The Ground returns to quiescence because the mature genital sexuality achieved by such integration, unlike the persistent sexuality of adolescence, is discretely intermittent in expression. When it is "on," it is on—as, too, are related sensations, feelings, and fantasies. When it is "off," however, it lies quietly within the Ground along with the other nonegoic potentials of the Ground. In this way, although sexuality remains awake in the sense of being arousable in response to sexual stimuli, the Ground otherwise returns to a relatively quiescent state. Psychoanalyst Peter Blos (1968) described this reorganization of the id as a second, higher form of latency.

THE MYSTERIOUS GRAVITATIONAL ATTRACTOR

Most people follow the spiral path only in its outward, worldly stages, only to the point of mature ego development. For most people, therefore, the id as reorganized in early adulthood is the final form of the Dynamic Ground. Some people, however, embark upon the inward turn of the spiral path, and for these people new forms of the Dynamic Ground begin to emerge. The first such form is that of a mysterious gravitational attractor. The Dynamic Ground assumes this form because, if we recall, the inward turn of the spiral path is initiated by an introversion of psychic energy, a reversal of flow that divests the world of aliveness and that concomitantly invests the Dynamic Ground with a heightened charge. Following the lead of introverting energy, the ego loses interest in worldly involvement and is drawn inward. It "dies to the world" and is beckoned by a mysterious *je ne sais quoi*, by an unknown center of gravity hidden deep within the psyche.

For explanatory purposes it will be useful to consider the extreme case of such introversion, the case in which the charge accumulating in the Dynamic Ground grows sufficiently strong that the Ground becomes a source of inescapable gravity, a black hole in psychic space. As a source of such gravity, the Ground affects the ego by inexorably drawing it away from worldly engagement and pulling it ever more deeply into disengaged introversion. The ego is aware of the relentless gravity acting upon it but has no understanding of the nature or source of this gravity. All the ego knows is that it experiences increasing difficulty in achieving contact with the world and is being pulled into dark depths. The ego feels enervated, sunken, and immobilized. Although the Dynamic Ground is gravitationally charged, it has not yet reawakened and, therefore, remains invisible to the ego. It is still the unconscious id. The Ground, however, despite its invisibility, is now the central reality of the ego's life. The ego is no longer "in the world" and is now subject to the inescapable pull of a hidden center of dynamic darkness.

Although black holes in psychic space may be rare, evidence of their existence can be found in the phenomenologies of clinical depression and borderline disorder. People suffering from depression, for example, report feelings of gloom, heaviness, inertia, and fatigue. Afflicted with such feelings, depressed people are unable to set themselves in motion. As much as they may want to resume normal activity, they feel as though they are unable to do so because they are weighed down and weakened by a dark gravity emanating from psychic depths. The following two personal narratives—the first one employing the black hole analogy—powerfully attest the gravitational character of the depressed condition:

> My moodiness got worse and worse, and I was constantly fighting with my boyfriend, through no fault of his. In my mind, I vividly saw myself teetering on the edge of a bottomless black hole. I felt that if I fell in, I would never stop falling. (Gray 1995)

> A darkness seems to arise in the basement [of the house of self]. It pervades upward into the level above, attracting the person's attention. It draws a person downward into the lower depths, as it were. The "eyes of the soul" or the person's inward attention become focused on these lower regions. All the happiness, joy, and brightness that attended the life on the first story disappear. The energy that accompanies the normal activities of life disappears. (Long 1998)

Introverting psychic energy can transform the Dynamic Ground into a black hole at the deepest center of psychic space. When such a hole is formed, one is pulled inexorably toward it (or toward the "dark basement of the house of self"), drained of energy, and rendered unable to live one's former life in the world.

Some symptoms of borderline disorder suggest an even closer encounter with a psychic black hole, for people suffering from borderline disorder are prone to dark, inert states that, on the edge of psychosis, augur the obliteration of self. According to Jerome Kroll (1988), these states are trancelike conditions of vacant absorption. This description fits well with our account, for it suggests that the borderline person has been taken in tow by a gravitational energy that slows the mind, reducing it to a condition of morbid blankness. Afflicted with states of deathlike emptiness, the borderline person is thrown into a panic, an annihilation anxiety, which Gerald Adler (1985) describes as "the threat of loss of self through psychological disintegration . . ." p. 29). The person in the throes of such anxiety suffers from a fear of being swallowed and destroyed in inner darkness.

Annihilation anxiety suggests that the borderline person is situated near the "event horizon" of an inner black hole and, in this proximity to the black hole, is subjected to gravitational forces of such magnitude as to induce states of mind-numbing, self-erasing stupor. These blank trances signal imminent danger of destruction by gravitational engulfment. Panic ensues. It seems as though all is lost, and yet the person in the borderline situation escapes ego death. The borderline person is somehow able to hover near the event horizon of a black hole without passing into the region of no return. Desperate measures, of course, are required to keep outside this region. For example, a person caught in the gravitational pull of an inner black hole might instigate interpersonal crises, engage in reckless behavior, use drugs, or commit acts of self-mutilation in order to create exciting scenes or to produce intense sensations and thereby pull free from the black hole. Seemingly against all odds, these desperate measures work, for a time. The borderline somehow escapes annihilation. Borderline disorder is aptly described as "stably unstable," for the person suffering borderline disorder is a survivor living on the edge of the abyss.

Although people in the depths of depression feel "dead to the world," they typically do not feel as though their existence as subjects of consciousness is on the verge of disintegration. They have been weakened by inner gravitational forces but remain safely distant from the gravitationally charged Ground. People suffering borderline disorder, in contrast, are dangerously close to the Ground and for this reason are terrified of being swallowed and torn to pieces by gravitational energies. Whereas depressed people find themselves in a dark, lifeless cellar of the psyche, borderline people find themselves in a cellar with a collapsing floor. People in the borderline situation, therefore, must make desperate overtures to others and must repeatedly summon crisis energies to keep from being sucked into a bottomless black pit at the base of the psyche.

Again, black holes are symptomatic of extreme conditions. Most people on the inward turn of the spiral journey, in experiencing the pull of the Ground as a mysterious gravitational attractor, probably do not encounter the dreadful gravity of an inner black hole. Serious depressive and borderline symptoms, then, are probably exceptions rather than the rule so far as the inward turn is concerned. That said, it is important to acknowledge the possibility of black holes and, therefore, of depressive and borderline symptoms as part of the inward turn of the spiral path. The inward turn is initiated by an introversion of psychic energy that disengages the ego from the outer world and imbues the inner Ground with a gravitational charge. When the flow of energy is especially powerful, a black hole can be created, and the ego can be afflicted with dark, depressed moods and even with annihilation anxiety. Depressive and borderline symptoms occurring in this developmental context pose a special challenge to the clinician, for how is the clinician to know whether such symptoms are pathologies on the path to awakening or simply pathologies without redeeming prospects? The diagnosis is not easy. The judgment must be based not only on the symptoms themselves but also on broader clinical and developmental data.

THE NUMINOUS CORE OF THE PSYCHE

Whether or not the Ground becomes a black hole, the introversion of psychic energy sometimes charges the Ground sufficiently to ignite the power of the Ground in its plenipotency. When this occurs the Ground ceases being an inert center of psychic gravity and becomes a dynamically active psychic core releasing *numinous energy.* Numinous energy, as Rudolf Otto (1917) explained, is the *mysterium tremendum et fascinans.* It is a seemingly supernatural energy that has overpowering, bivalent effects upon the ego: it both repels and fascinates, terrifies and exhilarates, eclipses and enraptures the ego. The ego, in experiencing the numinous, shudders with holy dread before an immensity that it is "wholly other" and that affects the ego in wildly opposing ways. In the next chapter we discuss Otto's account of the numinous and explain that, from a spiral perspective, numinous energy is a stage-related manifestation of the power of the Ground characteristic of initial spiritual awakening and regression in the service of transcendence. Here the focus is on the Dynamic Ground as the source of numinous energy rather than on numinous energy itself.

Earlier, we used the analogy of the genie in the lamp to illustrate how primal repression not only submerges but also quiets the Dynamic Ground, transforming it from a psychic source that is plenipotently active to a source that is greatly reduced in activity, "put to sleep." Here we can use the analogy of a volcano returning to life to illustrate the awakening of the Ground as numinous core of the psyche. Let us assume that a volcano has just become active after a long period of dormancy. It has not yet begun to spew lava, but it releases smoke and jets of fire and makes the earth tremble. This spectacle, let us assume, has numinous effects upon the people living at the base of the volcano: it causes them to shudder with dread; it petrifies them; it entrances them; it throws them into altered states of consciousness. Affected in these ways, the people of the volcano believe that a supernatural power originating deep beneath the earth has begun to manifest itself in the world. The ground under foot is still terra firma, but it now trembles. Moreover, the earth has ruptured at a central point, opening a duct to an invisible underground realm in which prodigious forces are astir.

Similarly, the person in whom the Dynamic Ground has just become active feels as though a supernatural power issuing from a point deep within the psyche has broken containment and has begun to manifest itself in the upper region of consciousness. The ego here resides near an inner volcano. The molten core of this volcano remains under ground and hidden from view, for primal repression, although ruptured at a central point, has not yet given way. The Dynamic Ground thus remains submerged, and primal repression continues to support the ego as terra firma and to shield the ego from the underlying Ground. The Dynamic Ground, however, is no longer dormant or inert, and a rupture has occurred. The Dynamic Ground is now not only the id but also a psychic core emitting plenipotent numinous energy, and primal repression is now rent in a way that allows some of this energy to rise into consciousness.

Our volcano story is not just a convenient analogy; it is a widespread mythological idea. People from cultures around the world have believed that volcanoes are openings to underground numinous forces or beings. Such a belief, for example, is evident in the Greek myth of the monster Typhon, said to be buried beneath Mt. Etna; in the Roman poet Virgil's account, in the *Aeneid*, of the entrance to the underworld, which he located in a volcanic region around Mt. Vesuvius; and in many popular beliefs about angry volcano deities, especially goddesses, for example, the Hawaiian goddess Pele and the Philippine goddess Darago. Active volcanoes are awesome, entrancing phenomena. It is understandable that they have captured the mythological imagination, which has seen them as portals to supernatural powers of a dark, hidden underworld.

The volcano, as mythological motif, belongs to a larger network of images known as the *axis mundi* group. According to scholars of the history of religion, people of widely differing cultures have believed that there is a world axis located at the center of the earth, which is marked by a cosmic mountain (e.g., Mount Meru of South Asian mythology, Mount Haraberazaiti of Iranian mythology, and Mount Himingbjör of Scandanavian mythology) or by a cosmic tree (e.g., Kiskanu of Babylonian mythology and Yggdrasill of Scandanavian mythology).[2] The cosmic mountain or tree, situated at the hub of the world, vertically intersects and thereby connects the three basic cosmic domains: underworld, earth, heaven. The roots of the cosmic mountain or tree sink deep into the ground, where primal energies are astir and gods and spirits of the underworld reside; and the upper reaches of the mountain or tree extend to the highest point on earth, where the mundane realm gives way to the realm of celestial gods and spirits. In thus connecting the three cosmic domains, the *axis mundi* is a channel through which the powers or beings of any one of these realms can pass into any other of the realms, which otherwise are separate spheres of existence.

Such a passage from one cosmic domain to another is what historian of religion Mircea Eliade (1969) called a "rupture of plane," a rent in the fabric of being that allows the powers native to one domain briefly to manifest themselves in another. According to the *axis mundi* cosmology, any such rupture of a cosmic plane is only an isolated or temporary opening and not a removal of the plane. Except for the point that opens—the *axis mundi* channel—the plane remains intact; and except for what passes through the opening from one cosmic domain to the next, the domains remain separate worlds. The *axis mundi* is the only channel connecting otherwise disconnected worlds. In the volcano analogy, the vent of the volcano is the *axis mundi*, and the smoke and fire indicate that a rupture of plane has occurred allowing forces of the underworld to enter the world above. The volcano has not yet erupted, and so the underground realm of molten rock remains hidden from view, a world apart. The underworld below and the world above, except for the smoke and fire released through the vent, remain separate worlds.

A similar conception of an underlying source of power connected by a central duct to a higher region of consciousness is found in Tantrism. In Hindu Tantrism the Dynamic Ground is represented by a bulb (*kanda*) at the base of the spine in which *kundalinī*, the "serpent power," is said to lie dormant in a coiled posture, ready to spring into action. Upon awakening, *kundalinī* can no longer be contained in its sleeping place and begins to ascend through a channel called the *sushumnā*, a primary energy conduit connecting the lower regions of the body to the head. Ascending through this channel, *kundalinī* manifests itself as the goddess Shakti, who awakens instinctual, emotional, and cognitive centers (*chakras*) and eventually unites with her consort, Shiva, at the crown of the head. Tantrism in effect incorporates the three cosmic domains within the body, with the *sushumnā* serving as the connecting axis. The lower world in which prodigious forces are astir—corresponding to the repressed but awakening Ground, the numinous core of the psyche—is situated at the lowest extremity of the body's trunk, and this lower world releases numinous energies into the upper world of consciousness through a central duct, corresponding to the *axis mundi*.

Whether pictured as an awakening volcano releasing smoke and fire through a vent, as a cosmic mountain or tree releasing energies and spirits through an *axis mundi*, or as a bulb at the base of the spine releasing *kundalinī* through a *sushumnā*, the awakening Ground is conceived as an underlying seat of supernatural power connected to the upper world of consciousness by a vertical channel, a channel through which the awakening power of the Ground ascends and, in doing so, ruptures the plane (primal repression) separating consciousness from the underlying deep unconscious. As the numinous core of the psyche, the Ground is no longer a sealed and dormant id, for the power of the Ground has been ignited. Currents of this awakening plenipotent energy rise through an aperture leading from the Ground below to the ego's psychic space above.

THE PSYCHIC UNDERWORLD

The volcano analogy is useful in representing the situation in which a reactivated but still submerged Ground releases numinous energy into the upper region of consciousness. The analogy presupposes both (1) that primal repression, although ruptured at a central point, otherwise remains intact and (2) that repressed nonegoic life, the "molten core" of the psyche, is still for the most part safely submerged beneath primal repression. The volcano analogy, useful for conveying this particular psychic situation, is less useful once development turns in the direction of regression in the service of transcendence, that is, once primal repression begins to give way. The volcano analogy ceases being apt in this new psychic situation because, once primal repression begins to give way, the ego no longer stands on solid ground. Primal repression is the terra firma that supports the ego "above ground" and keeps it from succumbing to the gravitational pull of the Dynamic Ground "below ground." Consequently, once primal repression begins to give way, the earth beneath the ego's feet opens, and the ego is drawn into a gravitationally charged underlying space. The volcano analogy—if revised, for the volcano is now an erupting volcano—remains accurate to the extent that this underlying space, the Dynamic Ground or psychic core, now begins to discharge potent energies across the entire range of nonegoic potentials (derepression). What is more evident from the ego's perspective, however, is the sense of losing the ground under foot and being pulled through a psychic chasm into an underlying realm. The Dynamic Ground is indeed now an erupting psychic core, but it is also a gravitationally charged underworld into which the ego is drawn.

Accounts of descent into the underworld are to be found in mythology, in spiritual literature, and in depth psychology. In mythology the descent is described in the many tales of the hero's journey, tales that Joseph Campbell (1949) summarized so brilliantly in *Hero with a Thousand Faces*. According to Campbell, the hero's journey is an odyssey that leads the hero into the underworld in search of a treasure or a special power. In the underworld the hero faces life-threatening tests and does battle with monstrous forces. The hero repeatedly faces destruction but somehow survives each encounter with death, usually by magical means or protection from the gods. In completing the journey, the hero returns to the natural world transformed, ready to perform extraordinary deeds. By virtue of having won the treasure or power of the underworld or simply by virtue of having survived the challenges of the underworld, the hero is now superhuman, like a god on earth.

To change the metaphor from under*earth* to under*sea*, the journey of descent into the underworld is expressed mythologically in accounts of a night sea journey of the sun. According to Leo Frobenius (1904), who gathered versions of this myth from many different cultures, the core themes of the myth are these: (1) the sun (representing the ego) descends into ocean depths; (2) the sun is then swallowed by a sea monster; and (3) the sun is released from the sea monster and rises for the dawn of a new day. Closely related to the myth of the night sea journey of the sun are myths of persons (e.g., Jonah) being swallowed by sea monsters only to be given a new lease on life. In general, the myth of the night sea journey and related myths are symbolic expressions of the need to descend into depths and therein to undergo a deathlike ordeal before being granted renewed or higher life.

Turning from mythological narrative to spiritual literature, the descent into the underworld is depicted as a spiritual seeker's passage through demonic realms, a passage during which the seeker is preyed upon by dark forces and subjected to an ordeal of trial and temptation. The seeker is tormented by evil spirits or apparitions: Satan's minions, *asura*s (Hinduism), the demon tempter Mara (early Buddhism), *makyō* or "diabolical phenomena" (Zen). In Western contemplative traditions, people at this stage of the spiritual path are counseled to exercise discernment and to pray for protection from God, angels, Jesus, Mary, or saints if they are to free themselves from evil and find their way to higher spiritual ground. In the primary Asian traditions, Hinduism and Buddhism, in contrast, people at this stage are counseled to exercise steadfast witness-consciousness or mindfulness so that they can liberate themselves from the snares of conditioned existence (*samsāra*) and achieve a higher, unconditioned plane beyond good and evil.

The best-known description of descent into the underworld in all of spiritual literature is Dante's account, in the *Comedy*, of the descent into hell. The pilgrim Dante, led by Virgil, descends through the many levels of hell, witnessing the afflictions of those condemned to eternal torment. This journey into the inferno is a necessary first stage of a longer journey that will lead Dante through purgatory to paradise. The pilgrim Dante must begin his journey by descending into hell because he learns essential lessons in hell, and in any case all above-ground accessways to higher spiritual realms are blocked. There is no way to ascend to higher spiritual realms without first descending into the depths. The *Comedy* locates the entrance to purgatory at the very bottom of hell. The descent into hell is thus a necessary stage of the pilgrim's eschatological journey.

In depth psychology, the descent into the underworld is a major thematic focus of the work of C. G. Jung. Indeed, it is Jung who first explained the archetypal significance of the idea of descent into the underworld. In Jung's interpretation, the many mythological and spiritual accounts of descent into the underworld are expressions of the archetypal imagination as it has tried to make sense of a fundamental reversal that occurs in the life course. According to Jung, we, especially at midlife, come to an impasse so far as our outer, worldly life is concerned and begin to hear a call beckoning us to explore the psychic world within. Responding to this call, we embark upon a journey of inwardness, a journey that retraces our developmental path to unconscious depths that were original sources of our existence. This return to origins begins at personal levels of the unconscious, disclosing the personal shadow and repressed biographical materials, and then proceeds to universal or collective levels, at which instinctual, numinous, and archetypal influences come powerfully into play. Both legs of this journey into underlying psychic realms are essential stages of what Jung calls the individuation process, a process that aims ultimately at whole-psyche integration.

In most accounts—whether mythological, spiritual, or psychological—the descent into the underworld or to the Dynamic Ground is not only a dangerous odyssey but also an essential stage of a longer journey. It is a dangerous odyssey because it poses the risk, variously conceived, of destruction, damnation, ensnarement, or psychosis. In posing such a risk, however, the descent into the underworld or to the Dynamic Ground is nonetheless an essential stage of a longer journey, for contact with the forces of the underworld is necessary for the attainment of higher life. In our examples, the hero must endure the challenges of the underworld if he is to be transformed from a mere human into a superhuman being; the sun must be swallowed by the sea monster if it is to be released for the dawn of a new day; spiritual travelers must pass through demonic realms if they are to free themselves from evil or liberate themselves from the snares of conditioned existence; the pilgrim Dante must learn about the torments of hell if he is to be ready for the lessons of purgatory; and the ego of Jungian depth psychology must encounter the energies and images of the collective unconscious if it is to move forward on the path of individuation.

THE SOURCE OF RENEWING LIFE

Once regression in the service of transcendence has run its course and the ego is in touch with the Ground, the introversion of psychic energy and the derepression of nonegoic potentials, the gravitational charging and the eruptive discharging of the Ground are complete. At this point, then—the beginning of regeneration in Spirit—the Dynamic Ground ceases being a dark underworld exerting an ineluctable downward pull, and it ceases as well being a psychic core ejecting pent-up, supercharged materials. The major negative effects of the Ground thus disappear, and the Ground begins to affect the ego in primarily positive ways.

If, however, the Ground now begins to affect the ego in primarily positive ways, it continues nonetheless to affect the ego violently. The awakened power of the Ground is still more than the ego can easily endure. The ego has not yet adapted to the plenipotency of the power of the Ground, and therefore the power of the Ground continues to violate, inflate, burst, arrest, and captivate the ego. It continues to be excessive, "too much." This excessiveness, however, is no longer perceived as harmful or malign and is perceived instead as a purgative-redemptive violence that is for the ego's own good. Accordingly, even though the power of the Ground continues to affect the ego violently, the ego now perceives the Ground and its nonegoic potentials as having restorative rather than destructive, regenerative rather than regressive effects. The Dynamic Ground, no longer a gravitationally charged underworld or an eruptively discharging psychic core, is now a source of naturally upwelling instinctual, affective, imaginal, and spiritual spontaneities. It is a source of healing and enlivening energies. In the terminology to be used here, it is "the source of renewing life."

As the source of renewing life, the Dynamic Ground has been depicted mythologically in symbols of fertile earth, a lush garden, and rejuvenating waters. The Ground is here the fertile soil of myths and rites of renewal. The Demeter-Persephone story, for example, gives clear expression to the idea of a deep source that releases a regenerating power of life. Demeter enacts this idea by allowing the grain to grow only during those seasons when Persephone, her daughter, is released from the underworld. In addition to their roles in Greek mythology generally, Demeter and Persephone (or Kore) were the central figures of the Eleusinian mysteries, which were secret rites of spiritual renewal. The Demeter-Persephone myth and many other myths of fertile soil and crop regeneration give not only literal expression to annual agricultural renewal but also symbolic expression to the inner renewal of regeneration in Spirit. During regression in the service of transcendence, the ego returns to the Ground; during regeneration in Spirit, the ego begins to take root in the Ground, which thus becomes the source of the ego's renewed life.

The Ground as source of renewing life is also depicted as a lush garden, especially a garden in which a sacred tree grows tall: the tree of life. The symbol of the tree of life is found not only in the Book of Genesis but also in mythologies around the world. As a symbol, the tree of life is similar to the images of the *axis mundi* group, discussed earlier, because the tree of life connects the three cosmic domains: its roots reach down from the surface of the earth deep into the ground, and its branches reach up from earth into heaven. The tree of life, however, differs from the images of the *axis mundi* group in that, in connecting the three cosmic domains, it integrates these domains as one world: the planes separating the cosmic domains have disappeared. The tree of life, in rooting beneath the ground, feeds upon underground energies and allows these energies fruitful expression in the world above; and the tree of life, in growing skyward, actually reaches into heavenly realms and is bathed in heavenly light. Moreover, in many versions the tree of life is twined by a climbing serpent or serpents, which symbolize vitality and health (e.g., the medical caduceus) and complete harmony of the instincts and Spirit (the serpent or serpents are climbing the tree rather than sleeping or lurking below). In these ways the tree of life, rather than rupturing the planes of otherwise disconnected worlds, brings worlds together in harmonious unity.

As source of renewing life, the Dynamic Ground is also depicted by images of water, for example, images of replenishing wellsprings, pellucid streams abounding in life, fountains of youth, and baptismal founts or basins. In this perspective the Ground is seen as a source of water possessing both cleansing and regenerating powers. The water possesses cleansing powers because it removes the accumulated stains of life, and it possesses regenerating powers because it gives renewed health, youth, and innocence to those who partake of it. The water of regeneration in Spirit washes away taint and sin, and it heals body and soul and stimulates new growth. It is a water of both purgation and redemption. One is made new again, without either the defilements or debilities of foregone years.

THE FERTILE-SACRED VOID

In its organization as psychic underworld, the Dynamic Ground is a separate cosmic domain. The ego, in descending into this nether world, departs from its own domain through a rupture of plane and enters what seems an alien world. In its organization as source of renewing life, the Ground is no longer a separate world, for the ego has established roots in the Ground. Still, as source of renewing life, the Ground is not completely native Ground. It is a Ground in which the ego has taken root and in which the ego is nourished and grows (regeneration), but it is not yet the ego's own Ground. The Ground does not lose all vestiges of otherness and become the ego's own Ground until integration is achieved.

The Ground that has become the ego's own Ground is a fertile-sacred void. It is a void because, unlike primal repression, the Dynamic Ground is not a terra firma. It is an open dimension of depth, which, as such, provides no solid under-footing for the ego. If, however, the Dynamic Ground is an open dimension of depth, it is not, as fertile-sacred void, an underlying space into which the ego is liable to fall. The ego need have no fear of falling, for the Ground is no longer a center of psychic gravity and is now instead a source of upwelling life. As fertile-sacred void, then, the Ground is a "full void" rather than an "empty void"; it is a dynamic plenum that buoys and uplifts the ego rather than a gravitational vacuum that might swallow the ego. This is not to say that the integrated ego is never drawn into the depths of the Ground, for indeed, at times, it is, for example, in moments of profound absorption and in the deepest states of sleep. The point, rather, is that the Ground, as fertile-sacred void, is not an underlying space that threatens to engulf the ego.

As *fertile*-sacred void, the Ground overflows with life. Although no longer a source of renewing life, it remains the source of life. It is the source from which life's myriad spontaneities—energies, impulses, feelings, images, and inspirations—arise. It is a source not only of instinctual life but also of creative and spiritual life. The spontaneities that arise from the Ground as fertile-sacred void begin as tiny bubbles that quickly expand and take on form as they ascend. These bubbles are not yet "things." Unlike fish in a pond, which have a stable form under water, the bubbles rising in the void are rapidly changing, self-organizing packets of energy. As such, they exist as bubbles only so long as they rise in the void. They burst once they reach the surface of conscious-ness and give psychic expression to their hitherto merely psychoid, implicit form. The fertile-sacred void, again, is a full rather than an empty void; although empty of things, it is teeming with emerging life.

As fertile-*sacred* void, the Ground is the source not only of life generally but also of spiritual life in particular. The awakened Ground is the seat of the power of the Ground in its plenipotent, free expression as Spirit, and the awakened Ground in its highest expression as fertile-sacred void is the seat of Spirit in its truest expression as transparent Spirit.[3] The emergence and unfolding expressions of the power of the Ground as Spirit are discussed in the next chapter. Here it suffices to say that the fertile-sacred void is the space through which transparent Spirit manifests itself in the soul. As a void that is full rather than empty, the fertile-sacred void is full above all with spiritual power. For the ego, the fertile-sacred void is the space through which God breathes the divine *pneuma* into the soul.

The emergence of the fertile-sacred void indicates that human development has come full circle or, rather, full spiral. End and beginning here coincide because the fertile-sacred void is a higher form of the primordial source of life experienced by the newborn. The fertile-sacred void and the primordial source of life are both expressions of the Dynamic Ground under conditions when (1) nonegoic potentials are fully awake and (2) the ego is harmoniously at one with the Ground. The fertile-sacred void and the primordial source of life are profoundly similar in these respects. Developmentally, however, these two expressions of the Ground differ by the widest possible margin, for the primordial source of life is a prepersonal organization of the Ground and the fertile-sacred void a transpersonal organization. The primordial source of life is a psychic womb from which the nascent ego is only beginning to emerge; the fertile-sacred void, in contrast, is a creation space and divine dwelling place with which the mature ego is completely integrated.

CONCLUDING OBSERVATIONS

In spiral perspective, the deep psyche is not an invariant source, structure, or realm. It is not an inherently prerational, instinctually governed unconscious, as Schopenhauer and Freud thought, or a constitutionally two-sided, pre-trans collective unconscious, as Jung thought, or an exclusively higher spiritual source, as some spiritual traditions have taught. Nor is the deep psyche in fact two separate psychic realms, one deep and one high, one a lower prepersonal unconscious and the other a higher transpersonal unconscious, as transpersonal theorists Roberto Assagioli and Ken Wilber have maintained. Rather, according to the spiral conception, the deep psyche or Dynamic Ground is a single psychic source that undergoes pre and then trans reorganizations in connection with the ego during the course of human development.

We have followed the developmental unfolding of the Dynamic Ground from its rudimentary prepersonal beginnings to its fully developed transpersonal expression. We have seen that the Ground manifests itself in many and markedly different ways, as primordial source of life, intrapsychic dimension of the Great Mother, split nurturant-dangerous Ground, id, mysterious gravitational attractor, numinous core of the psyche, psychic underworld or sea, source of renewing life, and fertile-sacred void. All of these manifestations, as we have seen, can be interpreted as developmental expressions of the same Dynamic Ground.

It is perplexing that the major theories of the deep psyche are so conspicuously at odds. The accounts of Schopenhauer, Freud, Jung, Assagioli, and Wilber and the accounts found in spiritual traditions such as Taoism and Buddhism are all profoundly insightful. Most of these accounts, however, are mutually exclusive as they stand. To affirm one is to rule out most of the rest. The discussion in this chapter moves in the direction of a more unified understanding. The spiral conception of development provides a framework within which major theories of the deep psyche can be fitted coherently, as stage-specific manifestations of the Dynamic Ground.

FOUR

ENERGY

HAVING IN THE last chapter presented a developmental account of the Dynamic Ground, we do the same in this chapter for one—the most important— of the nonegoic potentials of the Dynamic Ground: the power of the Ground. We explain how the power of the Ground expresses itself during the principal stages of the spiral path. As we shall see, the major developmental expressions of the power of the Ground correspond closely to those of the Ground itself.

TABLE 4.1

DEVELOPMENTAL EXPRESSIONS OF THE POWER OF THE GROUND

STAGE OF LIFE	THE POWER OF THE GROUND
Neonatal stage	Primordial reservoir
Early preoedipal stage	Reservoir opens; freely mobile plenipotent energy
Late preoedipal stage	Power of the Ground split into forces of light and darkness
Oedipal stage	From the splitting of the power of the Ground to the repression of the power of the Ground
Latency	Division of power of the Ground into latent libido (plenipotent, instinctually organized energy of the id) and active psychic energy (nonplenipotent, neutral energy of consciousness)
Puberty and adolescence	Libido awakens as intermittently active energy of sexual experience
Early adulthood	Stable differentiation of awakened libido and psychic energy
Crossroads	Introversion of psychic energy
Awakening	Awakening of power of the Ground as numinous Spirit

DEVELOPMENTAL EXPRESSIONS OF THE POWER OF THE GROUND *(CONTINUED)*

STAGE OF LIFE	THE POWER OF THE GROUND
Regression in the service of transcendence	Numinous Spirit intermixed with derepressing instincts
Regeneration in Spirit	Transforming Spirit
Ego-Ground integration	Transparent Spirit

THE PRIMORDIAL RESERVOIR

The archetypal motif of life emerging from a watery source has a twofold ontogenetic basis. First, the newborn as a physical being enters the world from the mother's womb, in which it had been enveloped in amniotic fluid; secondly, the newborn as a psychical being, as a nascent ego, continues even after birth to be enveloped in a fluidic medium: the power of the Dynamic Ground. The ego is at first an incipient ego still enfolded in the Dynamic Ground and, therefore, still immersed in the power of the Ground. It is enfolded in the Dynamic Ground organized as the primordial source of life; correspondingly, it is immersed in the power of the Ground organized as the "primordial reservoir."

Pooled as a reservoir, the power of the Ground is contained at its source in the Ground. It is gathered there as an untapped concentration of energy. The power of the Ground is not always pooled as a reservoir during the neonatal stage, for the newborn draws upon the power of the Ground—thus tapping the primordial reservoir—when awake and engaged in object-related activities. Many studies have shown that newborns are acutely aware of perceptual stimuli and preferentially attend to and eagerly engage select stimuli, especially those corresponding to the face, voice, and nurturing attentions of the caregiver. Newborns, then, when alert and engaged, channel the power of the Ground. Stimuli that capture the newborn's attention trigger a mobilization of the power of the Ground, which flows from its source in the Ground to the triggering stimuli, investing them with energy.

Although the power of the Ground is not always pooled as a reservoir during the neonatal stage, it is usually pooled in this way because newborns engage objects only intermittently and for brief periods of time. Newborns do not yet understand object permanence, and for this reason the objects they engage are only transient stimuli rather than enduring objects in a transcendent world "out there." Newborns have no awareness of an independently existing external world; consequently, they are prone to lapse into disengaged, inwardly absorbed states when attention-commanding stimuli disappear from awareness. In giving way to such states, newborns cease mobilizing the power of the Ground and yield to reimmersion in the power of the Ground, which regathers within the primordial reservoir.

The power of the Ground as experienced by the newborn is the power of the Ground in its *plenipotency*, that is to say, in its full intensity. In this plenipotent expression, the power of the Ground is an immense power that can easily overpower the ego—for example, by eclipsing, capturing, absorbing, inflating, or transporting it—and in relation to which the ego is inherently a lesser power. The ego, accordingly, is not only *the* subject of consciousness but also *a* subject of a superior power: the plenipotent power of the Ground. That it is thus related to a superior power is unknown to the ego throughout much of life because primal repression, in submerging the Ground, quiets the power of the Ground. During much of life the power of the Ground is active only in the diminished and usually invisible form of psychic energy.

The power of the Ground has four properties that need to be described before we can proceed further with the account of the primary organization and principal expressions of the power of the Ground during the neonatal stage. The properties in question are, strictly speaking, relational properties and, more precisely, causal powers. They are four basic ways in which the power of the Ground affects the ego, namely, (1) as an *amplifying* power, (2) as an *attracting* power, (3) as an *infusive* power, and (4) as a *dissolvent* power. The power of the Ground affects the ego by intensifying and magnifying the ego's experience (amplification), by exerting a gravitational or magnetic pull upon the ego (attraction), by inwardly energizing and inflating the ego (infusion), and, sometimes, by absorbing the ego or inflating it beyond the limits of self-cohesion (dissolution).

The power of the Ground is an *amplifying* energy because it intensifies the activity of psychic systems, accelerating and magnifying their objects. In the view presented here, the power of the Ground, in thus intensifying psychic systems, does not itself possess the character of any particular psychic system. It is not, therefore, inherently either a sexual energy (libido) or an aggressive energy, as classical psychoanalysis maintains.[1] To be sure, the power of the Ground energizes instinctual systems (along with other psychic systems), but it is not for that reason itself inherently instinctual in character. In the account that follows, then, neither libido nor aggressive energy in the original psychoanalytic sense is acknowledged. Still, it is useful to retain *libido* as a broadly inclusive term to designate the power of the Ground insofar as it is channeled through or contained in an instinctual system, be it sexuality or some other instinctual system. Understood in this inclusive sense, the term is useful because the power of the Ground, if not an instinctual energy by nature, is at least, as Freud explained, developmentally tied to basic instinctual zones. Libido, in the meaning just specified, is one of the three major expressions of the power of the Ground discussed in this chapter, the other two being psychic energy and Spirit.

The power of the Ground is an *attracting* energy because it exerts a gravitational or magnetic pull upon the ego. High concentrations of the power of the Ground (henceforth *energy cathexes*) and objects highly charged with the power of the Ground (henceforth *object cathexes*) elicit the ego's attention and can, if the accumulation of energy is sufficiently great, bind the ego in states of fascination or fixation. It is noteworthy that the ego is thus drawn to the power of the Ground irrespective of whether its perceived character or the perceived character of the objects in which it is invested is positive or negative. For example, things perceived as eerie or ghastly command attention despite being frightening. It is not so much the positive or negative charge of the energy affecting the ego as it is the intensity of the energy that draws the ego's attention.

The power of the Ground is an *infusive* energy because it acts not only upon the ego as a cathectic, attracting energy, but also within the ego as an energy that excites and inflates the ego. The ego is in some respects like a bubble, an elastic membrane that expands or contracts, becoming more or less energized, with fluctuations in air pressure, that is, fluctuations in degree of infusive charge. When the power of the Ground enters the ego, the ego is inwardly energized and expands, giving rise to experiences of highly charged spaciousness or effusiveness. The ego, in being infused by the power of the Ground, is at once stimulated and dilated. The inflowing energy has both amplifying and pneumatic effects: it not only charges the ego, intensifying its experience, but also inflates the ego, stretching and attenuating its boundaries.

The power of the Ground is also a *dissolvent* energy, an energy that can dissolve the ego. The power of the Ground can dissolve the ego in two ways, either cathectically, through absorption, or pneumatically, through inflation. Absorptive dissolutions occur when the ego is so drawn to an energy or object cathexis that it loses its separate boundaries and is absorbed without remainder in the accumulated energy or energized object. When the ego is absorbed within an energy cathexis, the resulting state can be called an "energy-based absorption"; when the ego is absorbed within an object cathexis, the resulting state can be called an "object-based absorption." In contrast to absorptive dissolutions, pneumatic dissolutions occur when the ego is inwardly inflated to the point at which its boundaries lose cohesion. Whereas absorptive dissolutions are states of envelopment or enstasy,[2] pneumatic dissolutions are states of unlimitedness or ecstasy. Pneumatic dissolutions are states of infusion that are so powerful that they burst the ego's elastic membrane.

Having set forth the four basic causal properties of the power of the Ground, we can now return to the discussion of the newborn and describe in a more precise way how the power of the Ground affects the newborn. The principal ways are these: (1) as a plenipotent amplifying energy; (2) as an attracting-dissolvent energy that draws the newborn into states of object-based fascination and absorption; (3) as an infusive-dissolvent energy that pneumatically inflates and bursts the newborn's ego; and (4) as an irresistible energy cathexis that repeatedly returns the newborn to absorption in the Dynamic Ground (reimmersion in the primordial reservoir, the oceanic experience).

As a plenipotent amplifying energy, the power of the Ground greatly heightens the newborn's experience. The newborn's senses and bodily tissues are supercharged with high-intensity energy, and the stimuli, sensations, and feelings experienced by the newborn for this reason possess great force and vivacity. Visual stimuli pulsate with rich, deep colors; bodily sensations pierce, gnaw, throb, soothe, or delight; and affective currents sweep through the body as powerful waves. The waking experience of the newborn, amplified by plenipotent energy, is superabundantly alive.

As an attracting-dissolvent energy, the power of the Ground magnetizes objects of the newborn's experience, rendering them cathexis objects. Because the objects thus magnetized are charged with an energy of plenipotent intensity, they have an especially strong allure: they fascinate the newborn and frequently draw the newborn into hypnotic absorption. These cathectically induced states are usually positive in tone, for the newborn has little attachment to self-possession and, therefore, usually gives way to the attracting-dissolvent effects of the power of the Ground without resistance, in experiences of delighted wonderment or captivation. In addition to having a positive tone, the fascinated and absorbed states in question are typically brief in duration. These states quickly pass because the objects that fascinate or absorb the newborn are only transitory groupings of stimuli. At one moment the newborn is entranced by one object, at another moment by another.

As an infusive-dissolvent energy, the power of the Ground affects the newborn by pneumatically inflating and, frequently, bursting its ego. The ego membrane of the newborn is delicate, and infusive currents of plenipotent energy easily expand it, often beyond the limits of cohesion. Most such pneumatic experiences, like the object-based cathectic experiences just described, are probably positive in tone. With little attachment to self-possession, the newborn likely yields to the infusive-dissolvent effects of the power of the Ground without resistance, in experiences of pleasureable expansion or effusion rather than experiences of painful distention or rupture.

States of intense amplification, object-based fascination or absorption, and infusive inflation or dissolution are distinctive of the newborn's experience when it is alertly awake. The newborn, however, is less often awake than it is asleep; and when awake, it is frequently in a disengaged, dreamy state. Despite being distinctive of the newborn's alert waking experience, then, the states discussed thus far are more the exception than the rule. None of them is the newborn's primary energic state. Rather, the newborn's primary state is a condition of energy-based absorption: immersion in the Dynamic Ground. Such absorption is the primary state because the power of the Ground, pooled as the primordial reservoir, is an immensely powerful concentration of energy, an energy cathexis, to which the newborn is irresistibly drawn and to which it yields, again and again. Because the newborn has little attachment to self-possession, it likely yields to reimmersion in the Ground, as it does to the object-based and pneumatic states discussed, without resistance. It probably experiences such reimmersion as a blissful return to the oceanic state from which it originally emerged.

THE RESERVOIR OPENS

The newborn, again, does not understand object permanence, and for this reason the sensory objects experienced by the newborn are only groupings of sensory stimuli, stimuli that cease to exist once they are no longer present to consciousness. When a previously noticed stimulus pattern reappears after having been absent from awareness, the newborn recognizes the pattern and responds to it, typically, as it did before. It does so, however, without understanding that the pattern corresponds to an entity that existed during the interval when it was not perceived.[3] The next two chapters discuss how an understanding of object permanence profoundly changes the nature of the infant's—and, later, the toddler's—experience. The focus here is on the power of the Ground, and the relevant point is this: Once the child begins to understand object permanence, the power of the Ground is no longer channeled only intermittently to transient stimulus patterns and begins being channeled in a sustained way to a world of transcendent, enduring objects.

Whereas the newborn is able to sustain attention upon objects only so long as they remain within view, the infant or toddler who understands object permanence is able to sustain attention upon objects even after they have disappeared from view. The child who understands object permanence can pursue objects after they leave the field of perception—at first by eye and mental projection (the infant) and then also by locomotion (the toddler)—and can search for new, hitherto unknown objects. Following the course of the child's attention, then, the power of the Ground now flows out from the Ground to the newly discovered world of transcendent, enduring objects. The power of the Ground is no longer contained primarily in the primordial reservoir, flowing out from this reservoir only for brief periods when the child is awake and focused on occurrent, passing stimuli, and now flows out to an independent, permanent world, a world upon which the child is intensely focused for extended periods during waking hours.

In flowing out to the newly discovered transcendent world, the plenipotent power of the Ground supercharges this world with amplifying, attracting, dissolvent energy, energy that at this point has a fundamentally positive character.[4] Charged with such energy, the newly discovered world is a realm that is pleasurably enhanced in its qualities and proportions (amplification), that is irresistible in its allure (attraction), and that is blissfully absorbing or enrapturing in its myriad pleasures (dissolvent effect). The new world that has opened up for the child is thus a fascinating, enchanted world. It is a radically new world that is full of treasures to discover, mysteries to delve, and marvels to behold. No wonder the practicing toddler has such a passion to explore! The world at this point is a prepersonal paradise, a garden of delight, as we explain in chapter 8.

Although the power of the Ground flows out to the world when the child is actively engaged, it flows back to the Ground when the child is fatigued.

When the child tires of exploration, the power of the Ground recedes from the world and regathers at its source, refilling the primordial reservoir. The power of the Ground is in this way both an outflowing and an inflowing energy. It is an energy that flows from its inner source to animate the world "out there" and an energy that flows back to its source so that the child can be rejuvenated in the bliss of sleep. Enticed by the outward flow of the power of the Ground, the child enthusiastically explores the external world as a garden of delight; and beckoned by the inward flow of the power of the Ground, the child yields pleasurably to reimmersion in the Dynamic Ground, its inner womb.

THE SPLITTING OF THE POWER OF THE GROUND INTO FORCES OF LIGHT AND DARKNESS

The child's unqualifiedly positive outlook, reflected in the reckless confidence with which it explores the world, is shattered at some point in the second half of the second year. The child loses its confidence at this point because the child discovers both (1) that the transcendent world "out there" is much larger and much more dangerous than previously was understood and (2) that the caregiver cannot always be relied upon to meet the child's needs. These discoveries destroy the child's self-confidence and trigger the defense mechanism of splitting, which is a thorough sundering of experience into positive and negative sides or realms. In the last chapter we learned that this preoedipal splitting is a splitting of the Dynamic Ground into two equal but opposite Grounds: a nurturant Ground and a dangerous Ground. We can now add that this splitting is evident in the child's experience of the power of the Ground as a division of this power into a power of light on the one hand and a power of darkness on the other.

The splitting of the power of the Ground is manifested in both its outflowing movement as the energy of the transcendent world and its inflowing movement as the energy of the primordial reservoir. The positive expressions of these oppositely directed currents of energy are just the expressions described in the last section, that is, those that pertain to the practicing child's delight in exploring the world and pleasure in returning to oceanic immersion. The principal way these positive expressions change after splitting occurs is that they are exaggerated by being set in contrast to equal but opposite negative expressions, with which they now alternate. To recapitulate, then, the positive expressions of the power of the Ground in its outflowing and inflowing movements are these: In its outflowing movement the power of the Ground is (1) a plenipotent amplifying energy that enhances sensory qualities in pleasing ways and invigorates the atmosphere of the world; (2) an attracting energy that renders the world irresistibly inviting, eliciting in the child an insatiable curiosity and passion to explore; and (3) a dissolvent energy that draws the child into pleasurable absorptions or that infusively enraptures the child. In turn, in its inflowing movement the power of the Ground is an energy that regathers as the restorative water of an inner womb (the nurturant Ground), to which the ego returns to enjoy the bliss of sleep.

The split-off negative expressions of outflowing and inflowing energy are the contrary opposites of these positive expressions. Accordingly, the negative expressions can be described as follows: In its outflowing movement the power of the Ground is (1) a plenipotent amplifying energy that magnifies sensory qualities in menacing (distorted, monstrous) ways and darkens the atmosphere of the world; (2) an attracting energy that renders the world morbidly fascinating, inducing obsessive preoccupation with invisible dangers and hidden monsters; and (3) a dissolvent energy that draws the child into dreadful absorptions or that infusively bursts the child's ego in painful or frightening ways. In turn, in its inflowing movement the power of the Ground is an energy that regathers as a lethally dissolvent energy or "acid" of an inner abyss (the dangerous Ground), an abyss that swallows and consumes the ego.

Generally speaking, whereas the outflowing power of the Ground in its positive expressions *enchants* the world, brightening its horizons and rendering it magical and delightful, the outflowing power of the Ground in its negative expressions *haunts* the world, darkening its horizons and rendering it monstrous and frightening. Correspondingly, whereas the inflowing power of the Ground in its positive expressions fills the Ground with life-renewing water, making the Ground once again a restorative inner womb (the nurturant Ground), the inflowing power of the Ground in its negative expressions fills the Ground with noxious fluid, making the Ground a seething inner abyss or witch's caldron (the dangerous Ground). When the outflowing and inflowing movements of the power of the Ground are in the positive mode, the child still lives in an enchanted world lovingly protected by the Good Mother. The child adventures with delight into a world that is appealing, invigorating, and, the child assumes, safe; and when the child rests from its adventures, it yields to the blissful, regenerating waters of the nurturant Ground. When, however, the outflowing and inflowing movements of the power of the Ground are in the negative mode, the child lives in a world of just the opposite character, a haunted world malevolently controlled by the Terrible Mother. The child shrinks back in fear from a world that is ominous and dangerous; and when the child wearies and is forced to let down its guard as it goes to sleep, it falls prey to the dark energies of the dangerous Ground.

PRIMAL REPRESSION AND THE DIVISION OF THE POWER OF THE GROUND INTO PSYCHIC ENERGY AND LATENT LIBIDO

As we know, the splitting of the Ground leads eventually to primal repression, which quiets the nonegoic potentials of the Ground. The power of the Ground in particular is quieted in this way. Moreover, in being quieted, the power of the Ground is divided into two separate energies: *psychic energy* and *latent libido.*[5] Psychic energy is a nonplenipotent neutral (i.e., noninstinctual) energy that circulates as the "fuel" of conscious life. Latent libido, in contrast, is a plenipotent instinctually organized energy that has been reduced from an active to an inactive default state. Psychic energy is the power of the Ground to the extent that it remains active despite primal repression and, therefore, is available to energize psychic systems generally. Latent libido, in contrast, is the power of the Ground to the extent that it has been restricted to an instinctual organization and "put to sleep," reduced to the potential energy of the Dynamic Ground organized as the id.

Clearly, primal repression does not completely deactivate the power of the Ground. If it did, the psyche would be depleted altogether of energy, and death would ensue. The power of the Ground, therefore, remains active to some degree. This active energy, not tied to any particular psychic system, is what psychoanalysis refers to as "neutralized" (i.e., deinstinctualized) psychic energy and what Jungian psychology refers to as "neutral" (i.e., general) psychic energy. Of these two conceptions, the view presented here is closer to the Jungian understanding; for the power of the Ground, as explained earlier, is not inherently the energy of any particular psychic system or systems, instinctual or other, and, therefore, is a neutral energy in a sense close to the Jungian usage. This neutral character of the power of the Ground, it should be stressed, does not mean that the power of the Ground lacks a nature of its own. The power of the Ground does have its own distinctive nature—which, as explained later in the chapter, can be defined in terms of its four basic causal properties—but this nature is not expressive of any particular psychic system or systems. If, then, the power of the Ground (and, therefore, psychic energy, too) is a neutral energy, that does not mean that it is featureless. Rather, it means only that it has a nature that is neutral with respect to psychic systems.

In agreeing with Jung that psychic energy is inherently neutral with respect to psychic systems, the view presented here departs from Jung in distinguishing between psychic energy as a diminished, nonplenipotent expression of the power of the Ground and the power of the Ground itself in its original plenipotency. To my knowledge there is nothing explicit in the Jungian corpus corresponding to this distinction, despite the fact that Jung describes the energy of the collective unconscious as a numinous—and, therefore, plenipotent—power. This apparent omission is significant, for the psychic energy of our conscious experience is not the awesome energy of the Jungian collective unconscious. It is, rather, something much less powerful, something much more safe. Psychic energy differs markedly from the power of the Ground in its plenipotency because primal repression greatly reduces the intensity level of the power of the Ground, somewhat as a vented covering placed over a fire reduces the intensity of combustion. Owing to primal repression, then, the power of the Ground in its original plenipotency is absent from conscious experience. It ceases being the active energy of consciousness and is reduced to an instinctually organized potential energy, latent libido, the "sleeping" energy of the id. Only a much-abated form of the power of the Ground continues to be active during waking consciousness. This diminished form of the power of the Ground, psychic energy, is an energy that retains the system-neutral character of the power of the Ground but not its original plenipotency.

Although the view presented here follows Jung in holding that the power of the Ground is system-neutral rather than inherently instinctual in character, it follows Freud in holding that the power of the Ground is nonetheless intimately linked with instinctuality. Primal repression is responsible for this connection, for primal repression, in quieting the power of the Ground, restricts it to its seat at the base of the bodymind. Primal repression thus confines the power of the Ground—except for what remains active as psychic energy—to an inactive instinctual organization. It reduces the power of the Ground to near dormancy within the lower instinctual regions. In being confined in this way, the power of the Ground assumes an acquired instinctual character. It becomes an instinctual energy by virtue of a restrictive developmental organization rather than by virtue of a system-specific inherent nature. Again, it becomes latent libido. In Tantric terms, it becomes *kundalini*, the sleeping serpent power lying dormant at the base of the spine.

According to the psychoanalytic view, latency signals a neutralization (i.e., deinstinctualization) of libido and aggressive energy. Freud believed that these instinctual energies are to a certain extent neutralized in the transition to latency so that, liberated from instinctual aims, they can be used by the ego in the exercise of its autonomous functions. According to the view presented here, in contrast, latency signals a change of just the opposite sort, namely, an instinctualization of a neutral energy rather than a neutralization of an instinctual energy or energies. This change, again, is only a restrictive instinctual organization of the power of the Ground, not a transformation of its inherent nature. Moreover, it is a restrictive organization that allows some part of the power of the Ground—namely, the part that remains active as psychic energy—to retain its neutral character. Nevertheless, the change *is* an instinctualization in that the power of the Ground is for the most part withdrawn from circulation and, reduced to a dormant state, forced to keep the exclusive company of the instincts.

In sum, primal repression divides the power of the Ground into active psychic energy on the one hand and latent libido on the other. Active psychic energy, nonplenipotent in intensity, is a system-neutral energy that circulates without restriction as the fuel of psychic systems during periods of waking consciousness. Latent libido, in contrast, is the potential power of the Dynamic Ground organized as the id. Latent libido is a plenipotent energy that has been reduced from an active to an inactive default state and that, although system-neutral by nature, possesses an acquired instinctual character by virtue of repressive confinement to the region of the root instinctual centers. The beginnings of the division of the power of the Ground into active psychic energy and latent libido occur in the late preoedipal stage, when the child first begins to struggle to overcome splitting. The division is not fully established, however, until the end of the oedipal stage, when the oedipal change of object forces the child to make a final commitment to primal repression.

PSYCHIC ENERGY AS THE INVISIBLE ENERGY OF CONSCIOUS LIFE

The consolidation of primal repression at the close of the oedipal stage introduces the stage of latency, which is a stage during which the power of the Ground, having been quieted, expresses itself only in the nonplenipotent form of psychic energy. Based as it is on a quieting of the power of the Ground, latency is a stage marked by a pervasive reduction in the intensity level of experience. Although this lowering of intensity is in significant respects a loss, it is on balance a gain, for primal repression, as we know, plays a positive developmental role. Primal repression is the necessary basis of the id-ego-superego structure of the latency period, a structure that allows the young ego to accelerate its development insulated from highly charged nonegoic potentials and with the assistance of internalized parental authority, the superego. The lowering of the intensity level of experience, accordingly, is a net gain at this developmental juncture.

Because psychic energy is an expression of the power of the Ground, it possesses the four basic causal properties of the power of the Ground, although not in their plenipotency. Psychic energy, then, is a power that amplifies experience, that attracts the ego's attention, that inwardly infuses the ego, and that, on rare occasions, if present at a sufficiently high degree of intensity, dissolves the ego. Psychic energy is an *amplifying* power because it is an energy that accelerates consciousness, magnifies psychic contents, and enlivens the world. Depending on the quantity of psychic energy in play, consciousness is quick or sluggish, stimuli are vivid or dull, and the world is vibrant or devoid of life. Psychic energy is an *attracting* power because, when channeled in the form of cathexes, it draws the ego's attention to the concentrations of energy thus created. Such cathexes are usually object (rather than energy) cathexes produced by conscious or unconscious desires, fears, or fixations. Psychic energy is an *infusive* power because, when active within the ego, it excites and inflates the ego and can induce highly energized, expansive states of mind. Finally, psychic energy is a *dissolvent* power because it can—again, on rare occasions, if present at a sufficiently high degree of intensity—dissolve the ego, either cathectically through absorption (e.g., consuming preoccupations, obsessions) or infusively through inflation (e.g., episodes of powerful effusive emoting).

Although the amplifying, attracting, infusive, and dissolvent effects of psychic energy are real and sometimes dramatic, they usually go unnoticed.

Psychic energy for this reason is usually invisible. It is invisible not only because it is a nonplenipotent energy, an energy with a lower intensity range, but also because it is almost always expressed through and, therefore, in the form of particular psychic systems or their objects. Psychic energy is almost always channeled through psychic systems and rarely expresses itself in a free, system-independent manner. The ego experiences psychic energy as the energy of psychic systems or their objects; it rarely experiences psychic energy on its own, as energy—whether in the form of energy cathexes or energy infusions. Cathexes of psychic energy are almost always object cathexes, and infusions of psychic energy are almost always channeled infusions, infusions expressed through particular nonegoic potentials or ego functions. Accordingly, psychic energy remains in the background not only because it is a nonplenipotent energy but also because it is almost always "in disguise," in the dress of particular psychic systems or their objects.

Because primal repression divides the power of the Ground into invisible psychic energy and latent libido, the child of the latency stage has little or no awareness of the power of the Ground. The power of the Ground in its plenipotency "slumbers" at the base of the spine in the form of latent libido, and psychic energy goes undetected as the energy of psychic systems. Both of the two organizations of the power of the Ground distinctive of the latency period, then, are unknown to the latency child. To construct a simile, the latency child can be likened to a fish swimming in a crater lake of a dormant volcano. The fish has no awareness of the prodigious energy that lies dormant beneath the floor of the lake (latent libido), and it has no awareness even of the water in which it swims (psychic energy). The water in which the fish swims is a transparent medium, not an object of which the fish is aware. The fish swims through the water and sees things in the water but does not—or only rarely, when the water is turbulent—notice the water itself.

THE AWAKENING OF LIBIDO DURING PUBERTY

The placid conditions of the latency stage come abruptly to an end with the awakening of sexuality during puberty. The id is agitated at this point, for the awakening of sexuality is an awakening of the slumbering power of the Dynamic Ground. This sexually triggered awakening of the power of the Ground, we should note, is an awakening of a limited sort. Specifically, it is an intermittent, partial, and system-specific awakening. That is—and here we begin with an abbreviated statement that will need elaboration—it is an awakening that expresses itself (1) *intermittently,* in discrete experiences of sexual arousal; (2) *partially,* in experiences of sexual arousal that usually but not always fall short of plenipotency (i.e., ecstasy, sexual orgasm); and (3) *in a system-specific way,* in the instinctually channeled form of libido. The following qualification should be added: Although the power of the Ground expresses itself during adolescence most evidently in intermittent discharges of libido connected with discrete experiences of sexual arousal, it also expresses itself in a more ongoing way as the energy of the awakening sexual drive, that is, as the erotically charged energy of importunate sexual desire. For the adolescent, if sexuality is not always "on" in the sense of arousal, it is rarely "off" in the sense of complete quiescence, abeyance of desire.

To clarify these points, let us fashion a variation on the fable of the genie in the magic lamp. Instead of a genie that manifests itself formlessly (representing unchanneled, free energy) or that manifests itself in ever-changing forms (representing energy channeled through many different psychic systems), imagine a genie that manifests itself only in a sexual way (representing the power of the Ground in the instinctually channeled form of libido). Additionally, instead of a genie that awakens and then remains awake, imagine a genie that awakens only intermittently and even then, usually, incompletely, not in the fullness of its power. Finally, instead of a genie that, when returning to the lamp to sleep, sleeps soundly, imagine a genie that slumbers restlessly, a genie that is disturbed by longing or desire even when asleep.

In this revised version of the fable, the times during which the genie is awake represent states of libidinal arousal. These states are sexually channeled high-energy states, which typically are brief in duration. The fact that the genie, when awake, is usually not completely awake indicates that these states of arousal, although high in energy, usually fall short of plenipotent, orgasmic intensity. As for the restlessness of the genie's slumber, it represents the persistence of the awakening sexual drive during adolescence, the nagging of sexual desire. It represents the fact that, for adolescents, libido is not only easily stirred but also, frequently, simply astir, active without having been activated by stimulation of the sexual system. If the sexual genie of adolescence usually does not awaken completely, neither does it sleep soundly.

On those occasions when sexual arousal culminates in orgasm, the power of the Ground expresses itself plenipotently and dissolves the ego in ecstasy. In sexual orgasm libido acting infusively within the ego inflates the ego and bursts it in euphoric outpourings. Although the ego still rests on primal repression and would be greatly threatened if the power of the Ground were to awaken outside the channel of sexuality, it still craves the plenipotency of the power of the Ground and for this reason, once sexuality begins to awaken, is impelled to experience sexual orgasm. Beginning in adolescence, sexuality becomes the vehicle for the reemergence of ecstasy in our lives. It becomes the means by which we begin, once again, to experience rapture, transport, bliss.

Sexual ecstasy and spiritual ecstasy have frequently been compared, and for good reason, for these two forms of ecstasy are similar not only in being experiences of ecstatic pneumatic dissolution but also in being expressions of the power of the Ground in its plenipotency. Related in these ways, sexual and spiritual ecstasy are sibling experiences. Sexual ecstasy, however, should be considered the junior of these siblings, owing to the following limitations: (1)

sexual ecstasy is an expression of the power of the Ground only in the limited form of libido; (2) sexual ecstasy is tied to the biological programs and personal preferences governing sexual arousal; and (3) sexual ecstasy is an experience that allows one, after orgasm, to return to one's former self, untransformed. Sexual ecstasy is an infusion of the ego with an instinctually channeled energy that, in the service of biological imperatives and personal desires, enraptures the ego without requiring it to grow. In contrast, as we shall see, spiritual ecstasy is an infusion of the ego with an unchanneled, free energy that, in the service of transcendence, transforms the ego in the direction of spiritual authenticity and wholeness.

If sexual and spiritual ecstasy differ in the ways just outlined, it follows that Reichian sexual therapy should not be considered a therapy that deepens spirituality, at least not under usual life circumstances. This is not to say that Reichian therapy is not good therapy. A robustly healthy sex life with strong, unconditional orgasms should be counted a blessing. The point, rather, is that a robustly healthy sex life should not—and again the qualification "under usual circumstances" is needed—be considered a means to spirituality. A healthy sex life typically occurs *within* the framework of the id-ego-superego structure. Sexuality usually is not a vehicle for *transcending* this structure. Sexual orgasm, then, although a sibling of spiritual ecstasy, usually is not a precursor of spiritual ecstasy. Sexuality gives expression to the "instinctual genie," and it does so, usually, in a way that does not lead to an awakening of the "spiritual genie," that is to say, the plenipotent power of the Ground in its free, unchanneled expression as Spirit.

Emphasis is placed on the qualification "under usual circumstances" because it is important to leave open the possibility of sacred sexuality, which is discussed in chapter 7. The spiral perspective stresses the intimate developmental interconnection between sexuality and spirituality and acknowledges that sexuality can be a gateway to profound spiritual experience.[6] In the spiral perspective, however, adolescence and even early adulthood are not stages during which such sexuality is likely to occur. The developmental context for such sexuality is, rather, the stages of spiritual transformation—initial awakening, regression in the service of transcendence, and regeneration in Spirit—which are stages during which spiritual and instinctual awakening are intimately interlinked. Accordingly, sexual arousal during these stages can lead beyond sexuality: the sexual genie can shed its sexual form and manifest itself as free plenipotent energy, or Spirit. Sexual arousal during stages of spiritual transformation can lead not only to sexual orgasm but also to spiritual transport. Again, however, experiences like these are stage related and would be premature if they were to occur during adolescence or even early adulthood. In the spiral view, then, Tantric, Taoist, and other practices of sacred sexuality have a special relevance for people who are near or in stages of spiritual transformation.

INTEGRATED LIBIDO: THE SECOND
LATENCY OF EARLY ADULTHOOD

Psychoanalyst Peter Blos (1968) held that the stable integration of awakened sexuality during early adulthood marks the beginning of a second and higher stage of latency. This second latency is like the latency of childhood in being a stage during which libido—and instinctual life generally—is usually quiescent rather than active or astir. It differs from the latency of childhood, however, in being a stage during which libido, although usually quiescent, is arousable, even plenipotently so, in response to sexual stimuli. For the young adult, the sexual genie awakens during sexual arousal and manifests itself plenipotently in sexual orgasm. Thereafter, however, the genie returns to the lamp (the Ground) to sleep more or less soundly. The genie never again sleeps as soundly as it did during the initial latency period, but it sleeps more soundly than it did during adolescence, when it was chronically astir.

The expression of libido during the second latency of early adulthood corresponds to the achievement of mature genital sexuality. The young adult usually experiences libido either as an energy that is awake in response to sexual triggers or that is at rest within the sexual system. For the young adult, libido ordinarily is not astir in nonsexual situations and, therefore, ordinarily does not, as it did for the adolescent, intermix with psychic energy in nonsexual situations to cause persistent sexual desire. By early adulthood, accordingly, the functional differentiation of arousable libido from psychic energy is more or less complete. Libido, now mature sexual libido, is an intermittently active energy confined for the most part to its "proper" system: the sexual system. It is an energy that is active nonplenipotently in sexual arousal and plenipotently in sexual orgasm but that otherwise is usually inactive, returning to quiescence as the potential energy of the id. As for psychic energy, it is now once again, as it was during the first latency of childhood, a neutral energy that is usually free of libidinal admixture. It is an active, nonplenipotent energy that serves as the fuel of psychic systems generally.

The organization of energy distinctive of early adulthood is stable and, once established, remains in place for most people throughout the rest of their lives. Because most people do not experience the power of the Ground in any form other than as intermittently aroused libido or as continuously active psychic energy, it is understandable that they would assume that the energies experienced during early adulthood include all of the energies available to us. This assumption, however, is incorrect, for many people, especially after finishing the developmental tasks of early adulthood, begin to experience energy of a radically unfamiliar sort: spiritual energy. In our terms this emergence of spiritual energy can be described as a second awakening of the power of the Ground, a second awakening following the second latency of early adulthood. This second awakening of the power of the Ground differs profoundly from the awakening that occurs during puberty in being an awakening that is not limited to instinctual triggers and channels of expression. Rather than being an intermittent awakening of the power of the Ground in the channeled form of libido, it is, as we shall see, a permanent awakening of the power of the Ground in unchanneled or free expression as Spirit.

EBB TIDE: INTROVERSION OF PSYCHIC ENERGY

Some people—frequently at the turn of midlife—become disillusioned with the world. Perhaps they have finished the developmental tasks of early adulthood and still lack a sense of fulfillment, or perhaps they feel as though the goals they have been working toward are unreachable. Whatever the reason, those who suffer deep disillusionment—not simply passing depression, however debilitating—begin to understand that the world cannot provide what they most deeply need; and for this reason they begin to thirst for something more than worldly rewards, something as yet unknown. This phenomenon of disillusionment is multidimensional and is discussed in ensuing chapters from several different perspectives. The next chapter discusses the effect of disillusionment on the ego system; chapter 6 discusses its effect on our perception of others; chapter 7 discusses its effect on the experience of the body; and chapter 8 discusses its effect on the life-world. The task here is to explain how disillusionment can be understood in terms of the energy system.

According to psychoanalytic theory, disillusionment and ensuing withdrawal from the world are symptomatic of an introversion of psychic energy. Psychic energy that previously had flowed out to the world, giving vibrancy to perception and zest to life, recedes from the world and returns to its source in the deep psyche, with the consequence that perception is dulled and lassitude sets in. The world, no longer invested with amplifying and attracting energy, loses its intensity and appeal; correspondingly, the Dynamic Ground, charged with introverted energy, becomes a deep center of psychic gravity. As we learned in the last chapter, the introversion of psychic energy, if sufficiently strong, can transform the Dynamic Ground into a black hole in psychic space.

According to Jung (1928), introversion of psychic energy sometimes occurs at or near midlife as a phase of a normal developmental process. In his view, the first half of life moves in an outward direction: At the beginning of life we differentiate ourselves from the inner collective unconscious; in childhood we explore the outer environment and learn basic interpersonal skills; and then in early adulthood we forge a worldly persona by committing ourselves to the responsibilities of work and relationships. Once this initial phase of our developmental journey is complete, according to Jung, we are ready for a one hundred and eighty degree turn in our basic life orientation. We are ready for an inward turn that would return us to the innermost bases of our being. This inward turn is ushered in, according to Jung, by a recession of psychic energy, which ceases flowing out to the world and begins flowing back to its source in the deep psyche. Psychic energy here undergoes a tidal reversal, changing from an outgoing tide that enlivens the world to an ebb tide that desiccates the world and gravitationally charges inner depths.

The introversion of psychic energy at or near midlife does not always lead to a new stage of life. For many people the introversion of psychic energy is only a temporary ebb tide, which is soon reversed. These people experience brief periods of withdrawal or depression and then become their "old selves" again. For others the introversion of psychic energy, rather than leading to a new, transpersonal stage of life, actually leads to prolonged struggles with psychic gravity, perhaps to chronic depressive or even borderline conditions. The introversion of psychic energy, then, is not itself sufficient to initiate stage transition to a higher developmental level. For such a transition to begin, it is necessary not only that introverted psychic energy draw one inward toward the Ground but also that introverted psychic energy trigger an awakening of the power of the Ground in its plenipotency. If transition to a higher developmental level is to occur, one must experience the power of the Ground not only as introverted psychic energy, a source of inner gravity, but also as awakening Spirit, a power that transforms and replenishes the soul.

THE AWAKENING OF THE POWER OF THE GROUND AS NUMINOUS SPIRIT

The Dynamic Ground usually remains quiet even when it is heightened in gravitational charge by introverted psychic energy. It remains the submerged, hidden id. It sometimes happens, however, that the concentration of psychic energy in the Ground is sufficient to ignite the prodigious potential power of the Ground. When such ignition occurs, the Ground ceases being an inert gravitational attractor and becomes an active psychic core emitting pulsations of plenipotent power, power no longer confined to—even if still closely linked with—sexual channels of expression. The ego, in experiencing such emanations, confronts what Rudolf Otto (1917) called the *numinous* and what is here called *numinous Spirit*. It is this awakening of numinous Spirit, not the introversion of psychic energy, that signals the true beginning of transition from personal to transpersonal stages of development.

To understand numinous Spirit, we need to develop more fully a distinction introduced earlier, namely, the distinction between *channeled* and *free* (system-independent) energy, which is not to be confused with the psychoanalytic distinction between bound and free energy.[7] Channeled energy is energy that is put to work as the fuel of psychic systems and their objects. Psychic energy—that is, nonplenipotent neutral energy—is the primary example of channeled energy because it is energy that is experienced primarily through and in the form of the psychic systems it energizes. As a channeled energy, psychic energy, as explained earlier, is rarely experienced on its own, as energy. Because psychic energy is almost always channeled rather than free, it rarely presents itself to the ego in any way other than as the energy of psychic systems.

Libido—that is, energy expressed through or contained in instinctual systems—is also an example of channeled energy. When libido is aroused, it manifests itself through instinctual systems and their objects, especially the sexual system and its objects. As a channeled energy, libido is usually invisible. One is usually aware of sexual feelings in relation to a sexually attractive person rather than of libido itself as the energizer of sexual experience. Libido, however, ceases being invisible on those occasions when sexual arousal culminates in sexual orgasm, for in sexual orgasm it is precisely the release of libido as a plenipotent, ecstatic energy that is at the forefront of the experience. Still, even though libido is experienced as energy during sexual orgasm, it remains a channeled energy, for sexual orgasm, as the culmination of sexual arousal, is an expression of the power of the Ground through a particular psychic system, the sexual system.

In contrast to channeled energy, free energy is energy that presents itself directly to the ego, without being expressed through psychic systems or their objects. Free energy can present itself to the ego in two principal ways, either (1) as a concentration of energy (an energy cathexis) acting *upon* the ego in amplifying, attracting, dissolvent (enstatic) ways or (2) as an infusive energy acting *within* the ego in amplifying, pneumatic, dissolvent (ecstatic) ways. Because free energy is not an expression of any particular psychic system or corresponding object, it is energy that, if experienced by the ego at all, is experienced *as energy*. Under conditions of primal repression, free energy is a rare exception to the rule. In our everyday experience, energy, whether psychic energy or libido, is usually expressed in channeled form and, therefore, is usually experienced in the dress of particular psychic systems and their objects rather than nakedly, as energy.

The situation changes dramatically, however, when introverted psychic energy triggers a reawakening of the power of the Ground, for the power of the Ground at this point begins to manifest itself in ways that are at once plenipotent and free. That is to say, it begins to manifest itself as Spirit.[8] The original plenipotency of the power of the Ground is restored, and the power of the Ground begins to emerge as an awesome power existing in its own right, apart from its channeled expressions as the energy of psychic systems. The ego, in experiencing this reawakening occurring in the depths of the soul, begins to sense the presence of a power that is immense (a plenipotent energy) and that is other rather than immanent to the ego (a free energy). Moreover, it begins to sense the presence of a power that, in addition to being plenipotent and free, has the more specific character of numinosity. The ego here, in becoming aware of Spirit, becomes aware more specifically of numinous Spirit.

The numinous, Rudolf Otto explained, is the *mysterium tremendum et fascinans*, a mysterious, immense, and fascinating power. Numinous Spirit is a *mysterium*, an unfathomable mystery, because the ego experiences numinous Spirit as an energy that arises from a source beyond the ego's own domain and that, in its manifest free form, is radically new and unrecognized by the ego.

Numinous Spirit is in these ways, to use Otto's expression, "wholly other." To be sure, the awakened power of the Ground has an uncanny trace of familiarity, for it is the same power that the ego long ago, in early childhood, experienced directly and on the most intimate of terms. This fact notwithstanding, when the power of the Ground is reawakened later in life, the ego perforce experiences it as something unprecedented. The mature ego has long since lost contact with free plenipotent energy, and for this reason it experiences the reawakened power of the Ground as wholly other.

In being a *mysterium,* numinous Spirit is more specifically a *mysterium tremendum,* a radically new power of prodigious magnitude. This immensity of numinous Spirit is what we have called the plenipotency of the power of the Ground. When the power of the Ground is awake, it is a power in comparison with which the ego's power is as if nothing, and it is just this immeasurably large difference in power that is first impressed upon the ego. The ego, consequently, is in awe of numinous Spirit. The ego, it is true, is at times exalted by the awakened power of the Ground. The ego, however, as Otto stressed, is also humbled, eclipsed, reduced to naught. Moreover, even the exaltations are a consequence of the immensity of the power of the Ground, which carries the ego aloft without anything the ego can do to resist, should it desire.

In addition to being wholly other and immense, numinous Spirit is compelling or fascinating (*fascinans*): the ego is irresistibly drawn to numinous Spirit. Numinous Spirit has this effect upon the ego because, as we have learned, the power of the Ground is an attracting force. It is a force that attracts the ego not only by binding its attention in states of fascination or fixation but also by drawing it into states of absorption, be they blissful entrancements or dreadful engulfments. When the ego gives way to absorption in the power of the Ground, it yields to the power of the Ground acting as an irresistible energy cathexis. The ego in face of numinous Spirit, then, stands before a power to which it is ineluctably attracted, a power from which the ego cannot look away, a power that draws the ego out of itself and beckons it to let go, to surrender.

The immensity and irresistibility of the power of the Ground explain another feature of the numinous stressed by Otto, namely, its *bivalence.*[9] The ego undergoing spiritual awakening is predisposed to experience the power of the Ground in two starkly contrasting expressions: as a power of light on the one hand and a power of darkness on the other. The ego undergoing awakening is prone to experience the power of the Ground in this bivalent, split manner because it is acutely ambivalent toward the power of the Ground. The ego is both drawn to the power of the Ground as an immensity that blissfully absorbs and exalts the ego and fearful of the power of the Ground as an immensity that dreadfully engulfs and otherwise violently overpowers the ego. The ego experiences the power of the Ground as a power that, it seems, could lead the ego either to higher life or to destruction, either to transcendence or to annihilation. The ego does not yet understand that these opposite possibilities are not "intentions" of the power of the Ground but are rather a consequence of its own unreadiness for the plenipotency of the power of the Ground. Accordingly, the ego projects its ambivalence toward the power of the Ground upon the power of the Ground and, therefore, misperceives this power as a bivalent, split power. The ego at least is strongly predisposed to misperceive the power of the Ground in this way.[10]

In perceiving the power of the Ground as a bivalent, split power, the ego perceives the power of the Ground as either (1) two separate powers, one a wholly good redemptive power and the other a wholly evil destructive power, or (2) as a single power with two equal but opposite, light and dark sides. In either case the ego misperceives opposite effects of numinous Spirit as an opposition inherent to numinous Spirit. It misperceives its own subjective ambivalence as an objective bivalence of the power of the Ground. Similar to the rapprochement child who, in its vulnerability, projects its ambivalence toward the Great Mother upon the Great Mother, thus splitting the Great Mother into the Good Mother and the Terrible Mother, the ego facing the reawakened power of the Ground is prone to experience this power in split fashion, as either two opposed powers or as opposed aspects of a single power.

Monotheistic spiritual traditions of the West, which assume the existence of an all-good supreme being, tend to interpret the bivalence of numinous Spirit in the first of the ways mentioned. They tend to attribute the light and dark dimensions of numinous reality to two separate and opposed forces: God and counter-God, conceived variously as Ahura Mazda and Ahriman, God and Satan, Allah and Shaitan. Major Asian spiritual traditions such as Hinduism and Buddhism also interpret the bivalence of numinous Spirit in the first of the ways mentioned, dividing numinous reality into realms of good gods or semi-divine beings (*devas*, *buddhas*, *bodhisattvas*) on the one hand and evil demons (*asuras*, Mara) on the other. Unlike Western traditions, however, Hinduism and Buddhism—or, more precisely, Vedanta Hinduism and Mahayana Buddhism—also posit an absolute ground of existence (Brahman and the Void, respectively) that is beyond good and evil.

In contrast to the main Western and Asian traditions, many animistic and ancestral forms of spirituality interpret the light and dark dimensions of numinous reality in the second of the ways mentioned, attributing both of these dimensions to the same spirits or ancestors. Spirits or ancestors in these traditions, accordingly, tend to have both good and evil aspects. They are usually beings who, if propitiated, can bestow favors and good fortune but who, if unheeded or defied, can be malevolent. This way of interpreting the light and dark dimensions of numinous Spirit is also found in polytheistic traditions such as those of ancient Egypt and classical Greece and Rome, although the gods of these traditions, in having both good and evil aspects, tend to be more diffusely, less exaggeratedly good and evil.

Otto's well-known definition of the numinous as the *mysterium tremendum et fascinans* applies most evidently to the numinous insofar as it acts upon the ego as an ego-transcendent, cathectic power. It also, however, applies to—and Otto, in terms different from those used here, has much to say about—the numinous insofar as it acts within the ego as an ego-immanent, infusive power. Although these latter effects differ from the former in being infusive rather than cathectic, they, too, exhibit the major features of the numinous: otherness, immensity, irresistibility, and bivalence.

Otherness: Infusively, numinous Spirit is wholly other or mysterious because it differs dramatically from psychic energy and libido, the only kinds of inwardly active energies with which the adult ego is familiar. The energic organization of adult life, as we know, includes only psychic energy and libido as active energies, and these energies are usually nonplenipotent in intensity and channeled in expression. Awakening Spirit, in contrast, is plenipotent in intensity and free in expression and, therefore, is experienced by the ego as a radically new and unrecognized energy, even though it is the very same energy as psychic energy and libido in a markedly different manner of expression.

Immensity: Infusively, numinous Spirit is immense because it is a plenipotent power that inwardly affects the ego in ways the ego is powerless to resist. Numinous Spirit pierces, dilates, inflates, and pneumatically bursts the ego irrespective of the ego's will. Numinous Spirit is a prodigious power not only in its ego-transcendent manifestation as a force that beckons, overawes, and absorbs the ego but also in its ego-immanent manifestation as a force that energizes the ego inwardly in intense, highly volatile ways.

Irresistibility: Infusively, numinous Spirit is irresistible because it intoxicates the ego and induces an unquenchable thirst for numinous infusion, a thirst that drives the ego to open itself to numinous Spirit even when the movements of numinous Spirit are "too, too much," so intense that they cause agony rather than ecstasy, wounding rather than opening. In those instances in which the plenipotent intensity of numinous Spirit causes agony or wounding, the ego's drivenness to experience numinous infusion is similar in some respects to addictive pathology.[11] The yearning for numinous infusion and the craving for the euphoria induced by drugs are similar because both are unappeasable needs for something that causes pain, needs that cause those who experience them to do "anything necessary" to satisfy, or at least placate, the needs. Similar in these ways, the thirst for numinous Spirit and addiction to drugs are, of course, otherwise utterly dissimiliar. In particular, they differ entirely in their long-term effects: whereas addiction to drugs has no redeeming value, thirst for numinous Spirit has precisely redeeming—that is to say, redemptive, salvific—value.

Bivalence: Infusively, numinous Spirit is bivalent because the ego undergoing initial awakening, when violently pierced, agitated, or burst by the power of the Ground, is prone to perceive this power as an inherently destructive or malign power or as a power that has an inherently destructive or malign side. Again, the ego is prone to this perception because it has not yet adjusted to the plenipotency of the power of the Ground. The ego, overwhelmed by the immensity of the power of the Ground, experiences strong ambivalence toward the power of the Ground and is for this reason prone to project bivalence upon the power of the Ground. During initial awakening, then, the ego is prone to experience the infusive movement of the power of the Ground not only as a movement of a redemptive power that opens, transports, and enraptures the ego but also as a movement of a dark power that wounds, dislocates, and ruptures the ego. (See note 10.)

In sum, introverted psychic energy can trigger a reawakening of the power of the Ground, which begins to express itself in plenipotent and free form as Spirit and, more specifically, as numinous Spirit. In experiencing numinous Spirit, the ego is exposed, both from without (ego-transcendently, cathectically) and from within (ego-immanently, infusively), to a power that is wholly other, immense, irresistible, and bivalent. The ego is cathectically drawn to this power and summoned to yield to it, and it is inwardly infused by this power and dilated, inflated, and "blown away" by it. Owing to its unreadiness and consequent ambivalence, the ego perceives the power of the Ground as having a bivalent, split nature—a nature that, it seems, confronts the ego with opposite possible destinies: salvation or damnation, transcendence or psychosis. When the power of the Ground is reawakened, then, the ego's world is profoundly changed. The ego discovers that it is a powerless subject in the presence of a *mysterium tremendum et fascinans,* and it feels as though its ultimate fate lies in the balance.

SPIRITUAL AWAKENING AND INSTINCTUAL DEREPRESSION

Because primal repression restricts the power of the Ground to an instinctual organization as libido, the awakening of the power of the Ground as numinous Spirit is also, eventually if not at first, an awakening of libido. The qualification "eventually if not at first" is inserted because the awakening process in its initial phases may show no signs of instinctual derepression. An awakening volcano typically releases hot gases before it begins to erupt and discharge lava; similarly, the awakening Dynamic Ground typically releases numinous "vapors" before it begins to derepress and discharge libido. The initial awakening of Spirit, then, is typically signaled by a manifestation of numinous energy that is without significant instinctual coloration. As initial awakening deepens, however, the underlying association of the power of the Ground with instinctual life begins to be revealed; and at this point numinous energy begins to be intermixed with instinctually channeled energy, libido. This intermixing of numinous Spirit with libido indicates that initial spiritual awakening has come to an end and regression in the service of transcendence has begun.

If the awakening of Spirit is thus eventually also an awakening of libido, it is an awakening of libido of a special sort; for unlike the awakening of libido that occurs during puberty, this awakening does not leave the power of the Ground organized as libido. On the contrary, it is an awakening of libido that is at the same time a liberation of the power of the Ground from its instinctual organization, an awakening, therefore, that allows the power of the Ground to begin expressing itself as a free rather than a channeled energy. The instinctual coloring of numinous Spirit that occurs in the awakening process thus reflects the undoing of the instinctual organization imposed upon the power of the Ground by primal repression. An image frequently used in South Asian spiritual traditions to express this rising of spiritual life from lowly instinctual origins is that of the lotus emerging from a swamp. Spirituality in this and other ways is an intimate companion of the instincts.

The bivalence of numinous Spirit becomes all the more dramatic once instinctual derepression begins, for the dark dimension of numinous Spirit is now associated with instinctuality and the light dimension, in consequence, with anti-instinctuality. During regression in the service of transcendence, then, numinous Spirit in its dark dimension is perceived as a power that is not only destructive and malign but also primitive and rapacious. In the mythological imagination, this dark instinctual power is depicted as a beast of the underworld or undersea, and the awakening of this power is depicted as an awakening of the beast from its slumber. Again, however, this awakening is an awakening of a special sort, for it is not only an awakening of a beast of the underworld or undersea but also an awakening of this beast from its bestiality. It is an awakening that progressively reveals that the power of the Ground is not inherently bestial but is rather a power that, in no way opposed to instinctuality, is itself pristinely spiritual in nature.

This fact, however, is not fully understood until regression in the service of transcendence has completed its work. During regression in the service of transcendence, then, the ego is prone to perceive recrudescing instinctuality as a bestial power opposed to spirituality. In Tantric terms, the ego does not yet understand that the awakening serpent power *kundalinī* is an initial aspect or phase of the manifestation of the goddess Shakti and, therefore, perceives *kundalinī* as a lower power in opposition to Shakti. In our terms, the ego does not yet understand that derepressing libido is an initial aspect or phase of the liberation of Spirit and, therefore, perceives libido as a lower power in opposition to Spirit. Regression in the service of transcendence is a stage during which the ego is predisposed to superimpose an instinctual–anti-instinctual bivalence upon the dark-light bivalence of numinous Spirit and, consequently, to perceive instinctuality as opposed to the spiritual process.[12]

FROM NUMINOUS SPIRIT TO TRANSFORMING SPIRIT

Numinous Spirit eventually gives way to *transforming Spirit*, the power of spiritual regeneration. If numinous Spirit is the power of the Ground experienced as wholly other, immense, irresistible, and bivalent, transforming Spirit is the power of the Ground experienced as immense and irresistible but no longer as wholly other or bivalent. Transforming Spirit is the power of the

Ground experienced as kindred rather than wholly other and as univalent (i.e., wholly redemptive, no longer destructive or malign) rather than bivalent. In this section we discuss the kindredness and univalence of transforming Spirit, beginning with the latter. We discuss one other aspect of transforming Spirit as well, namely, its excessiveness.

The ego experiences transforming Spirit as a univalent power because, having weathered the challenges of initial awakening and regression in the service of transcendence, the ego is much better able to tolerate the plenipotency of the power of the Ground and is able, looking back, to see that the long-term effects of the power of the Ground have been salutary. The ego in this way loses its fear of the power of the Ground and is able to see that even the most painful and highly instinctualized manifestations of the power of the Ground have been for the ego's own good. The ego, that is, is able to see that these manifestations were not evil doings of a dark force or dark side of Spirit but were rather initial expressions of the purgative and regenerative work of Spirit. As the ego increases its capacity for and understanding of Spirit, then, it gradually outgrows its ambivalence toward Spirit and is able finally, at the transition from regression in the service of transcendence to regeneration in Spirit, to cease projecting bivalence upon Spirit.

The ego experiences transforming Spirit as a kindred power because, by the time regeneration in Spirit begins, the awakened power of the Ground is no longer radically new to the ego's experience and, as we have just seen, is no longer perceived as a power opposed to the ego's interests. The power of the Ground, as transforming Spirit, is still mysterious—although now more in the sense of being miraculous than in the sense of being strange—and it is still an immense power that frequently overpowers the ego. The power of the Ground, however, is no longer wholly other either in the sense of being foreign or in the sense of being menacing. The ego no longer experiences the power of the Ground as other in either of these senses because the ego is now well familiar with the power of the Ground and has already accepted the power of the Ground as the sovereign power of the soul. By the beginning of regeneration in Spirit, then, the ego has begun to perceive Spirit as a superior ally or partner rather than as something alien or inimical. It has begun to perceive Spirit as a power that, although not yet wholly self, is no longer wholly other, which is just to say that it has begun to perceive Spirit as a kindred power. The ego, for example, may here begin to perceive Spirit as a counselor, guardian, or lover. These manifestations of Spirit are discussed in the next chapter.

Although the power of the Ground, as transforming Spirit, is no longer either bivalent or wholly other, it continues to be violent, that is to say, excessive in its effects. To be sure, the psychic atmosphere is now much less turbulent than it was during regression in the service of transcendence. The eruptive derepression of nonegoic potentials is over; and the ego, as noted, is much better adapted to the awakened power of the Ground. The ego, however, is still not fully adapted to plenipotent energy and, therefore, is still frequently overpowered by it. The intensity of the power of the Ground, as transforming Spirit, still frequently exceeds the ego's tolerance. The intensity of the power of the Ground is thus excessive. It is both "too much" in the sense of being unbearably pleasurable and "too, too much" in the sense of being agonizingly painful.

Despite being affected violently by the power of the Ground, the ego no longer fears the power of the Ground. The ego now perceives the power of the Ground as a univalent power and, therefore, perceives the excessiveness of the power of the Ground as having beneficial—healing, rejuvenating, redemptive—long-term effects. The ego understands that the pain inflicted by transforming Spirit is caused by a power that is the ego's own superior ally and, therefore, is a pain that is a necessary part of the ego's own spiritual growth. The ego for this reason does not resist transforming Spirit, even when the consequences of doing so are frightening or seemingly dangerous. Should, for example, transforming Spirit manifest itself as an immense energy cathexis, the ego yields to absorption, despite fears of engulfment; and should transforming Spirit manifest itself as a highly charged infusive current, the ego surrenders to the inner movement of energy, however excruciating the experience might be.

The pleasurable-painful excessiveness of transforming Spirit is well documented in mystical literature, especially in writings on contemplative prayer. St. Teresa of Avila, the preeminent representative of this genre, provides a rich account of the delectations and devastations that transforming Spirit can inflict. Teresa speaks of being abducted, captivated, absorbed, pierced, cauterized, ravished, transported, and enraptured by Spirit. As a cathectic power, transforming Spirit irresistibly attracts and lays claim to the ego, drawing the ego—whether by "abduction" or "seduction"—into spiritual absorptions; and as an infusive power, Spirit dilates, penetrates, violates, inwardly caresses, burns, intoxicates, euphorically excites, and enraptures the ego. Donald Blais (1997), who has written an illuminating account of Teresa's mystical transformation, stresses that for Teresa—and for others, too—the effects of Spirit can be so excessive as to appear pathological. Still, the ego continues to yearn for Spirit.

Although transforming Spirit is excessive in the ways just described, we should stress that this excessiveness is most pronounced in the early phases of regeneration in Spirit. The excessiveness of transforming Spirit is a consequence of the ego's incomplete adaptation to plenipotent energy, and it therefore gradually becomes less severe as the ego's adaptation improves. During regeneration in Spirit, then, the violent effects of the power of the Ground steadily decrease. Unbearable pleasures and agonizing pains gradually disappear, and the ego, accordingly, is less often overpowered and more often empowered by the power of the Ground. As regeneration in Spirit unfolds in the direction of integration, the ego is increasingly better able to function in the high-intensity environment of plenipotent energy. It becomes an increasingly effective agent of Spirit.

In sum, regeneration in spirit is a stage during which the power of the Ground, as transforming Spirit, is no longer bivalent but still affects the ego in a violent manner. The ego surrenders to transforming Spirit as a wholly redemptive power and cooperates with it as it transforms the ego in pleasurable-painful ways. The ego yearns for transforming Spirit even when it knows that the intensity of transforming Spirit will be painful. The ego accepts the painful effects of the power of the Ground because it realizes that they are a necessary part of the spiritual growth process, and in any case these painful effects, along with violent effects generally, occur less often as the ego's tolerance for the awakened power of the Ground grows. Intense pleasures and pains gradually give way to states of composed intensity as the ego becomes better able to function in the rarified atmosphere of Spirit.

FROM TRANSFORMING SPIRIT TO TRANSPARENT SPIRIT

Numinous Spirit, as we have seen, emerges during initial awakening and then is intermixed with derepressing instincts during regression in the service of transcendence. As a particular form of Spirit, numinous Spirit is distinguished primarily by its stark otherness, its bivalence, and its connection with instinctual derepression. Numinous Spirit gives way to transforming Spirit once regression in the service of transcendence has run its course and regeneration in Spirit begins. Transforming Spirit is like numinous Spirit in having an intensity that exceeds the ego's tolerance, but it differs from numinous Spirit in being kindred rather than wholly other, univalent rather than bivalent, and free for the most part of instinctual intermixture. In turn, transforming Spirit gives way to *transparent Spirit* once the regeneration process has completed its work and the ego is fully integrated with the Dynamic Ground. Reflecting the seamless ego-Ground unity of the stage of integration, the primary distinguishing features of transparent Spirit are complete "non-otherness"—for transparent Spirit is not other even in the sense of being kindred—and nonexcessiveness or nonviolence. Under integrated conditions the awakened power of the Ground is no longer to any degree other in relation to the ego, and it no longer, or only rarely, affects the ego in a violent manner.

Free of all vestiges of otherness, transparent Spirit is the ego's own Spirit or higher Self. It is the ultimate "I" and, because we all share this higher Self, the ultimate "We." Whereas numinous Spirit is wholly other in relation to the ego and whereas transforming Spirit is kindred to the ego but still other to some degree, transparent Spirit is the ego's very self or, rather, Self. Transforming Spirit, in being closely related to the ego, is a kindred Spirit; nevertheless, as a power that *affects* the ego, it is not yet a power that *is* the ego. Transparent Spirit, in contrast, is just such a power. Because the integrated ego gives itself completely to Spirit, Spirit, as transparent Spirit, gives itself completely to the ego.

As is explained more fully in the next chapter, the integrated ego and transparent Spirit form a completely unified system, an ego-Spirit or self-Self system.

The intense enstasies and ecstasies of the early phases of the regeneration process are dramatic phenomena, but they are symptomatic of spiritual immaturity. They indicate that the ego is not yet fully adapted to the plenipotency of Spirit and for this reason is not yet a fully capable instrument of Spirit. The disappearance of these phenomena in later phases of regeneration in Spirit, therefore, is by no means a loss. On the contrary, it is an indication of spiritual growth. In growing in Spirit, then, the ego is affected less and less violently by Spirit. It is increasingly empowered and decreasingly overpowered by Spirit. In arriving at integration, the ego is fully developed in its own functions and firmly anchored in the Ground and, therefore, is seldom taken captive or inflated wildly by the power of the Ground. Especially strong emanations of the power of the Ground can overpower the integrated ego, as, for example, occurs in experiences of profound mystical rapture. Experiences like these, however, are rare gifts. Usually, Spirit, as transparent Spirit, is a nonviolent power, a power of which the ego is an effective instrument.

The point was made earlier that the power of the Ground does not have the inherent character of any psychic system and, in particular, that it is not inherently a sexual energy or an aggressive energy, as classical psychoanalysis maintains. The power of the Ground energizes all psychic systems without itself possessing the nature of any of them. In other words, it is a system-neutral energy. If, however, the power of the Ground is a system-neutral energy, it is not for that reason a completely featureless energy, an energy without a nature of its own. The power of the Ground does have an intrinsic nature, a nature that is revealed through its basic causal properties. This nature, however, is camouflaged throughout most of human development and does not become evident until integration is achieved. It is only after integration is achieved that the power of the Ground manifests itself transparently. Spirit manifests itself as transparent Spirit only to the integrated person.

To recall, the power of the Ground has four basic causal properties: it is an amplifying energy, an attracting energy, an infusive energy, and a dissolvent energy. The power of the Ground has these causal properties in all of its modes of expression: plenipotent, nonplenipotent, channeled, free, libidinal, neutral, bivalent, univalent, overpowering, empowering, wholly other, kindred, non-other. However, although the power of the Ground has these four properties in all of its modes of expression, it reveals itself transparently through these properties only when it expresses itself (1) *plenipotently,* in the fullness of its power; (2) *freely,* without taking on the dress of particular psychic systems or their objects; (3) *integrally,* under integrated conditions, without being hidden by repression or obscured by otherness; and (4) *nonviolently,* without distortions arising from disruption or derangement of faculties. In its forms as numinous Spirit and transforming Spirit, the power of the Ground expresses itself in ways that satisfy the first two of these conditions but not the last two.

Both numinous Spirit and transforming Spirit are plenipotent and free in expression; they also, however, are at least to some degree other in relation to the ego and violent in the manner they affect the ego. Numinous Spirit is wholly other in relation to the ego and bivalent in its violent effects; and transforming Spirit, although closely allied with the ego, is still other in relation to the ego and, although univalent, is still excessive and disruptive in its effects. Only in its manifestation as transparent Spirit does the power of the Ground express itself in a way that satisfies all four of the conditions stated. Only in its manifestation as transparent Spirit, then, does the power of the Ground fully reveal itself through its causal properties.

The four causal properties of the power of the Ground reveal four inherent dimensions of the power of the Ground. These dimensions are introduced here by stating them in the abstract, and then each of the dimensions is discussed in turn. The four dimensions are these: (1) *light:* as an amplifying energy, the power of the Ground is an energy that irradiates the world and incandesces consciousness; (2) *love:* as an attracting energy, the power of the Ground is an energy that increases the attractiveness of—and thereby our attraction to—the world and other people; (3) *connection:* as both an attracting and an infusive energy, the power of the Ground is an energy that brings us into intimate contact with the world and others; and (4) *union:* as a dissolvent energy, the power of the Ground is an energy that releases us from self-boundaries and allows us to experience our underlying oneness with the world and others.

As an amplifying energy, the power of the Ground reveals itself under integrated conditions to be an energy that irradiates the world and incandesces consciousness. The power of the Ground, as transparent Spirit, flows out from the Ground and bathes the world in radiant light, giving the world and everything in it a sparkle, freshness, richness, and depth. Amplified by transparent Spirit, the sky scintillates and sensory qualities gleam with a brilliant yet soothing luster. In thus lighting up the world, transparent Spirit lights up consciousness as well. Conciousness glows with incandescent clarity, for the nonviolent plenipotency of transparent Spirit amplifies consciousness without agitating or obscuring it, making it at once intense and clear, keen and lucent. The integrated person is in this way *enlightened* by the power of the Ground. Such enlightenment does not consist of moments— or days or weeks—of heightened consciousness (e.g., *satori* flashes, episodes of intense clarity), which are characteristic of less mature, preintegrated stages of the spiritual process. The enlightenment of the integrated person is not an intermittent switching on of interior light; rather, it is an achieved higher level of illumination.

As an attracting energy, the power of the Ground reveals itself under integrated conditions to be an energy that enhances the attractiveness of—and thereby our attraction to—the world and other people, which is to say that it reveals itself as the power of love. The world, charged with plenipotent attracting energy, is beautiful and precious beyond measure. It is a world that is perfect just as it is, a world that elicits our affirmation, our reverential gratitude. Imbued with transparent Spirit, everthing in the world possesses sacred value, not only objects but also people. Indeed, people especially possess sacred value because they are themselves sources of this value. They are not only objects on which the power of the Ground is projected but also subjects from whom the power of the Ground emanates—whether in plenipotent and free expression, as Spirit, or in nonplenipotent or channeled forms, as psychic energy or libido. Under integrated conditions, then, not only the world but also and especially people possess love-eliciting sacred value. The integrated person is well aware of the dangers of nature and the shortcomings of human beings, but this awareness in no way detracts from the integrated person's unconditional love of the world and love of others.

As both an attracting and an infusive energy, the power of the Ground reveals itself under integrated conditions to be an energy that establishes connections, spiritual linkages, between self and world and self and others. As an attracting energy, the power of the Ground not only enhances the value of the world and others but also draws us out of ourselves to make intimate contact with the world and others. In turn, as an infusive energy, the power of the Ground inwardly expands the ego and then overflows ego boundaries, pouring into the world. Such infusion, in expanding the ego, is not experienced by the ego as an enlargement of its stature or value. That type of expansion, ego inflation, is symptomatic of spiritual immaturity. For the spiritually mature person, infusive expansion, rather than swelling the ego within itself, carries the ego beyond itself. It carries the ego into the world and enhances the ego's sense of belonging to the world. In thus enhancing the ego's sense of belonging to the world, infusive expansion also enhances the ego's sense of belonging with others, who are now perceived—as is explained in chapter 6—as siblings in Spirit. Transparent Spirit is the Spirit of connection, of belonging to the world and belonging with others as members of the human family.

Finally, as a dissolvent energy, the power of the Ground reveals itself under integrated conditions to be a power that allows us to experience our underlying oneness with the world and others. As a dissolvent energy, the power of the Ground sometimes completely eliminates the boundaries of individuated selfhood—whether cathectically, by drawing the ego into absorption, or infusively, by expanding the ego beyond delimitation—and thereby enables us to experience not only a sense of connection but also a sense of identity (nondual unity) with the world and others. No good purpose would be served, of course, if this experience of identity were to undermine individuated existence. That would lead only to regression, and the work of Spirit is progressive rather than regressive. Spirit, then, in leading us to union, leads us to a transcendence in which we temporarily let go all differences so that, having savored oneness, we can increase our appreciation of diversity once we return from union to individuated awareness.

Corresponding to the distinctive ways in which it reveals itself to the integrated person through its causal properties, the power of the Ground as transparent Spirit can be said to have the fourfold character of light, love, connection, and union. Transparent Spirit is a power that illuminates the world and consciousness, that elicits love of the world and others, that moves us to reach out to the world and others, and that allows us to savor our underlying oneness with the world and others. Although, in my opinion, we cannot know the ultimate origin of the power of the Ground—whether it is a metaphysical energy that descends from a heavenly "above" or a this-worldly energy that arises from a biological "below"—we can know the basic character of the power of the Ground as light, love, connection, and union. Whatever its ultimate origin may be, the power of the Ground, as transparent Spirit, is the sacred power to which the religions of the world have prayed and in which they have rejoiced. It is the luminous, loving, connecting, and unifying power that is our shared highest Self and ultimate good.

FIVE

THE EGO

THE EGO IS the main subject of this book. It is the "self" about which we are principally concerned, even though it is a lesser self in relation to Spirit, our higher Self. It is the ego's experience about which we have been speaking and about which we will continue to speak. In previous chapters we considered the ego's unfolding interaction with the Dynamic Ground and the power of the Ground, and in subsequent chapters we consider the ego's unfolding relationships with others, the body, and the world. In this chapter we focus on the ego directly; our main subject takes center stage. We discuss the ego not only as a psychic center and agency but also as a larger psychic system, plotting the development of this system as it emerges and is reconstituted at critical junctures along the spiral path.

TABLE 5.1

DEVELOPMENTAL ORGANIZATIONS OF THE EGO SYSTEM

STAGE OF LIFE	EGO SYSTEM
Neonatal stage	Incipient ego
Early preoedipal stage	Prepersonal body ego
Late preoedipal stage	Split body ego
Oedipal stage	From a split body ego to a unified mental ego
Latency	Fully formed ego system: self-representation, ego ideal, and superego; repressed shadow
Puberty and adolescence	Latency ego system outgrown and disowned; shadow derepressed
Early adulthood	Ego system reconstituted on basis of identity project
Crossroads	Ego "dies to the world"; self-representation deanimated; shadow derepressed

DEVELOPMENTAL ORGANIZATIONS OF THE EGO SYSTEM *(CONTINUED)*

STAGE OF LIFE	EGO SYSTEM
Awakening	Liminal ego on the threshold of the supernatural
Regression in the service of transcendence	Split between "higher" and "lower" selves; archetypal shadow derepressed
Regeneration in Spirit	Ego harnessed to Spirit; Spirit is ego's counselor, guardian, lover
Ego-Ground integration	Ego wedded to Spirit; Spirit is ego's higher Self

ONTOLOGICAL CONSIDERATIONS

The ego is the center of consciousness. As such, it is a singular perspective from which psychosensory data are experienced and organized. On the most fundamental level, the ego is what the eighteenth-century German philosopher Immanuel Kant called the *unity of apperception*. Unpacking Kant's terminology, this means that the ego is a singular perspective that serves (1) as the abiding reference point in relation to which changing moments of consciousness are held together as moments of a single temporally extended consciousness (unity), and (2) as the owner or proprietary subject of consciousness, that is, the subject that, at some level, recognizes experience as its own experience (apperception). The ego, then, is the abiding reference point in relation to which consciousness is at once *one* consciousness and *someone's* consciousness. It is a unified first-person perspective, a temporally synthesized proprietary point of view.

The ego is not only a unity of apperception but also a psychic agency. It is not only an ongoing focal perspective from which experience is witnessed but also a subject that acts upon experience. As an active subject, the ego is the executor of the so-called ego functions: synthesis, reality testing, discursive cognition, impulse control, and intentional action. It is the ego that ties together disconnected or opposing elements of experience, that distinguishes between reality and imagination, that classifies, correlates, and makes inferences, that controls urges and feelings, and that engages in purposive activity. At the outset of life many of these functions are completely absent and others are present only in the most minimal way; still, they are functions that, once they begin to develop, belong to and are performed by the ego as an active subject situated at the center of consciousness. The ego, then, is not only an abiding subjective point of view but also an agency that performs essential psychic functions.

The ego thus described is the *nuclear ego*. Henceforth, when the term *ego* is used, the reader should understand that it is the nuclear ego to which reference is being made. The nuclear ego is the basis of the larger ego system, which includes, in addition to the nuclear ego, the self-representation, superego, and ego ideal. These three latter components of the ego system emerge in precursory ways during preoedipal and oedipal stages of development and then are integrated as elements of a fully established ego system in the transition to the stage of latency. This initial ego system, as we shall see, is only the first of several ego systems that are formed during the course of spiral development.

The ego exists in essential relation to the Dynamic Ground. The ego is rooted in the Ground and could not exist apart from the Ground. The ego remains dependent upon the Ground even under conditions of primal repression, when the nonegoic potentials of the Ground are markedly reduced in activity. The ego depends upon the Dynamic Ground not only as the source of instinct, feeling, and imagination but also and most importantly as the source of energy. We learned in the last chapter that the major forms of energy upon which the ego depends—psychic energy, libido, and Spirit—are all expressions of the power of the Dynamic Ground. The ego could perhaps exist without some of the nonegoic potentials of the Ground, but it could not possibly exist without the power of the Ground.

The implication is clear: the ego is not a self-subsistent entity; rather, the ego exists only in relation to the Dynamic Ground, in which it is rooted and of which it is an agency. The ego exists only as a side of an ego-Ground duality. Moreover, the ego is the lesser (subject) side of this duality; the Ground, and in particular the power of the Ground, is the greater (sovereign) side. Although the ego goes through much of life unaware of the Dynamic Ground—which, quieted and submerged by primal repression, is organized as the unconscious id—it is nonetheless inherently tied to and dependent upon the Ground. If the ego were completely uprooted from the Ground, it would cease to exist.

Does the ego's dependence upon the Dynamic Ground preclude the continued existence of the ego after the death of the body? This question is in all likelihood unanswerable. In the last chapter no position was taken on the ultimate ontological status of the power of the Dynamic Ground. In particular, no position was taken on the question of whether the power of the Ground is a this-worldly power arising from a biological "below" or a cosmic power descending from a heavenly "above." Correspondingly, in this chapter no position is taken on the ultimate ontological status of the ego. In particular, no position is taken on whether the ego is something that exists only as a perishable product of biological evolution or something that might have an existence beyond the biological order. It is not clear what would count as evidence on either side of this issue. The only ontological point to be made here, then, is that the ego is a side of an ego-Ground duality and, therefore, is not a self-subsistent entity.

THE INCIPIENT EGO

When the newborn is awake and alertly focused on objects, it is a proprietary, active subject of consciousness, a unity of apperception that performs precursory ego functions. The newborn, then, *does* have an ego, that is to say, a nuclear ego. The newborn's ego, however, is only an incipient ego, and in particular it is only a minimal and intermittent ego.

The newborn's ego is a minimal ego for two principal reasons. First, it is minimal because the newborn's apperception is minimal: it is an apperception that is entirely prereflective and lacking in any sense of I-not-I boundaries. Daniel Stern (1985) has helped dispel the misunderstanding that the newborn is altogether without a sense of self. The newborn does have a sense of itself as the center of a field of experience and, therefore, a sense, however primitive, of the "mineness" of its experience. This sense of being the center and owner of experience, however, is a merely felt sense preceding any mental self-representation and preceding even any immediate perceptual awareness of self-boundaries. The neonatal self, therefore, is a self with a proprietary center but no circumference. The newborn is not yet able to thematize itself—mentally or even perceptually—as an object of consciousness for itself.

Secondly, the newborn's ego is minimal because ego functions are in play only in a minimal way. The newborn, for example, knows no difference between reality and the imagination and, therefore, does not seek to test the reality of things; nor does the newborn actively explore the environment; nor, quite evidently, does it exercise impulse control. This is not to say that the newborn is a completely inactive witness. The newborn *does* act. For example, it tracks salient stimuli; it engages in sensorimotor manipulations centered in the mouth (rooting, sucking); and it may participate in interactional synchronies with the caregiver. These actions, however, are of the most rudimentary sort. Moreover, they are primarily reactions—reflexive actions—rather than actions proper: the newborn *follows* salient stimuli, *responds* to tactile stimulation with rooting and sucking manipulations, and is *drawn into* interactional synchronies with the caregiver. We learned in chapter 3 that most of the nonegoic potentials of the Ground are fully active at birth. Here we can add that almost the opposite is true of ego functions. At birth, the ego is active, but only in a few primitive and reactive ways.

In addition to being minimal, the newborn's ego is intermittent, also for two principal reasons. It is intermittent, first, because it requires the support of an occurrent stimulus. The newborn is able to hold itself together as a singular subject only so long as it is given a stimulus to engage or track. Without such a stimulus serving as anchor, the newborn tends to lose focus and fall into disengaged, un-unified states, states of trancelike suspension. For the newborn, accordingly, ego-centered consciousness must be consciousness *of* some object; and as we know, the only objectlike things that exist for the newborn—who does not yet understand object permanence—are occurrent stimuli. For the newborn, accordingly, ego-centered consciousness must be consciousness *of* an occurrent stimulus (or stimulus pattern). Occurrent stimuli, however, are only temporary phenomena—and, therefore, so, too, is the newborn's ego-centered consciousness. The ego of the newborn is repeatedly formed and dissolved in response to arising and passing stimuli.

For the newborn, then, the unity of apperception is sustained by occurrent stimuli. The ability to hold consciousness together as a unity without the support of an occurrent stimulus develops only gradually as the child masters the object concept and thereby becomes able to keep an object in mind—and, correlatively, to sustain itself *as* mind (i.e., as ego-centered, focused consciousness)—even after the object has exited the sensory field. The newborn, having no understanding of object permanence, is not able on its own to sustain itself as an ego-subject. It is dependent upon the stimulus or stimulus pattern of the moment to serve as support.

The second reason for the intermittence of the newborn's ego is that the newborn is subject to the pull of the power of the Ground organized as the primordial reservoir. The primary organization of the power of the Ground at this point, if we recall, is as a pool of plenipotent energy that acts upon the nascent ego as a powerful attractor (an energy cathexis). Responding to the pull of this inner reservoir of energy, the newborn is prone to lose its hold on individuated consciousness, giving way either to trancelike states (when an occurrent stimulus disappears) or to the bliss of oceanic dissolution (sleep). The newborn experiences periods of alert, ego-centered wakefulness, but these periods tend to be followed by extended periods of drowsiness or unconsciousness. Much of the newborn's time is spent in either semi-egoless or completely egoless states, states in which the newborn is either yielding to or completely enveloped in the water of the primordial reservoir.

THE PREPERSONAL BODY EGO

The child begins to understand object permanence at approximately four or five months of age (Baillargeon 1987). At this age, then, the child becomes able actively to hold itself together as the subject of consciousness by holding in mind objects that have disappeared from the sensory field. The child is at first able to do this only for brief moments, but before long it is able to keep absent objects in mind and, therefore, to sustain unified ego-consciousness for significant periods of time. In achieving this ability, however, the child does not wholly overcome its previous dependence upon occurrent stimuli, for the child needs sensory cues to remind itself of absent objects. For example, the child needs the so-called transitional object to remind itself of the absent caregiver. The child, then, is still dependent upon sensory stimuli to sustain object consciousness and, therefore, apperception or ego-consciousness. The child is not able to evoke representations of absent objects without the aid of sensory cues until approximately the middle of the second year.

If, however, the child is still dependent upon sensory stimuli, it now has a significant degree of control over which stimuli it will experience. The four to eight month old child is much more active as an ego subject and has learned how to excercise control over sensory cues representing objects. The transitional object can again serve as an example. The child, in clinging to the transitional object, actively selects the content of its experience. Rather than passively waiting for whatever stimulus might happen to appear, the child chooses to focus on the transitional object and the comforting images and feelings it occasions. The child in this way exercises much more control over its object choice and, therefore, has much greater stability as an apperceiving subject. The child's unity of apperception may still be dependent upon sensory stimuli, but this dependence is now an active, controlled dependence upon stimulus representations of objects rather than a passive, uncontrolled dependence upon the presence of the corresponding objects themselves.

As the child learns to crawl and then walk, ego functions rapidly develop, and the child begins to exercise even greater control over experience. In becoming mobile, the child becomes able to pursue objects that have exited from awareness and, therefore, is less dependent upon sensory reminders of those objects. Piaget believed that the understanding of object permanence itself first emerged in the period coinciding with the achievement of locomotive abilities, around eight months of age. Subsequent research (see Mandler 1990) has shown that Piaget was mistaken in this view. Many more recent studies have demonstrated that the child understands object permanence earlier than Piaget realized—as early as four months of age or even earlier—but lacks the motor skills to put this understanding into effective practice until about the time Piaget specified.

In any case, eight months of age is about the time at which the child enters a period of markedly increased activity. This period—which in Mahler's account of childhood development is the practicing subphase of the separation-individuation process—is a time during which the child explores the environment with reckless abandon and delight, always assuming that the caregiver is close by to rescue the child from danger. This period of exploration is a stage of dramatic advance in sensorimotor cognition and corresponding object-directed intentional action. It is a stage of greatly increased control of object consciousness. It is, therefore, also a stage of greatly strengthened apperception; for the more the ego exercises cognitive, intentional, and other functions in relation to objects of consciousness, the better able it is to sustain itself as the subject of consciousness. Subject-anchored consciousness is still dependent upon object consciousness, but it is now dependent in a much less passive and precarious way.

In opening the child to a world that exists even when not perceived, the understanding of object permanence at the same time throws into relief for the child the limited and local boundaries of its immediate experience. As a world lying beyond the boundaries of perception is disclosed to the child, so, too, by contrast, is the child's own sphere of existence lying within those boundaries. Corresponding to the discovery of a transcendent world "out there" is the discovery of an immanent I (infant, toddler) "here." This distinction between child "here" and world "out there" is the first demarcation between self and other, between the ego as center and subject of experience and the outer world as objective realm.

The boundary of this demarcation is the child's body, for the body is a physical object that is unique both in being a locus of sensations and in never being absent from the child's experience. The body is a sensorium the surface of which is especially sensitive to the play of stimuli. Moreover, the body is always present and available to the child; unlike other objects, it never disappears from the field of awareness. For these reasons, then, the ego at this developmental juncture prereflectively identifies with its corporeal existence. As Freud (1923) said, "it (the conscious ego) is first and foremost a body ego" (p. 27). In fact, as we have seen, the first ego is an incipient ego unaware of a transcendent world "out there" and, therefore, of a body-bounded immanent sphere distinct from such a world. This fact notwithstanding, the ego becomes a body ego very early in life, perhaps as early as the middle of the first year.

The young body ego—that is, the body ego from approximately five to eighteen months of age—is like the incipient ego of the newborn in apperceiving itself directly and prereflectively, without the mediation of a self-representation. This fact is noteworthy considering that the body ego, unlike the incipient ego, is capable of representational thinking. The body ego has this ability because the ability is presupposed by even the most rudimentary understanding of object permanence. A representation of some sort is required in order to keep an object in mind after it has exited the sensory field. In the absence of the caregiver, for example, the transitional object evokes images, feelings, and sensations that are of the same sort as those elicited by the caregiver when the caregiver is present. These images, feelings, and sensations coalesce as a mental formation that refers to something beyond itself, the absent caregiver, and, therefore, that has a representational character. The network of experiences evoked by the transitional object, then, is a representation of a primitive sort, and so, too, are other groupings of experiences evoked by other sensory cues. The young body ego may not be able to evoke mental representations without the aid of sensory signals, but it is able to form representations on the basis of such signals.

Why, then, does the young body ego not form a representation of its own bodily self? The answer is that the body ego has no need for such a representation. Representations are initially formed as substitutes for absent objects, and the body, again, is never absent from experience. The first representation is the representation, prompted by the transitional object, of the absent caregiver. This representation is formed so that the child can hold in mind images, feelings, and sensations related to the caregiver when the caregiver is absent. The child, then, forms a representation of the caregiver because it has a need for such a representation. It does not, however, have a need for a representation of itself as a bodily being. Because the body is never absent from experience, the child has no need to form a mental construct to stand in the stead of the body. Rather than forming a representation of itself *as* the body, then, the young body ego simply senses itself to *be* the body.

In being without a self-representation, the young body ego, a fortiori, is without an ego ideal and without a superego as well. In having no representation of what it *is*, the young body ego does not project an ideal of what it *could* be, nor does it command itself to meet a norm defining what at least it *should* be. Rather, the young body ego, without self-regulation, acts in a completely spontaneous, pleasure-seeking manner. The young body ego, then, neither defines nor supervises itself. It directly discerns its bodily nature, and it gives immediate, pleasure-seeking expression to its polymorphously sensual life. The young body ego enthusiastically enjoys the newly discovered world "out there" as a garden of delight, and it enjoys its own bodily self as an organ of delight. The young body ego is an ungoverned hedonic being whose actions give expression to the pleasure principle.

SPLITTING AND THE EMERGENCE OF THE SELF-REPRESENTATION

According to Piaget, the object concept is not fully developed until approximately the middle of the second year, for it is not until this age that children are able to evoke and sustain representations of absent objects without the aid of sensory cues. It is not until about sixteen to eighteen months of age, then, that children are able to hold succeeding moments of consciousness together for lengths of time limited only by their own interest and energy. The absence of a stimulus object or sensory signal need not break up the unity of apperception. Jerome Kagan (1989) makes this point: "I believe that a central change of this period [the middle of the second year and thereafter] is the ability to sustain ideas and action plans. The psychological stage on which schemata interact and guide action does not collapse every half-minute or so as it did previously" (p. 237). To be sure, the "psychological stage" does still collapse; discontinuities of consciousness (lapses, absorptions) still frequently occur. The unity of consciousness is never an uninterrupted absolute. Discontinuities in the synthesized flow of experience, however, now occur much less often than they did before.

The full achievement of the object concept is marked not only by the ability to evoke representations without the aid of sensory cues but also by an understanding that the world is vastly larger than previously realized. If the ability to evoke representations without the aid of sensory cues has the positive consequence of consolidating the unity of apperception, the understanding of the vastness of the world—and, therefore, of the possible inaccessibility of the caregiver—has the negative consequence of terrifying the child and triggering the defense mechanism of splitting. We discussed preoedipal splitting briefly in chapter 3 and learned that this splitting affects the child's perception of the Dynamic Ground by dividing the Ground into a nurturant

Ground (a replenishing inner womb) on the one hand and a dangerous Ground (a frightening abyss) on the other. We then learned in the last chapter that preoedipal splitting affects the power of the Ground in particular by dividing it into opposing forces of light and darkness. We can now consider more fully the causes of preoedipal splitting and, focusing on the ego, learn how preoedipal splitting affects the child's awareness of itself. As we shall see, preoedipal splitting forces the child to begin thinking about itself and, more specifically, to begin thinking about itself in split, opposite ways. Splitting, that is, forces the child to begin forging its first self-representation, which has the fate of being a split self-representation. In first beginning to reflect upon itself, the child thinks of itself as being either all good or all bad, as being either a "good child" or a "bad child."

Studies by Piaget and others (see Bower 1982) have shown that, before about sixteen to eighteen months, children assume that objects absent from view exist at nearby locations, either at locations where they are usually found or at locations where they were last seen. Between approximately six and ten to twelve months of age, children will look for an object at the location where the object has been found on repeated occasions in the past. Children tie the object to this location so strongly that they will look for it there even when they have just seen it being hidden in another place. By about ten to twelve months children cease making this particular placement error but continue to assume that objects are bound to specific locations in space. This assumption is evident in children between ten or twelve and sixteen or eighteen months in a failure to understand invisible displacements of objects. For example, if a child in this age range sees an apple being placed under one of two cloths and then watches as the positions of the two cloths are transposed, the child will look for the apple under the cloth that is in the place where the apple was originally hidden. The child makes this mistake even though the cloth with the apple under it has a conspicuous lump in it, whereas the cloth that the child selects is flat.

Before about sixteen to eighteen months, then, children assume that objects out of view, including most importantly the caregiver, remain close by and can be found at familiar locations. They believe that objects that are unperceived are still effectively present at locations where they previously have been found or were last seen. Although objects are understood to have an existence beyond immediate experience, the location of this existence, it is assumed, is still tied to experience in a way that guarantees that the objects are nearby and accessible if needed. This assumption is what allows the practicing toddler to explore the world with reckless abandon. The toddler need not worry, for the caregiver, even if out of sight, is always close by to rescue the toddler from danger—or so the toddler assumes.

The picture changes dramatically, however, once the child understands that objects are not inherently local and can exist anywhere in a vastly enlarged space, for this insight dashes the child's assumption about the caregiver's accessibility and, therefore, about its own safety. The child is no longer in a small, local world overseen by an ever-present guardian and is suddenly thrust into an immense world in which it could be alone. The child is for this reason suddenly afflicted with abandonment anxiety. The caregiver that the child had taken for granted is now seen as a being who could be lost, as a being who, indeed, could abandon the child if the child is not what the caregiver expects it to be. The child becomes acutely aware of its vulnerability and dependence upon the caregiver, and it now seeks desperately to remain within the caregiver's good graces.

For this reason the child begins to try to control its behavior in a desire to be a "good child," a child who fulfills the caregiver's expectations and, therefore, is deserving of the caregiver's love. The child's behavior is not easily changed, however. The child remains to a large extent its former spontaneous body-self, which is a self that frequently violates the wishes and even the imperatives of the caregiver. Wanting to be good, the child now sees this uncontrollable side of itself as bad. It is so important to the child to be a good child—its very existence, it seems, is at stake—that the child cannot accept this bad side of itself. The child, accordingly dissociates itself from this bad side, which is separated off as a "bad child." In this way the child begins thinking about itself in split fashion as not only an all-good good child but also an all-bad bad child in the faith that, because it can at any time reappear as good child, it will not be abandoned by the caregiver, no matter how bad it might have been as bad child. The child's abandonment anxiety in this way causes the child to begin forming a self-representation, and this first self-representation is a split self-representation.

The child, then, goes from being an undefined, ungoverned body ego to being a defined, good-bad split personality. The good child is a child who is obedient and, therefore, deserving of the caregiver's devotion. This child is defined and governed to a significant extent and, therefore, is no longer the wholly spontaneous body ego of the practicing subphase of the separation-individuation process. The good child, to be sure, is an impulse-motivated, body-identified ego. The good child, however, is also an impulse-monitoring, behavior-identified ego, an ego that yields only to "good" impulses and that fashions its behaviors in ways that, it believes, will elicit the love of the caregiver. The bad child, in contrast, is a body ego that yields to impulses that transgress the caregiver's expectations and, therefore, that defines itself in negative terms. The bad child is a negatively defined, ungoverned, completely impulsive body ego, the complete opposite of the good child.

The splitting of the body ego into a good child and a bad child is a serious cleaving of the child's experience. In effect, the child becomes two children, and it perceives itself thus. The good child perceives itself as a wholly good child; the bad child perceives itself as a wholly bad child. These two personalities are disjoined from each other. Although the child knows both personalities, it does not relate to them as subpersonalities of a single self; rather, it relates to them as separate persons. Accordingly, when the child is the good child, it is exclusively the good child; and when the child is the bad child, it is exclusively the bad child. It is crucial to splitting as a defense mechanism that the child keep its opposite personalities separate, for it is only by means of such separation that the child is able to do whatever it pleases as bad child without in any way detracting from its perfection and worthiness as good child.

Preoedipal splitting of the self-representation has an ironic aspect because it occurs at the same time that the unity of apperception is consolidated. Just when the ego becomes able to sustain unified, subject-anchored consciousness without the aid of sensory cues, it suffers a splitting that divides it into two unified, subject-anchored consciousnesses. The gain in the unity of apperception remains, but it is now distributed over two egos. Consciousness does not fall into egoless lapses or absorptions as easily as it did before. The body ego is now able to maintain itself for long periods *as ego*. The body ego, however, now switches back and forth between two opposite personalities. The good child and the bad child are both unified within themselves as stable ego-subjects, but the two are not unified between themselves in a way that would make them parts of a larger, integrated ego system.

FROM A SPLIT BODY EGO TO AN INTEGRATED MENTAL EGO

Preoedipal splitting is a defense mechanism that soon becomes a problem worse than the one it is supposed to solve. Preoedipal splitting, then, must eventually be brought to an end, and in particular the split in the original self-representation must be mended. In the next chapter we explore reasons why splitting must be overcome and present an account of how this is accomplished during the late preoedipal and oedipal stages. Here the focus is on the surmounting of splitting insofar as it mends the child's self-representation and otherwise brings into being a unified ego system.

The mending of the child's split self-representation occurs because the child gradually learns that, abandonment anxiety notwithstanding, the caregiver is in fact almost always present to care for the child when it is in need, even when it has been a bad child. Over time, the child comes to see that although many things in the world are out of range or have become lost, the caregiver is in fact almost always available for the child, even if on occasion the child must wait patiently for the caregiver to appear. Moreover, the child comes to see that perfectly good behavior on its part is not required for the caregiver's loving attentions. Although the caregiver may punish the child when it misbehaves, the caregiver does not abandon the child and continues to meet the child's needs. For these reasons the child is gradually relieved of abandonment anxiety and begins to understand that it does not need to be perfect but needs only to be "good enough" in order to be safe in the large world of unanchored objects in which it lives.[1] In coming to understand that it need not be perfect, the child is able to repair the split in its self-representation. It ceases being a split good-bad child and becomes an integrated good enough child.

The integrated self-representation that emerges here, in being a good enough self-representation, is a realistic compromise between the previous good child and bad child self-representations. In being a compromise between these two self-representations, however, it is not an equal compromise, for "good enough" here means "more good than bad." It means, in the child's mind, that the child has a sufficient net positive value to be worthy of the caregiver's love. The good enough child, therefore, remains closer to the former good child self-representation than it does to the former bad child self-representation. It no longer identifies with the former good child self-representation, but it still associates itself with it, namely, as an ideal goal, as a representation of what the child ideally *could be* rather than as a representation of what the child *is*. In contrast, the good enough child dissociates itself from many, although not all, of the features of the former bad child self-representation, especially the more extreme features. Whereas the former good child self-representation is retained and projected as an ideal self, becoming thereby the ego ideal of psychoanalysis, much of the former bad child self-representation is rejected and repressed as not-self, becoming thereby the shadow of Jungian psychology. Primal repression buries much of the former bad child self-representation, hiding it from view. Because the shadow is repressed, it is technically not a part of the integrated ego system that is here emerging. It is, however, inherently tied to this system, as an unconscious anti–ego ideal.

Emerging concomitantly with the ego ideal and the shadow is the super-ego. As an inner agency regulating behavior, the superego is not entirely new. A precursor of the superego can be found in the preoedipal good child's attempt to be a perfectly good child. This initial attempt at self-regulation, of course, is almost wholly ineffective because the preoedipal child, as a primarily hedonic being, is incapable of behaving in a perfectly good way and in fact is incapable of much self-control at all. Still, the preoedipal good child does desperately want to control its behavior, and this desire is the seed of the superego. Although the preoedipal good child requires of itself behavior that it cannot remotely approximate—and this is why the good child so quickly metamorphoses into the bad child—it does require behavior of itself and, therefore, has a precursory superego.

If the precursory superego of the preoedipal good child is ludicrously ineffective because it requires perfect behavior from a child who has very little self-control, the superego that emerges as splitting is overcome is effective because it requires much less from a child who has much more self-control. It requires much less from the child because it requires only good enough rather than perfect behavior, and the child has much more self-control because, as we shall see, primal repression subdues the impulses over which the child needs to exercise control. Let us consider both of these points.

The child, in overcoming splitting, realizes that it does not need to be perfect to meet the expectations of parents. The child, accordingly, ceases requiring perfection of itself and begins requiring of itself only what parents in fact require: good enough behavior. Disburdened of the belief that it must be perfect, the child, as noted, projects perfection beyond itself as the ego ideal; and requiring of itself now only that it be good enough, the child internalizes parental standards of acceptable, achievable behavior: the superego. The superego and ego ideal are in this way differentiated from each other and emerge as fully formed components of the ego system. The superego now becomes the inner voice by which the child exhorts itself to approximate the ego ideal in a good enough way so that it can be a good enough child.

Although the emerging superego requires only good enough rather than perfect behavior, it still requires that the child exercise considerable self-control, indeed much more self-control than earlier would have been possible. It requires, essentially, that the child go from being a primarily hedonic being acting according to the pleasure principle to being an effectively self-governing agent who can be relied upon to be a good enough child. How is such a change possible? The answer: primal repression. The child in all likelihood would not be able to regulate its behavior as required by the emerging superego were it not for the fact that primal repression weakens the impulses that the child is required to control. Primal repression, which is gradually consolidated during the oedipal stage, quiets the power of the Ground and related nonegoic potentials and in doing so significantly reduces the intensity of desires and feelings. The child's inner experience, thus subdued, becomes much more manageable. The child, then, is able to become a good enough child not only because it submits itself to a more realistic standard, the superego, but also because primal repression eliminates the most powerful challenges to the child's will. In this way primal repression plays an essential role in the overcoming of splitting and the unification of the ego system.

As the ego ideal and superego emerge in the ways explained, they also begin working in unison to motivate proper behavior. The ego ideal provides the child with telic or "pulling" motivation, offering the child an inspiring ideal toward which to strive; and the superego provides the child with impelling or "pushing" motivation, exhorting the child to achieve a good enough approximation of that ideal. The ego ideal is the carrot, the superego the stick. The ego ideal entices the child toward an ultimate goal as something to be desired, and the superego commands the child to keep moving toward this goal even when desire flags. The child, of course, never reaches the goal it pursues. The carrot always remains beyond reach; the ego ideal always remains ideal. All that is necessary is that a good enough effort is made to keep moving toward the goal.

The ego, then, unifies the larger ego system (1) by forging a good enough self-representation that integrates features from both the former good child self-representation and the former bad child self-representation;

(2) by projecting the former good child self-representation as a higher ideal self, thereby creating the ego ideal; (3) by repressing many of the features of the former bad child self-representation, thereby creating the shadow; (4) by internalizing parental standards of acceptable behavior, thereby creating a superego unburdened by expectations of perfection; and (5) by repressively subduing nonegoic potentials, thereby greatly increasing the ego's self-control and the ability to comply with superego demands. The ego in these ways overcomes the split in the preoedipal self-representation and brings into being an ego system that is both fully formed and fully integrated. The principal components of the ego system—self-representation, ego ideal, and superego—are now differentiated from each other, and they work together effectively to give the ego definition (the self-representation), justification (the self-representation is a good enough self-representation), and motivation (the inspiring motivation of the ego ideal and the disciplining motivation of the superego).

Occurring simultaneously with the integration of the ego system is a differentiation of the ego from the body. As the child changes from being a split good-bad child to being an integrated good enough child, it also changes from being a public body ego to being a private mental ego. If, as we have seen, primal repression plays an essential role in the former of these changes, the interpersonal correlate of primal repression, primal separation, plays an essential role in the latter change. Primal separation plays an essential role in transforming the child from a body ego to a mental ego because it is not only an act by which the child withdraws from symbiotic intimacy with the caregiver but also an act by which the child, in withdrawing from the caregiver, thereby withdraws from the body into psychic space. As a body ego, the child is completely open to the world and to others; it lacks an outer layer of protective shielding or buffering. It exists wholly in the public domain, nakedly, defenselessly exposed to radically intimate interpersonal contact. If, then, the child is to withdraw from symbiotic intimacy with the caregiver, it perforce must withdraw from the body. In fact, the child does just this. The child pulls back from embodied openness, retreating from physical, public space; and in doing so it enters a safe inner realm of which before it was unaware: private psychic space. As soon as the child has thus discovered the inner sanctuary of psychic space, it is no longer an exclusively bodily being. It has broken its exclusive identification with the body and has become a private mental ego.

The mental ego that emerges at this point is not a disembodied Cartesian ego. The ego here *differentiates* but does not *dissociate* itself from the body. The body remains integral to the ego's self-representation, but it is now reduced in status: it ceases being the self, the whole self, and nothing but the self and becomes instead an outer extension of an inner self. The ego is no longer exclusively a bodily being and is now an inner private subject that has a body. As the research of John Broughton (1978, 1980, 1982) has shown, children, starting at about four years of age, begin to think of themselves in terms of a vague head-body dualism. The ego at this age has contracted inwardly to a place somewhere in the head, somewhere behind the eyes and between the ears. To be sure, the ego—that is to say, the child—can come out from its "hiding place" in psychic space and reinhabit the whole of the body, as it does, for instance, when it engages in physical play or embracing. When the child does this, however, it is ever at the ready, should it feel threatened, to return to the inner haven inside the head, which is now the child's primary abode. When the child occupies this inner space, it feels as though it is hidden from view and, therefore, safe from others.

In sum, the process by which splitting is overcome has two primary consequences so far as the ego is concerned: (1) it differentiates and integrates the principal components of the ego system: self-representation, ego ideal, and superego; and (2) it differentiates the ego from the body as an inner subject that *has* rather than *is* a body. In light of these two outcomes, we can say that the transformation by which splitting is overcome changes the ego from being a split body ego to being an integrated mental ego. This transformation does not happen all at once. Indeed, the process begins before the beginning of the oedipal stage, in the subphase of the separation-individuation process that Mahler calls "on the way to object constancy" (twenty-four to thirty-six plus months). The transformation, however, is accelerated and brought to a final close during the oedipal stage, as we explain in the next chapter.

THE MENTAL EGO DURING LATENCY

The mental ego that emerges in the late preoedipal and oedipal stages is not fully established until the child makes a final commitment to primal repression and primal separation, that is to say, to primal closing. This commitment marks the end of the oedipal stage and the beginning of latency. Latency is for this reason the first major stage of the mental ego's tenure.

Because it is based on primal closing, latency is a stage of both calm (primal repression subdues nonegoic potentials) and safety (primal separation provides the child with privacy and defensive covering). Moreover, as psychoanalyst Peter Blos (1967) observed, latency is a stage during which the ego is inwardly supported—both protected and motivated—by parents. The latency child is inwardly protected by parents because it enjoys a sense of safety based on the implicit belief that parents can be trusted to take care of the child, even when the child misbehaves. At the same time, the latency child is inwardly motivated by parents because both the latency ego ideal and the latency superego embody parental norms: the ego ideal, as we have seen, embodies parental norms of perfect behavior, the superego parental norms of good enough behavior. The ego of the latency stage, then, is not only free of the intrapsychic storms and interpersonal entanglements that had plagued the later prelatency years but is also invisibly guarded and set in motion by parents. Owing to these favorable conditions, latency is a stage during which the ego is able to develop at an accelerated pace.

As a stage of accelerated ego development, latency is a time during which the child makes dramatic progress in mastering ego functions, in particular reality testing, preoperational and operational cognition, and exercise of will. The child now tests reality more effectively for two principal reasons. It does so, first, because it is no longer prone to the distortions characteristic of pre-oedipal splitting. The child is no longer prone to perceive itself or others as either all good or all bad and is able to see itself and others—and the world generally—in a more realistic way, as possessing both positive and negative qualities in varying combinations and weightings. Secondly, the child tests reality more effectively because the lower-intensity (i.e., nonplenipotent) atmosphere of latency allows the child to engage in uninterrupted investigations of the world. The child is no longer prone to be captivated or swept away by plenipotently charged persons, objects, or events and is able to remain gathered and focused as it explores the world. Whereas the prelatency child tends to be overpowered by plenipotent energy, the latency child is empowered by nonplenipotent energy. The latency child, therefore, is better able to keep its head clear and its faculties effectively engaged.[2]

The latency child makes dramatic progress in preoperational and operational cognition, as is well known. Early latency (from approximately five to seven years of age) is a period during which the child begins intuitively to understand general meanings independently of perceptual or imaginal instances (Piaget's intuitive substage of the stage of preoperations). With this intuitive understanding of general meanings achieved, middle and late latency are periods during which the child begins learning how to operate on general meanings—albeit only with concrete instances at hand—by mapping their scopes and following out their implications. Although the latency child is able intuitively to grasp many general meanings independently of concrete instances—primarily because such meanings are acquired through learning language—it is not yet able to operate on general meanings except by manipulating concrete instances. For this reason the operational cognition that is mastered during latency is a concrete operational cognition; it is a cognition that operates on abstract meanings but only in a concrete way.

Corresponding to the rapid progress made in reality testing and cognition during the latency stage is a rapid progress in self-control. As a consequence of primal repression, upwelling impulses and feelings are now significantly subdued; and as a consequence of primal separation, interpersonal vulnerabilities are defended. The child, therefore, is now much less often overwhelmed by psychic upheavals and by the actions and feelings of others and for this reason has much more relative self-control. Moreover, the child is now strongly motivated by the ego ideal and superego, which work in effective unison to keep the child moving forward on the right path. The latency child is still impulsive in many ways; compared with the prelatency child, however, the latency child is a model of compliance and control.

THE MENTAL EGO DURING ADOLESCENCE

Adolescence is a stage during which we are impelled to break free from basic parental influences so that we can find our own way in the world. The awakening of sexuality initiates a search for a new primary other or love object to replace the parent, typically the mother, who has played this role. The need to begin forging an adult identity triggers a disavowal of the parentally defined self-representation of the latency period and a corresponding disavowal of the parents as role models or ego ideal figures. In disavowing the parents as role models, adolescents begin to search for new role models to serve as guides in the exploration of new identity possibilities. Girls typically search for someone to replace the mother as ego ideal figure and boys for someone to replace the father. Additionally, as adolescents search for people to replace parents in the roles of primary other and ego ideal figure, they at the same time struggle to break free from the latency superego, which, as the internalized voice of parental—and especially paternal—authority, is now perceived as an oppressive, foreign voice. Adolescence is a stage during which the parentally derived ego system of latency, having been outgrown, is disowned, and initial steps are taken toward the formation of a new ego system.

Adolescents disavow all of the major components of the latency ego system: ego ideal, superego, and self-representation. The ego ideal of the latency ego system is an ideal of a perfectly good child, but adolescents are no longer children. The superego of the latency ego system is an inner agency enforcing parental authority over a child, but adolescents need to break free from parental governance so that they can begin governing themselves. The self-representation of the latency ego system, too, is tied to childhood: it is a representation of a good enough child. Again, however, adolescents are no longer children. From the perspective of adolescence, the latency ego ideal is a false ideal, the latency superego is an alien and stifling authority, and the latency self-representation is a representation of an immature former self. Adolescents are alienated from the whole of the ego system that had served them so well during the latency years. They no longer want to be good enough little girls or boys and want instead to be themselves, whatever that might be.

Disavowal of the latency ego system is deeply unsettling, for it undermines adolescents' sense of being and justification. Adolescents lose the identity that went with the latency self-representation. Moreover, in losing this identity, they lose both the sense of being and the sense of justification, the sense of good enough earned value, that went with it. The loss of their former identity thus makes adolescents susceptible to anxieties of both nothingness (loss of being) and worthlessness (loss of justification). Adolescence, as psychoanalyst Erik Erikson (1950, 1956) explained long ago, is a time of existential insecurity. Few adolescents may experience a full-fledged identity crisis, but most adolescents are prone to experience anxieties arising from a sense of nonbeing and lack of value.

Adolescents are also prone to experience another kind of anxiety, a distress arising from a sense not only of lacking earned positive value but also of possessing inherent negative value, that is, of being a "bad person." Anxiety of this sort can erupt because the shadow, which had been hidden beneath the latency ego system, is derepressed and exposed to consciousness. The split good-bad self-representation of the late prelatency stages, if we recall, becomes the ego ideal–shadow complex of latency. Of the two sides of this complex, the ego ideal is in principle accessible to consciousness during latency. It is prereflective but thematizable; aspects of it can be brought explicitly into awareness. The shadow, in contrast, in being repressed, is inaccessible to consciousness. The disavowal of the latency ego system at the beginning of adolescence, however, loosens the repression of the shadow, allowing it to emerge from darkness into light. In consequence, adolescents tend to suffer from disturbing self-denigrations. They are prone to see themselves not only as lacking in earned value but also as ungrateful and selfish. Some are even prone to see themselves as malevolent.

As adolescents separate from the latency ego system, they at the same time take initial steps that, in early adulthood, will lead to a new ego system. They explore possibilities for a new ego ideal by fantasizing about idols; they prepare for the formation of a new superego by steadfastly exercising self-will; and they test possible new self-representations by experimenting with lifestyles and fashions. Adolescents do all of this without making long-term commitments. Idols quickly become passé and are replaced by new idols; the exercise of self-will tends to be more an end in itself—an insistence upon freedom and difference—than a sustained resolve to meet long-term goals; and the testing of lifestyles and fashions has the character, to use existential philosopher Jean-Paul Sartre's (1956) expression, of "playing at being." Adolescence is a stage during which we rehearse for life. The rehearsal is necessary for the ensuing performance. It is by admiring idols, exercising self-will, and trying out lifestyles and fashions that we prepare ourselves to make the commitments that will bring into being the new ego system of early adulthood.

THE MENTAL EGO DURING EARLY ADULTHOOD

If adolescence is a time of rehearsal, early adulthood is the time when the curtain goes up on life. In making the transition from adolescence to early adulthood, we move from lifestyle experiments to long-term commitments and, thereby, from a transitional ego system to a reconstructed ego system. The two commitments that typically mark the movement from adolescence to early adulthood are commitments to a significant other or life partner and to a type of work or social contribution (whether in the public or private sphere or both). By means of these and other commitments—for example, commitments to political parties, churches, occupational organizations, interest groups, ethnicity—young adults embark upon an *identity project*, which is a project that rebuilds the ego system. By making long-term commitments, young adults cease adolescent "playing at being" and strive actually "to be." In thus setting out on the identity project, young adults refashion the principal components of the ego system: ego ideal, superego, and self-representation. They project new ideals to pursue, thereby reenvisioning the ego ideal; they enjoin upon themselves new responsibilities and obligations, thereby reengaging the superego; and in doing these things, they redefine who they are, thereby reconstituting the self-representation. The identity project is the vehicle for the rebuilding of the ego system in early adulthood.

As an example of how the identity project reconstructs the ego system, let us consider the hypothetical case of Carlos, a young Hispanic American. Carlos, let us assume, commits himself to being a husband, father, social worker, representative of Latino ethnicity, and Catholic. In committing himself to these categories of social participation, Carlos projects new ideal goals: he envisions what it would be like to be a perfect husband, father, social worker, and so forth. In thus envisioning new goals, Carlos fashions a new ego ideal. Carlos prereflectively understands that his new goals, as ideal goals, are not fully realizable. Moreover, he is aware that he sometimes loses motivation and sometimes is diverted from his commitments by competing desires and tendencies. To remain faithful to his commitments, then, Carlos motivates himself not only by fantasizing about his newly chosen goals and experiencing their inspiring "pull" but also by inwardly issuing imperatives to himself and experiencing their impelling "push." In speaking to himself in this manner, Carlos drives himself to persevere in the pursuit of his goals. He does not require himself perfectly to achieve these goals, but he does require himself to make sufficient progress toward them, progress that is good enough. If Carlos's new goals are components of a new ego ideal, the inner imperative voice by which Carlos keeps himself on his chosen course is the voice of a new superego. No longer the inner voice of parents, the oedipal father in particular, this superego voice is now Carlos's own voice. It is Carlos speaking to himself in the voice of self-discipline.

As Carlos is thus motivated by a new ego ideal and superego, he forges a new self-representation, a representation of himself as husband, father, social worker, Hispanic American, and Catholic. This self-representation is not created all at once; it is forged over time as Carlos continues to persevere in the direction of his ideals. Because Carlos does not require perfection of himself, the self-representation that he forges, like the self-representation of latency, is a good enough self-representation. It is a self-representation that falls considerably short of its corresponding ego ideal but that is nonetheless a sufficiently close approximation of that ideal to confer not only a solid sense of being but also a secure sense of net earned value. This at any rate is the norm. Some young adults, to be sure, are afflicted with a chronic anxiety of lack of worth. Such anxiety, however, is more characteristic of adolescents and older adults going through midlife transition than it is of young adults. For most young adults, serious doubts about self-worth are temporary effects of outer causes—for example, the loss of a job, the breakup of a relationship, a shameful incident, a brush with the law—rather than chronic symptoms of deficiencies inherent to the ego system. Most young adults, acknowledging their faults and shortcomings, believe that they are good enough. They believe that their balance sheet shows a net positive earned value.

This balance sheet of net value, however, is not based on a complete self-inventory, for it omits any features of the self that are inconsistent with being good enough. These features are repressed as a reconstituted shadow. Once again, as at the beginning of latency, the ego not only projects a perfect ego ideal and identifies with a good enough self-representation but also represses a bad or evil—a not good enough—shadow. The shadow of the young adult is of course no longer the parentally defined "bad child" shadow of latency; rather, it is a "bad adult" shadow, a personality fragment unacceptable to the young adult because it fails to meet the young adult's own standards of what is good enough. The young adult, then, in forging a new self-representation, creates a new shadow as well.

Assuming that the shadow is securely repressed, young adults typically earn an increasingly solid sense of being and value so long as they continue to make satisfying progress in the identity project. The ego ideal, although remaining ideal, becomes less vague and remote and more realistically articulated. The voice of the superego becomes less sternly commanding and more quietly effective. At the same time, the sense of identity and sense of good enough value embodied in the self-representation become less subject to doubt and more taken for granted. So long as a person continues to make satisfying progress in the identity project, the ego ideal, superego, and self-representation work increasingly well together as complementary components of the ego system. Moreover, because the commitments and goals of the identity project change as one grows older, passing from young to middle to later adulthood, there is no reason why one cannot continue to make satisfying progress in the identity project until the end of life. For this reason the ego system based on the identity project, forged in its initial form in early adulthood, is for most people a system that remains intact for the rest of life.

THE ALIENATED MENTAL EGO

Some people, however, reach a crossroads at which the ego system based on the identity project ceases being viable. We have discussed this crossroads in earlier chapters in terms of an introversion of psychic energy, a reversal of flow that divests the outer world of its aliveness and at the same time invests the deep core of the psyche, the Dynamic Ground, with gravitational charge. Here we consider how the ego system is affected when a person, approaching the crossroads in question, gets caught in this ebb tide of psychic energy.

Some people reach a point in life at which they cease making satisfying progress in the identity project and begin thinking that the project is impossible or futile. This pessimistic thinking may arise from a failure to achieve the realistic objectives of the identity project, or it may arise because these objectives have been achieved without, however, bringing a sense of meaningfulness or fulfillment. In either case a person might ask, "What's the use?" In the former case a person might say, "No matter how hard I try, I'll never be able to accomplish my goals," concluding that happiness is an unattainable goal. In the latter case a person might say, "I've accomplished what I set out to do in life, and nothing has changed," concluding that happiness is an illusory goal. In either case one begins to suffer frustration, loss of motivation, and a sense that life is without meaning or purpose. One finds oneself at an impasse from which, it seems, there is no escape.

Coinciding with this impasse is the introversion of psychic energy we have described. Perceiving that the identity project is impossible or futile, one ceases investing the world with psychic energy, and psychic energy, receding from the world, regathers at its source in the Dynamic Ground. Thus divested of energy, the world loses its aliveness and its positive and negative values and becomes arid, flat, absurd, a desert or barren wasteland. Many people who arrive at this difficult place in life suffer only temporarily. They endure a period of depression or existential dissatisfaction, a "midlife crisis," and then return to the identity project—perhaps now restructured—with renewed motivation. Others, however, suffer from a deeper alienation. Their sense of hopelessness does not go away; their world remains dead, devoid of motivating values. Their malaise is not a passing depression or crisis but a profound and transforming despair. For these people there is no possibility of resuming the identity project, even in new form, for the identity project and its corresponding ego system have been irrecoverably undermined.

The effect of such alienation is evident in all of the ego system's major components: ego ideal, superego, and self-representation. The ego ideal now loses its power to inspire. Ideals to which one had been powerfully drawn now seem unimportant, and persons previously perceived as embodying those ideals—former ego ideal figures—now seem merely ordinary or even ridiculous rather than exemplary or heroic. Concomitantly, as the ego ideal thus loses its power to inspire, the superego loses its power to impel or "push." The sense of futility is so pervasive that the voice of the superego has little if any effect. It becomes an impotent, nagging, or self-deprecating voice, which may sound like a broken record or a caricature of authoritarian command. The alienated mental ego in these ways utterly loses the motivation that, previously, the ego ideal and superego had provided.

This loss of motivation is at the same time a loss of the sense of being real, for the self-representation is deanimated and reduced to a mere persona, a lifeless mask. One no longer feels one's old self, and one's old self for this reason is thrown into relief as only a façade, a repertoire of habits and poses.

Attempts to return to normal are of no avail because withdrawal from the world is at the same time withdrawal from one's worldly self. In "dying to the world," one—as Søren Kierkegaard (1849), adopting a biblical expression (John 11:4), said—also undergoes a "sickness unto death." The worldly self in effect dies, and one is reduced to a nonentity, to a mere perspective looking out on a remote and alien landscape.

The deanimation of the self-representation divests the ego of its sense of being and earned value. The situation faced by the alienated person is similar in significant respects to that faced by the adolescent who, in outgrowing the latency self-representation, loses the sense of being and earned value based on that self-representation. The situation of the alienated person, however, differs from that of the adolescent in that whereas the adolescent is eagerly rehearsing for a new self-representation, the alienated person is vainly struggling to resuscitate an old, dying one. The adolescent is excited about future prospects in the world and is already testing possible new identity commitments. The alienated person, in contrast, is simply "dead to the world." This difference notwithstanding, the situations of the alienated person and the adolescent are similar in that both have lost their previous sense of being and earned value and, consequently, are prone to suffer from anxieties of lack of being and lack of value.

As happens during adolescence, the anxiety of lack of value is exacerbated by the resurfacing of the shadow. So long as the adult ego lives its self-representation, the shadow remains safely repressed and hidden from view. Once the ego begins to die to its self-representation, however, the shadow is derepressed and rises into consciousness, plaguing the ego with unwelcome self-insights. Traits and tendencies that had been denied now present themselves before consciousness. These previously excluded elements can no longer be kept buried in the basement of the ego system. The ego, therefore, is forced to confront them and, then, to acknowledge them. No longer able to be its old self, the ego is here forced to accept a self, a negative alter ego, that it had refused to recognize. The deanimation of the self-representation in this way leads to an animation of the shadow, which springs to life as if it were the ego's real self, much to the ego's dismay.

The shadow, however, is short-lived, for the introversion of psychic energy eventually deanimates it, too. The shadow, like the self-representation, is a worldly identity. It is a negative worldly identity but a worldly identity nonetheless. Accordingly, the withdrawal of energy from the world, in deanimating the ego's worldly existence, deanimates not only the self-representation but also, eventually, the shadow. The shadow, however, usually has to be derepressed and animated before it can be deanimated. The process, then, unfolds as follows: (1) the self-representation is deanimated, depriving the ego of its sense of being and earned value; (2) the shadow is derepressed and animated, exacerbating the ego's sense of lack of value; and (3) the shadow is deanimated. The deanimation of the shadow leaves the ego in a completely alienated, bereft condition. The ego no longer has any being or value in the world, good enough or otherwise.

THE EGO AWAKENS TO THE NUMINOUS

The alienated person, as we said, is at a crossroads. This crossroads, however, looks like a cul-de-sac, for the alienated person feels utterly at a loss and is seemingly without options. The alienated person is for this reason a despairing person. Again, this despair is not a depression caused by particular life circumstances but is rather a fundamental "sickness unto death" that no worldly developments could conceivably cure. The alienated person, then, is completely without hope so far as the known world is concerned. For this very reason, however, the alienated person is radically open to faith in the unknown. Despite its dark emptiness, despair is a condition pregnant with faith.

Despair is ripe with faith not only because it renders one receptive to the unknown but also because it draws one to the unknown, to an irresistible *je ne sais quoi*. This "I know not what" is the Dynamic Ground experienced as an invisible attractor to which one is drawn by introverted psychic energy. Having died to the world, one is drawn inward toward a center of gravity hidden deep within the psyche. One experiences the dark night that St. John of the Cross called the "night of the senses," a period of aridity and alienation during which one yearns for a redemptive power that one cannot begin to understand.[3] Despair is at once a loss of appetite for things of the world and a thirst for a power from the beyond.

As we know, introverted psychic energy sometimes accumulates sufficiently in the Ground to trigger an awakening of the power of the Ground in its plenipotency. The power of the Ground, thus awakened, manifests itself as numinous Spirit, the *mysterium tremendum et fascinans*. This awakening of the power of the Ground as numinous Spirit initiates a profound transformation, for one suddenly finds oneself in the presence of a prodigious power, a power that is bivalent and "wholly other." One confronts numinous Spirit as a power pervading the world and as a power acting intimately within the soul. In experiencing numinous Spirit as a power pervading the world, one is exalted and eclipsed, exhilarated and petrified, filled with reverence and struck down with fear and trembling; and in experiencing numinous Spirit as a power acting within the soul, one is pierced, inflated, intoxicated, enraptured, ruptured, and dissolved. Both without and within, one is aware that an immense, irresistible, light-dark Other has entered one's life.

The immensity and irresistibility of numinous Spirit alter the ego system in fundamental ways. The ego is shaken at its foundations because, in becoming aware of numinous Spirit, the ego discovers that it is not the unchallenged master of its own existence. Far from being master of itself, the ego here finds itself a small, weak subject whose fate is to be decided by Spirit's changing, bivalent winds. The ego here realizes that it is not the sovereign power of the soul but is instead a mere subject, a subject subservient to sovereign Spirit. The ego, although awakened to Spirit, has not yet been reborn in Spirit and, therefore, although no longer a worldly ego, is not yet a spiritual ego. Spirit does not yet play a role internal to the ego system. The ego is thus betwixt and between mundane and spiritual orders. Having died to the world of everyday life, it stands at the entrance to supernatural realms.

THE EGO RETURNS TO THE DYNAMIC GROUND

The journey into supernatural realms that begins at this point, as we know, is a difficult journey of return to the Dynamic Ground. It is a transformational journey of instinctual derepression as well as spiritual emergence, of regression as well as transcendence. It is a journey of *regression in the service of transcendence*. We have considered some of the difficulties inherent to this journey in earlier chapters. Here we focus specifically on difficulties that bear upon the ego system.

A primary difficulty plaguing the ego's return to the Ground is a new form of splitting. The ego, having awakened to Spirit, now begins to sense that it is somehow linked to Spirit. To be sure, the ego continues to perceive Spirit as a power that is wholly other. Spirit is still numinous Spirit. In continuing to perceive Spirit as a power that is wholly other, however, the ego now perceives Spirit as a power to which it is somehow tethered and toward which it is being pulled, as if led by Spirit in the direction of Spirit's otherness. Despite the mysterious otherness of Spirit, then, the ego here feels as though it has come under the influence of Spirit—indeed, that it has been "reborn" in Spirit— and, consequently, as though it has begun to change in ways that eventually would make it like Spirit. The point, though, is that this transforming rebirth in Spirit is problematic for the ego because the Spirit that the ego would become like is not only wholly other and mysterious but also bivalent. It is a numinous power that has both light and dark sides. The ego, consequently, here senses that it is being pulled in opposite, light and dark directions. Reflecting this inner conflict, the ego's self-representation is split along bivalent, good and evil lines.

This splitting of the self-representation differs from the splitting that occurs during the late preoedipal and oedipal periods, for it does not cleave the self-representation entirely. The ego, in sensing that its nature has begun to divide along numinously bivalent lines, sees itself as having both light and dark propensities and corresponding potentialities, not as having both light and dark actual natures. The ego here thinks of itself as a single ego that has been taken in tow at once by opposite forces, not as two egos, one completely good and the other completely evil. It thinks of itself as an ego that, having just been reborn in Spirit, has an undeveloped spiritual nature that could unfold in contrary ways. The ego during regression in the service of transcendence is both inspired by good and tempted by evil but is itself neither wholly good nor wholly evil. The ego here senses that it could develop along one or the other of two opposite paths depending upon whether it responds in faith to the encouragements of grace or succumbs in doubt to the enticements of evil.

The ego undergoing regression in the service of transcendence is not yet able to revive its previous worldly identity, the self-representation of the identity project. This identity, which was deanimated during the alienation process, remains out of play throughout much of regression in the service of transcendence. It remains in the background as an unsettled developmental issue because the ego that has just been reborn in Spirit is starting a new life, a life that is moving toward a future that is at once wholly other and split between opposite possible outcomes. The ego undergoing regression in the service of transcendence does have the basic identity of being a nascent spiritual self. Otherwise, however, it is unsure of what it is and what it will be, and for this reason it is not in a position to come to terms with its old self. Although no longer an alienated nonself—for it is now a nascent spiritual self—it is still too much of a new self facing a mysterious and divided destiny to be able to reclaim any significant part of its old self.

We learned in the last chapter that the awakening of the power of the Ground as numinous Spirit is an awakening that leads—eventually if not immediately—to a derepression of the instincts. This return to life of the instincts has significant consequences for the nascent spiritual ego. As we know, it gives a dramatic new cast to the bivalence of numinous Spirit, changing numinous bivalence from a "simple" good versus evil bivalence to a more complex bivalence of anti-instinctual good on the one hand and primitively instinctual evil on the other. Otherwise stated, it changes numinous bivalence into an opposition between disembodied angelic spirituality on the one hand and embodied demonic instinctuality on the other. The ego is strongly affected by both sides of this bivalence, for, again, having been reborn in Spirit, it experiences itself as being internally linked, however remotely, to both. In its self-representation, then, the ego here conceives of itself as a nascent spiritual self that wants to be "pure" (i.e., uncorrupted by the body) but that, in its weakness, is susceptible to "evil" temptations of the flesh. The ego prays to be uplifted by a power of light shining down from on high; simultaneously, it is prey to primitive urges arising from dark depths.

The splitting of the self-representation brought about by the ego's rebirth in Spirit—especially after instinctual derepression has pitted spirituality against instinctuality in the way just described—has several important consequences for the ego system. Among these consequence are (1) the emergence of a new superhuman (angelic) ego ideal, (2) the emergence of what Jung called the archetypal shadow, and (3) the emergence of a new superego, which exhorts the ego to keep to the straight and narrow path leading in the direction of the new ego ideal.

The new ego ideal, reflecting the disembodied spirituality to which the ego now aspires, is an ideal of angelic perfection, of eros-less agape. In thinking about its ideal possible self, the ego now fantasizes about purging itself of the instincts and becoming thereby a completely "pure" spiritual being. The ego thus elaborates in fantasy a new ultimate goal. This goal, however, is one-sided because the ego is inherently a spiritual *and* an instinctual being—even though the ego at this point experiences spirituality and instinctuality, agape and eros, as antagonistic contraries. Owing, then, to the bivalence of numinous Spirit and the corresponding split in the self-representation, the ego projects a self-stunting ego ideal. The ego sets its sights on a one-sided ideal of angelic perfection, believing that this is the telos toward which it will grow if it perseveres on the path of goodness, guided and inspired by grace.

In setting its sights on this ideal, the ego hopes that it will escape the seductions of the instinctual-as-demonic underside of the soul, which now emerges as the archetypal shadow. This archetypal shadow is to be distinguished from the personal shadow, which, as we have seen, surfaces during adolescence and again in adulthood during the stage of alienation. The personal shadow is the opposite of the worldly ego ideal. The personal shadow, therefore, is itself a worldly shadow; it is a representation of mundane, merely human evil. The archetypal shadow, in contrast, is the opposite of the angelic ego ideal that emerges during regression in the service of transcendence. The archetypal shadow, therefore, is an otherworldly shadow; it is a representation of supernatural, instinctually depraved evil. As the opposite of immaculate angelic goodness, the archetypal shadow is a representation of obscene demonic evil.

If the ego ideal of angelic goodness is a one-sided, false ideal, the archetypal shadow is an equally one-sided, false anti-ideal; for the instincts are not inherently evil, let alone demonically evil. The instincts are burdened with the appearance of evil only because primal repression sets them against the ego. Primal repression reduces the power of the Ground to instinctual libido and the Ground itself to the primitive id, stigmatizing both in the process. It is primal repression, then, that transforms nonegoic life into a primitive, malign "it" or not-self and, therefore, that is responsible for the fact that nonegoic life, during regression in the service of transcendence, expresses itself as a dark instinctual adversary. Having been reduced to libido, the power of the Ground returns to consciousness not only as awakening Spirit but also as derepressing, "impure" instinctual energy; and having been reduced to the id, the Dynamic Ground returns to consciousness not only as the seat of nonegoic potentials but also as a dark and primitive underworld or sea. The power of the Ground, however, is not inherently libido, and the Dynamic Ground is not inherently the id. It is primal repression that organizes the nonegoic sources of life in these ways.

As primal repression is lifted, then, and as the derepressive awakening of the Ground runs its course, the nonegoic bases of life are relieved of the taint of impurity and evil. Awakened instinctuality is relieved of its lewd, menacing character and begins to disclose itself as a natural dimension of life, a dimension that coexists harmoniously with redemptive spirituality. The process of instinctual derepression that occurs during regression in the service of transcendence is thus an essential precursor to the process of whole-psyche integration that occurs during regeneration in Spirit. The instincts, in awakening, necessarily assert themselves against the ego, for they must do so to eliminate what remains of primal repression. The manifestation of the archetypal shadow during regression in the service of transcendence is an unavoidable phase of the reactivation of instinctual life. Instinctual life must express itself as the archetypal shadow before it can be disburdened of this negative guise and be integrated within a larger, healthier psychic economy.[4]

Caught between an ego ideal of angelic perfection on the one hand and an archetypal shadow attracting it to demonic evil on the other, the ego of regression in the service of transcendence is importuned by contrary voices. One of these voices is a new superego voice, which entreats the ego to persevere in the direction of the ego ideal. The other voice is an anti-superego voice, which goads the ego to yield to the archetypal shadow.[5] The superego voice summons the ego to be pure and selfless. It warns the ego against falling prey to instinctual temptations, demonic seductions, and other risks leading to destruction (i.e., damnation, ensnarement, psychosis), and it praises or castigates the ego depending on how strong the ego is in resisting enticements to evil. In complete contrast, the anti-superego voice speaks to the ego in ways that encourage it to succumb to evil. It dares the ego to submit to dangerous desires; it unmasks the ideal of angelic purity as a sanctimonious illusion; and it applauds, mocks, or disparages the ego depending on how willing the ego is to yield to its "real" instinctual-demonic urges. The ego is caught between powerful opposing forces, and it hears opposite sorts of voices, both angelic and demonic, urging it to choose between absolute good and absolute evil. Regression in the service of transcendence for this reason is a stage requiring discernment and unremitting exercise of will.

THE EGO IS TRANSFORMED BY SPIRIT

We learned in the last chapter that the bivalence characteristic of initial awakening and regression in the service of transcendence is finally overcome in the transition to regeneration in Spirit. Bivalent numinous Spirit gives way to univalent (i.e., wholly redemptive) transforming Spirit. The ego that has endured regression in the service of transcendence is better adapted to nonegoic life in its awakened, plenipotent expression and has come to understand that nonegoic potentials are not alien or malign, as they had seemed. In particular, the ego no longer perceives the power of the Ground as wholly other or dark, and it no longer perceives the instincts as impure impediments to spiritual life. The ego now perceives the power of the Ground as a superior ally, as a power that, even when violent, is redemptive in its effects; and the ego now perceives the instincts as essential dimensions of life lived in its fullness. The conflict between spirituality and instinctuality and, with it, the splitting of the self-representation are in this way overcome. The split between a wholly good potential self defined by an angelic ego ideal and a wholly evil potential self defined by the archetypal shadow is mended.

Embodied instinctual life is no longer perceived as a dark adversary to which the ego is dangerously attracted and becomes an integral dimension—indeed, the organic basis—of awakened spiritual life.

The overcoming of the splitting of the self-representation brings into being a new, integrated self-representation. Like the self-representations of latency and early adulthood, this integrated self-representation is a good enough self-representation. The ego no longer thinks of itself as a spiritual infant split between angelic aspirations and demonic susceptibilities and thinks of itself instead as a maturing spiritual being who is at once spiritual, without thereby being anti-instinctual, and instinctual, without thereby being evil. The integrated self-representation that emerges in the transition to regeneration in Spirit is thus a representation of a person who is not angelically perfect—and, indeed, is even far from being humanly perfect—but who is nonetheless fundamentally good as a spiritually awakened human being. It is a representation of a person who is driven both by agape, sometimes to the point of overlooking self-needs, and by eros, sometimes to the point of overlooking the needs of others. Moreover, it is a representation of a person who experiences no inherent conflict between these two drives.

In addition to integrating the spiritual and instinctual dimensions of life, the self-representation of regeneration in Spirit also resuscitates many of the features of the self-representation forged during early adulthood. That is to say, it resuscitates many of the features of the self-representation of the identity project. This worldly self-representation, if we recall, is deanimated during the alienation process, and it remains moribund after the alienation process comes to an end, during initial awakening and throughout regression in the service of transcendence. During initial awakening the ego is a liminal ego that, caught between mundane and supernatural worlds, is unable to return to its old worldly self; and during regression in the service of transcendence the ego, having just been reborn in Spirit, is too new and too divided a spiritual self to have any idea how its old worldly self might fit with the self that it is to become. Once regeneration in Spirit begins, however, the ego is no longer subject to these limitations. The ego of regeneration in Spirit is well on its way to integrating the spiritual and earthly dimensions of life and has made significant progress toward spiritual maturity. It is an ego, therefore, that is able to see how and to what extent its old worldly self is properly a part of the spiritual self that it has become.

The person undergoing regeneration in Spirit, then, begins to see that the self-representation of the identity project is not after all a completely inauthentic or false self, as it had seemed. Many of the features of this old self now once again begin to seem "real" (i.e., animated, alive) and "fitting" (i.e., authentic). Many of these features, therefore, once again begin to be accepted as features proper to the self. There is, however, this difference: the features in question are no longer, as before, core features of the self-representation and are instead authentic but secondary forms of self-expression. In thus being reduced in status, these features make up an outer, peripheral layer of the self-system. They now seem fitting once again in somewhat the same way that articles of clothing that had been put in the back of the closet can be tried on and found once again to be suited to one's own style. The features in question, then, in being resuscitated, become integral but not central features of the self-system. They become authentically self-expressing "clothing" of an inner spiritual self.

The personal shadow, which was derepressed during the alienation process, and the archetypal shadow, which was derepressed during regression in the service of transcendence, are also integrated within the new, good enough self-representation of regeneration in Spirit. The substantive features of the personal shadow—namely, those that embody real traits, tendencies, or capabilities rather than only false negative judgments—are relieved of stigma and accepted as features of a more inclusive, realistic self. These features are incorporated within the self-representation as strengths that had been denied, eccentricities that had been hidden, weaknesses that need to be overcome, or selfish or aggressive tendencies that need to be controlled. The personal shadow is thus rehabilitated, and at the same time the archetypal shadow, as already discussed, is redeemed. Instinctual life, which had been condemned as a demonic adversary of spiritual life, is embraced as the organic basis of earthly existence in all its dimensions, including the spiritual dimension. In thus incorporating the substance of both the personal and archetypal shadows, the self-representation of regeneration in Spirit is the first self-representation that is fully inclusive, that is not based on repression, personal or primal. It is the first self-representation that is able to be good enough without having to disown any part of the psyche.

Once regeneration in Spirit begins, then, the psyche no longer has a repressed, "evil" underside. No part of the psyche is rejected. This does not mean that everything in the psyche is accepted as completely good, for, again, weaknesses, susceptibilities, and perhaps selfish or aggressive tendencies are acknowledged. The self-representation of regeneration in Spirit is the representation of a good enough but imperfect self, a self that does not condemn any part of itself as evil but at the same time recognizes that it could be, and should strive to be, much better than it is. Rather, then, than meaning that everything in the psyche is accepted as completely good, the fact that the psyche no longer has a repressed underside means that what stands apart from goodness is no longer an alienated adversary of goodness and is instead simply a falling short of full goodness. Good-evil dualism is thus replaced by a *privatio boni* orientation according to which evil is not anything in opposition to the good but is instead only a privation, that is, a falling short of the good.

The redemption of the archetypal shadow is at the same time a humanization of the ego ideal, which is relieved of its unrealistic angelic character and brought down to earth as an ideal of a spiritual but also instinctually grounded human being. In thus being humanized, the ego ideal, paradoxically, is at the same time more truly spiritualized, for it ceases being a far-fetched ideal fabricated by an ego new to the life of Spirit and becomes a much more realistic ideal projected by a spiritually more mature ego in intimate communication with Spirit. The ego ideal is still the *ego's* ideal and continues for that reason to be part of an ego system to some degree separate from Spirit. The ego ideal, however, is now forged by the ego on the basis of the transformative influence of Spirit as Spirit works moment by moment within the ego's domain. The ego no longer projects a remote, exaggerated ideal of otherworldly purity and instead places before itself attainable worldly goals as Spirit guides the ego in facing the challenges of daily life. In guiding the ego in this intimately intercommunicative way, Spirit—that is to say, transforming Spirit—becomes the ego's counselor. The ego consults with Spirit, and Spirit advises the ego on what is required—not only ultimately but also in the exigencies of the here and now—if one is fully to live the life of Spirit.

As the ego ideal is thus rooted in Spirit, so, too, is the superego. Spirit becomes not only the ego's counselor but also its guardian. Spirit not only guides and inspires the ego toward greater growth in Spirit; it also impels the ego to grow in Spirit. As guardian, Spirit is an enforcer that challenges, purges, or harnesses the ego when it resists spiritual growth. The ego, in being disciplined by Spirit in these ways, still speaks to itself in the voice of the superego, exhorting itself to be more open to Spirit, lecturing itself when it fails a test of Spirit, or praising itself when it does as Spirit would have it do. This superego voice, however, is now the lesser of two disciplining powers in the ego's life; for even if the ego does not exhort, lecture, or praise itself, Spirit will force it to grow. In being the counselor that guides the ego in envisioning an ideal of a fully spiritual life, Spirit is also the guardian that ensures that the ego stays the course in making sufficient, good enough progress toward this ideal. The ego ideal and superego, although remaining agencies of the ego system, are now both rooted in Spirit. Spirit now counsels the ego as the ego projects the ego ideal and acts as guardian of the ego as the ego struggles with its own self-disciplining efforts.

In its roles as counselor and guardian, transforming Spirit is a powerful inner presence that the ego cannot ignore. When the ego is lost, transforming Spirit sharpens the ego's vision; when the ego is weary, transforming Spirit rekindles the ego's strength and desire for spiritual growth; when the ego is resistant, transforming Spirit impels the ego to act; when the ego is defensive, transforming Spirit forcibly opens the ego; and when the ego is arrogant, transforming Spirit humbles the ego. In these and other ways transforming Spirit is a motivating power internal to the ego system, a power that both inspires and disciplines the ego. Transforming Spirit both illuminates the path on which the ego is traveling and insists that the ego keep moving forward on this path.

The rooting of the ego ideal and superego in Spirit marks a fundamental change in the bases of these agencies of the ego system. Whereas, during

latency, these agencies are grounded in internalized parental goals and requirements and, during early adulthood, in the ego's own self-chosen goals and
requirements, they are, during regeneration in Spirit, grounded in Spirit's
goals and requirements. The fundamental motivations driving the ego thus
change from parent-based motivations to the ego's own self-motivations to
Spirit-based motivations. The parent-based motivations of the latency stage
suffice until the ego, during adolescence, disowns the ego ideal and superego
of the latency ego system, and the self-motivations of early adulthood suffice
until the ego ceases making satisfying progress in the identity project. Arriving
at this impasse, the ego must again ground itself in something greater than
itself if it is to regain sufficient motivation to resume moving forward in life.
Without parents any longer available to fill this need, it is Spirit that emerges
as inner counselor and guardian.

There are many metaphors for transforming Spirit. In addition to being a
counselor and guardian, transforming Spirit is also a life-giver, comforter, gift-
giver, and lover. The metaphor of lover captures an especially powerful role of
transforming Spirit in some people's lives and is a leading idea in bhakti
Hinduism, contemplative Christianity, and devotional spirituality in other
religions. In contemplative Christianity, transforming Spirit—or, rather, the
Holy Spirit or Christ within—is experienced as spiritual bridegroom, as a
lover whose advances cause both ecstasy and agony. St. Teresa of Avila is best
known among Christian contemplative writers who describe transforming
Spirit in this way. Teresa speaks of transforming Spirit as a lover who enters
the soul, causing transporting rapture and excruciating pain in preparing the
soul for the divine marriage. The soul pines for Christ and utterly yields to
Christ even when Christ's actions are hurtful—for the pain is a good pain, the
pain of spiritual growth. According to Teresa, the courtship between the soul
and transforming Spirit is a tempestuous one because the bridegroom is
sometimes violent and the soul is hypersensitive and consumed with desire for
the divine. The soul, then, is unstable during this period of spiritual betrothal.
It is subject to wild fluctuations because, lovesick, it is passionately affected by
every advance and retreat of Spirit. For those who experience transforming
Spirit in these ways, Spirit is not only a motivator (i.e., a counselor and
guardian) and a sustainer (i.e., a life-giver, comforter, and gift-giver), but also
a love partner in one's transformation.

THE INTEGRATED EGO

As regeneration in Spirit approaches integration, transforming Spirit gives
way to transparent Spirit. Transparent Spirit, as we learned in the last chapter, is the power of the Ground once it has ceased being to any degree other
in relation to the ego and has ceased as well being excessive or violent in its
effects. It is the power of the Ground as it appears to an ego that is entirely in
accord with the Ground, namely, as Spirit in the highest sense of the term: the

dynamic essence of light (the power of the Ground as amplifying energy), love (the power of the Ground as attracting energy), connection (the power of the Ground as both attracting and infusive energy), and union (the power of the Ground as dissolvent energy). The full integration of the ego with transparent Spirit marks the final reconstitution of the ego system, this time as a larger self-Self system. The ego-Spirit system of regeneration in Spirit here matures into a system in which the ego, now a completely integrated vehicle of Spirit, is a lesser self, the ego *of* Spirit, and in which Spirit, no longer to any degree other in relation to the ego, is a superior Self, the ego's own higher Self. This self-Self system is the spiritual marriage, the *hieros gamos*. It is the marriage of the soul with Christ (mystical Christianity), the yoga or yoking of *ātman* to Brahman (Vedanta Hinduism), the union of Shakti and Shiva (Tantric Hinduism), and the alchemical *coniunctio* or conjunction of opposites. It is the transpersonal integration of the ego and the Dynamic Ground.

This reconstitution of the ego system as a self-Self system is evident in all of the elements of the ego system: self-representation, ego ideal, and superego. The self-representation here changes to reflect the fact that Spirit, as transparent Spirit, is now wholly self—or, rather, Self—rather than wholly other (numinous Spirit) or an ally of self but not yet wholly self (transforming Spirit). The ego now relates to Spirit as its own vital power and as the higher essence of its own being. The power of the Ground remains the plenipotent, sovereign power of the soul in relation to which the ego is "mere" subject, in both relevant senses of the term: ego-subject and servant-subject. In its plenipotent sovereignty, however, the power of the Ground is no longer to any degree a foreign or external power and is instead a power to which the ego is married and with which the ego has become one in a higher, integrated life. The ego's self-representation, then, is now a self-Self representation. It is a representation of the ego as agent of Spirit.

The ego ideal is also reconstituted in a way that reflects the ego's relationship with Spirit as higher Self. Specifically, it ceases being a projection fashioned by the ego after the ego has listened to the counsel of Spirit and becomes an immediate expression of the wisdom of Spirit channeled through the ego acting as vehicle of Spirit. The ego ideal, then, here becomes as much Spirit's as the ego's ideal; correspondingly, the wisdom of Spirit here becomes as much the ego's as Spirit's wisdom. Spirit, in other words, ceases being the ego's counselor and becomes the ego's own spiritual vision. The ego no longer needs to project an ideal goal on the basis of the counsel of Spirit and instead simply sees with Spirit's eyes. This spiritual vision is not bestowed upon the ego all at once in arriving at the goal of integration; rather, it is gradually conferred as regeneration in Spirit approaches integration. Integration is only the point at which the ego becomes fully sighted with the eyes of Spirit.

The superego, too, reflects the integrated unity of self and Self. The superego here ceases being a voice by which the ego disciplines itself in response to the goadings of Spirit, for Spirit's goadings are now the ego's own prompt-ings. Correspondingly, Spirit here ceases being the ego's guardian, for a guardian is other than the guarded, and Spirit is here the ego's higher Self. What had been the independent voice of the superego, then, here becomes the quiet commitment of the ego to obey Spirit's imperatives as its own imperatives. Correspondingly, what had been the guardian function of Spirit here becomes an impelling force by which the ego pushes itself to move for-ward in growth in Spirit. In being impelled by Spirit, the ego is now self-impelled or, rather, Self-impelled. The integrated ego in this way not only sees with Spirit's eyes but also acts with Spirit's will. The ego no longer needs either to project its own ideal or to discipline itself apart from Spirit because it now inherits both the inspiring wisdom and the driving force of Spirit.

For those who relate to Spirit as lover, the transition from regeneration in Spirit to integration is a transition that transforms the perceived nature of spiritual love: this love ceases manifesting itself as the ego's lover and begins manifesting itself as the ego's love of others. During regeneration in Spirit, the ego betrothed to transforming Spirit relates to a tempestuous lover who afflicts the ego with ecstasies and agonies of intense, intimate passion. This love relationship becomes increasingly intimate until it ceases being a betrothal in which the ego is in love with and impassioned by Spirit and becomes a marriage in which the ego becomes the means by which Spirit's love enters the world. The spiritual marriage, as a marriage of self to Self, is a relationship that creates a higher unity, a unity in which the ego no longer experiences Spirit as lover—for a lover is other than the beloved—and instead experiences Spirit as the attracting, uniting energy of love itself. In becoming the married partner of Spirit, the integrated ego is filled with the love of Spirit in a way that more channels this love through the ego as lover of others than it directs this love to the ego itself as beloved-lover of Spirit. The integrated ego, united with Spirit, is filled with the love of Spirit in a way that overflows into the world. The love of Spirit flows out from the ego to others as siblings in Spirit. In this way, then, the integrated ego not only sees with Spirit's eyes and acts with Spirit's will but also reaches out to others with Spirit's love.

SIX

THE OTHER

THIS CHAPTER TRACKS the changing ways in which we experience others as development unfolds along the spiral path. A major theme that emerges from the discussion is that interpersonal development mirrors intrapsychic development at major stages of the spiral path. The newborn's radical intimacy with the caregiver mirrors the newborn's unconditional openness to the Dynamic Ground. The loss of radical intimacy caused by primal separation mirrors the quieting of the Dynamic Ground caused by primal repression. The awakening to others as objects of sexual desire, of course, mirrors the awakening of sexuality during puberty. The perception of others as partners or co-workers in life's tasks mirrors the reorganization of the ego system on the basis of the identity project in early adulthood. The perception of others as inauthentic actors, which is symptomatic of the alienation that can occur at midlife, mirrors the deanimation of the self-representation, which is also symptomatic of this alienation. Finally, the perception of others as spiritual beings—whether as guides to the supernatural, as representatives of angelic or demonic realms, or, for those nearing spiritual maturity, as siblings in Spirit—mirrors the awakening and unfolding of the power of the Ground as numinous, transforming, and transparent Spirit.

TABLE 6.1

DEVELOPMENTAL EXPRESSIONS OF THE PERCEIVED OTHER

STAGE OF LIFE	OTHER
Neonatal stage	Caregiver as wholly immanent other
Early preoedipal stage	Immanent-transcendent Great Mother
Late preoedipal stage	Split Good-Terrible Mother
Oedipal stage	Oedipal change of object; final steps on the way to object constancy
Latency	Transcendent others; private self and private others

Developmental Expressions of the Perceived Other *(CONTINUED)*

STAGE OF LIFE	OTHER
Puberty and adolescence	Sexually attractive others; transitional ego ideal figures (idols, mentors)
Early adulthood	Partner in life's tasks
Crossroads	Inauthentic actors
Awakening	Psychopomps, gurus, guides
Regression in the service of transcendence	Splitting of others into saints and sinners, angels and demons
Regeneration in Spirit	On the way to higher object constancy
Ego-Ground integration	Siblings in Spirit

THE OTHER AS WHOLLY IMMANENT OTHER

Freud (1911a) and many older-generation psychoanalysts held that the newborn is autistically self-encapsulated and cut off from the world. This view is rejected by most psychoanalysts today, who stress a relational perspective; and it is rejected as well by most nonpsychoanalytic theorists and researchers focusing on early childhood development. The prevailing view at this time is that the newborn, far from being self-encapsulated, is a partner in a profoundly intimate relationship with the caregiver, a relationship that is essential not only to the newborn's existence but also to its incipient sense of self. In earlier chapters we have spoken of this relationship and have stressed its bidirectionality, the fact that the newborn's intimacy with the caregiver is at the same time an openness to the Dynamic Ground, the nonegoic potentials of which are projected upon the caregiver. Life's first relationship is a relationship with the caregiver as imbued with the plenipotent power and other nonegoic potentials of the Dynamic Ground. Given this bidirectionality, it will at times be necessary to refer to the newborn's relationship with the caregiver as a relationship with the "caregiver-Ground."

Although life's original relationship is one of great intimacy and power, it is not a relationship in the full sense of the term. The newborn is only partially differentiated from the caregiver-Ground and, therefore, is related to its principal other in a manner that is better described as "not yet apart" than as "closely joined." This incompletely differentiated state, we should stress, does not imply that the newborn lacks a subjective center within itself. We learned in the last chapter that the newborn has an incipient nuclear ego, which is a unity of apperception and center of psychic agency. The newborn, then, does have a subjective center within itself. In having such a center, however, the newborn does not have any boundaries that differentiate it from the rest of existence.

The newborn, lacking an understanding of object permanence, has no inkling that a world exists beyond its immediate experience and, therefore, in effect assumes that everything exists within its immediate experience. The newborn has a subjective center within itself, but it has no circumference. Rather than being cut off from all existence, then, the fact is that the newborn in effect includes all existence.

This all-inclusiveness of the newborn's consciousness has the following implication bearing upon its relationship with the caregiver: the newborn's relationship with the caregiver is a relationship with a wholly immanent other. So far as the newborn knows, the caregiver exists only as an intermittent stimulus configuration. The caregiver does have the status of "object" in the sense of being a datum within, rather than the subjective center of, the newborn's consciousness. In being an object in this sense, however, the caregiver is not an object in the more complete sense of being a transcendent entity existing independently of the newborn's consciousness. Although located outside the subjective center of the newborn's consciousness, the caregiver falls within the unbounded all-inclusiveness of the newborn's consciousness.

This immanence of the caregiver takes nothing away from the profundity of the newborn's relationship with the caregiver. It means only that this relationship, in all its profundity, is an incomplete relationship. The newborn's relationship with the caregiver is a profound relationship in being a radically intimate connection tapping the deepest sources of the newborn's being. It is at the same time, however, an incomplete relationship in being a connection between an unbounded, merely incipient ego and a wholly immanent, not yet independent other.

THE OTHER AS IMMANENT-
TRANSCENDENT GREAT MOTHER

Beginning at approximately four or five months of age, the child begins to understand object permanence. It begins to understand that objects exist even when not perceived and, therefore, that objects are transcendent entities. As the child thus begins to understand the transcendent existence of objects, it begins in particular to understand the transcendent existence of the caregiver. This initial sense of the caregiver's independence is frightening to the child, and the child, consequently, begins to cling to the caregiver and to suffer stranger anxiety (Spitz 1965). The distress experienced by the child at this point—coinciding with the differentiation subphase of the separation-individuation process—is considerable but short-lived. The child soon overcomes its anxiety and enters the practicing subphase of the separation-individuation process, the subphase from approximately eight to eighteen months of age during which the child explores the world with reckless abandon and delight, always assuming that the caregiver, when out of sight, is accessible in case of need.

In changing in status from an immanent stimulus configuration to a transcendent entity, the caregiver comes into focus as the Great Mother.[1] This Great Mother is a complex and paradoxical being, a being possessing both transcendent and immanent dimensions, both primitively human and superhuman aspects. The Great Mother, although understood to be a transcendent entity, is also a being with roots within the child; for the Great Mother is not only the outer caregiver but also a projection of the child's inner Ground. Furthermore, the Great Mother, although in some ways perceived as less than a complete human being, is in other ways perceived as more than a human being; for the Great Mother, enhanced by plenipotently charged projections, is a seemingly all-powerful provider of whom the child is in awe.

The Great Mother, like the caregiver as perceived during the neonatal stage, is the bidirectional caregiver-Ground. The Great Mother, then, is a being possessing both outer and inner, both objectively derived and subjectively projected dimensions. As such a bidirectional being, the primary way in which the Great Mother differs from the caregiver of the neonatal stage, as just explained, is that the Great Mother in her outer or objective dimension is understood to exist beyond consciousness. Whereas the objectivity of the newborn's principal other is an immanent objectivity of a stimulus configuration, the objectivity of the Great Mother is a transcendent objectivity of an independent entity. If, however, the Great Mother's objectivity is thus a transcendent objectivity, this does not mean that the Great Mother is a wholly transcendent being. Although the Great Mother is transcendent in her objective dimension, she is—or, as bidirectional caregiver-Ground, remains—immanent in her subjective dimension, as the focal object of the child's deep psyche. Although the Great Mother is understood to be a transcendent being, much of what the Great Mother is derives from within the child, from the Dynamic Ground. The Great Mother, then, is a paradoxical being, an independent existent with roots deep within the child.

We cannot know exactly how the child perceives the Great Mother, but it is unlikely that the child perceives her as having any more than a rudimentary human form. A good deal of research has demonstrated that infants and even newborns respond preferentially to the caregiver and interact with the caregiver in social, distinctively human ways.[2] Such behavior implies that from the outset of life the caregiver is perceived as having a distinctively human character. It does not imply, however, that the caregiver is perceived as having a fully human character, and the fact of course is that not only infants but toddlers, too, lack the cognitive abilities needed to recognize many human features and capabilities. Infants and toddlers, then, likely perceive the Great Mother as a being who is human only in basic, limited ways, for example, in particular vocalizations, facial expressions, gestural displays, and other communicative behaviors. Except for responding preferentially to distinctively human expressions such as these, infants and toddlers probably perceive the Great Mother primarily as a prepersonal being, as a source of warmth, food, protection, and comfort.

If the Great Mother is perceived as less than a full human being, she also, paradoxically, is perceived as more than a human being. Again, the Great Mother is a seemingly all-powerful being of whom the child is in awe. As the child's principal provider and protector, the Great Mother is the primary focus of the child's attention; and as an "object" imbued with plenipotent power and overlaid with archetypal images, the Great Mother is a being of irresistible magnetism, immense proportions, and compelling guises. The Great Mother for these reasons is not only a primitive but also a supernatural being, a being in the presence of whom the child is eclipsed or exalted, enchanted or astounded, captivated or dissolved. The Great Mother, in short, is a prepersonal goddess.

THE OTHER AS SPLIT GOOD-TERRIBLE MOTHER

Let us recall the background leading to preoedipal splitting: (1) The reason why the child quickly overcomes the anxiety accompanying the initial discovery of the caregiver's transcendent objectivity is that the child tacitly assumes that the caregiver, even when not perceived, is close by and accessible in case of need. (2) This assumption is shattered at approximately sixteen to eighteen months of age when the child comes to understand that objects, and the caregiver in particular, are not necessarily tied to the child's region of experience and can, therefore, exist anywhere in a vastly enlarged space. (3) This insight into the full independence of objects in turn afflicts the child with abandonment anxiety: the caregiver, whom the child had taken for granted, is now seen as a being who could be lost and, indeed, could abandon the child.

The insight into the full independence of objects and the abandonment anxiety that arises from it trigger preoedipal splitting. We already know from the discussion in the last chapter that this splitting forces the child to begin thinking of itself as both a "good child" and a "bad child." Here we can add that this splitting of the emerging self-representation is a subject-side correlate of a splitting of the child's primary object representation, the representation of the caregiver. The caregiver here ceases being the taken-for-granted Great Mother and, in the child's perception, is split into contrary opposites: the *Good Mother*, who unconditionally loves and omnipotently protects the child, and the *Terrible Mother*, who dislikes and punishes the child and who might leave the child to fend for itself. The Good Mother consists of all of the positive qualities of the Great Mother thrown into relief and exaggerated, and the Terrible Mother consists of all the opposite qualities, also thrown into relief and exaggerated. The Good Mother is all good, the Terrible Mother all bad. There is no middle ground.

The genius of preoedipal splitting as a defense mechanism is twofold, for it allows the child to believe both (1) that, irrespective of its behavior, it remains a good child, deserving of the love and protection of the caregiver; and (2) that, irrespective of the caregiver's behavior, the caregiver remains a Good Mother, a being who unconditionally loves and omnipotently protects the child. As for the first of these points, we already know that preoedipal splitting allows the child, as good child, to remain untainted by bad behavior. The child is unaffected by its own bad behavior because, in the child's mind, this behavior belongs to another, bad child. No matter how bad the child might be as bad child, it can always reappear as good child with a clean slate. This impeccability of the child, we can now add, is possessed by the caregiver as well: no matter how harsh or neglectful the caregiver might be as Terrible Mother, the caregiver can—and indeed will, the child assumes—reappear as the loving and protecting Good Mother. Because the Terrible Mother and the Good Mother are in effect separate people, the negative qualities of the former do not detract from the perfection the latter. Just as, then, splitting allows the child to believe that, appearances to the contrary, it is always worthy of love and protection, it also allows the child to believe that, appearances to the contrary, it will always in fact receive love and protection.

Although splitting is a brilliant defensive strategy, it cannot work in the long run because both the Good Mother and the Terrible Mother, like the good child and the bad child, are unsustainable exaggerations. The caregiver is not perfect, and so when the child reaches out hoping to be embraced or rescued by what it thinks is the Good Mother, its hopes are frequently dashed. The child for this reason finds it increasingly difficult to sustain belief in a perfect Good Mother. At the same time, however, the child finds it increasingly difficult to sustain belief in a completely bad Terrible Mother, for if the caregiver is not perfect, neither is the caregiver completely bad— indeed, far from it. The child, then, is frequently surprised to be treated well when, having misbehaved, it thought it was in danger of being punished by the Terrible Mother. The child in this way learns that the caregiver, although not perfect, nonetheless almost always meets the child's needs. The child eventually learns that the caregiver is neither perfectly good nor completely bad but is, rather, "good enough." Just as the child eventually overcomes the splitting of its self-representation by learning that it need not be perfect to be good enough to merit love and protection, so it also eventually overcomes the splitting of its principal object representation by learning that the caregiver need not be perfect to be good enough to provide love and protection. Splitting is based on unsustainable exaggerations, and the child is eventually disabused of these exaggerations and brought to a more realistic understanding of both itself and the caregiver.

THE OVERCOMING OF SPLITTING AND THE ACHIEVEMENT OF OBJECT CONSTANCY

According to a leading view of psychoanalytic object relations theory, the child overcomes splitting by giving up its fantasy about a "good object," the idealized caregiver. The child, in somewhat the manner just described, begins to understand that the caregiver is not perfect but is nonetheless primarily good, good enough to meet the child's needs. In arriving at this new understanding of its principal other, the child achieves *object constancy:* its primary object representation ceases being split, exaggerated, and wildly shifting and becomes integrated, realistic, and stable.

This psychoanalytic account of the overcoming of preoedipal splitting focuses primarily on cognitive factors. It is by learning more about the caregiver and about life in general that the child is able to mend not only its split representation of the caregiver but also its corresponding conflicting feelings for the caregiver. This account is undeniably accurate as far as it goes. In focusing primarily on cognitive factors, however, it does not give sufficient weight to crucial psychodynamic and intersubjective factors—namely, primal repression and primal separation, respectively—which underlie and facilitate the child's cognitive advance toward object constancy. The point is this: It would be much more difficult for the child to surmount splitting and achieve object constancy, if it would be possible at all, without the defensive infrastructure established by the consolidation of primal closing.

Otto Kernberg (1976, 1987) has hypothesized that the overcoming of splitting makes it possible for repression to become the child's primary defensive strategy. He says:

> *It is suggested that this consolidation of the ego establishes repression as the central defensive operation, in contrast to splitting of the earlier ego.* (1976, p. 41; emphasis in original)

> *The synthesis of identification systems* [the overcoming of split object representations and self-representations] *neutralizes aggression and possibly provides the most important single energy source for the higher level of repressive mechanisms to come . . . .* (1976, pp. 45–46; emphasis in original)

According to Kernberg, repression not only follows splitting but also is made possible only by the overcoming of splitting. The first of these points is unproblematic. The second, however, is not, for repression, as we have seen, rather than being made possible only by the overcoming of splitting, is in fact a means—perhaps an indispensable means—by which splitting is overcome.

Repression—primal repression, that is—is such a means because it divests the caregiver of projected plenipotent powers and in doing so reduces the caregiver from the caregiver-Ground, a prepersonal goddess, to the caregiver only, a being of considerably smaller stature and with considerably less impact on the child. Thus reduced in magnitude and effect, the caregiver, in the child's perception, is no longer so angelically good when good or so monstrously evil when not. The caregiver thus ceases possessing the awesome positive and negative qualities of the Good and Terrible Mothers, respectively, which could not coexist in a single being, and comes to possess instead much less pronounced positive and negative qualities, which can coexist in a single, imperfect (though primarily good) being. The child's cognitive advance, its ability to dispense with the fantasy of the Good Mother, is in this way facilitated by primal repression.

Were it not for primal repression disjoining the Ground from the caregiver, it is doubtful whether the child would be able to overcome splitting as quickly and effectively as it does, if it would be able to overcome splitting at all. Were it not for primal repression, the child might never be able to make the cognitive advance upon which object constancy is based.

Interestingly, in helping bring an end to preoedipal splitting, primal repression is responsible for a splitting of a new sort, namely, a splitting of the psyche into conscious and repressed, unconscious realms, into a realm of the conscious ego on the one hand and a realm of the submerged unconscious Ground on the other. The ego, that is, overcomes the "horizontal" splitting of consciousness into good and bad sides by perpetrating a "vertical" splitting of the psyche into conscious surface and repressed unconscious depths.[3] This two-tiered division of the psyche, once established, remains firmly in place. Indeed, for most people it remains in place for the rest of their lives. Primal repression, then, as a means by which preoedipal splitting is overcome, is no mere means in the sense of temporary expedient. It is a means that becomes a deep, long-lasting structure of the psyche.

In reducing the caregiver-Ground to, simply, the caregiver, primal repression at the same time renders the caregiver a wholly transcendent being. Primal repression, in withdrawing nonegoic potentials from the caregiver, severs the caregiver's line of immanence within the child. The child ceases projecting its inner Ground upon the caregiver, and the caregiver, correspondingly, ceases existing in part within the child. The caregiver is uprooted from the child's inner Ground and thus becomes exclusively an outer, transcendent being. Primal repression, then, not only divests the caregiver of plenipotent, overawing powers; it externalizes the caregiver as well.

This externalization of the caregiver can also be understood from the perspective of primal separation, which is the intersubjective correlate of primal repression. If primal repression is the act by which the child severs its internal connection with the caregiver, primal separation is the act by which the child puts safe distance between itself and the caregiver. Before primal separation, the child is a body ego without private inwardness. It is unconditionally open, living completely without defenses in the public domain. Open in this way, the child has no protection from powerful emotions flowing from the Great Mother. Such unprotected openness, of course, is not a problem in stages preceding splitting because it is the basis of nurturing exchanges between the child and the caregiver. After splitting occurs, however, this openness becomes deeply problematic because it becomes the basis not only of nurturing but also of hurtful exchanges. It becomes the basis not only of the child's intimacy with the Good Mother but also of the child's vulnerability to the Terrible Mother. The child cannot enjoy the former without also suffering the latter.

If vulnerability to the Terrible Mother is the price the child must pay for intimacy with the Good Mother, then forfeiture of intimacy with the Good Mother—that is to say, of radical, wholly open and undefended intimacy—is the price the child must pay for overcoming vulnerability to the Terrible Mother. Splitting must be brought to an end, and so the child pays this price. It draws back from the caregiver and in doing so discovers a private inner space in which it is safely distant from the caregiver and in which it can, should it feel the need, close itself to the caregiver. Whether, then, by primal repression or by primal separation—which in any case, again, are two sides of the same act, primal closing—the child disengages itself from the caregiver, reducing the caregiver from an immanent-transcendent other to an exclusively transcendent other. Whether by primal repression or primal separation, the child cuts its psychic umbilical cord and establishes within itself a sphere of protected privacy. The child, related now to a wholly transcendent, non-plenipotent other and safe within the exclusively immanent sphere of its own psychic space, is no longer so powerfully or deeply affected by the caregiver. The child, therefore, is able to see the caregiver in more realistic light, as a single, imperfect but good enough parent. The child, in other words, achieves object constancy.

The child does not commit itself to primal closing in one decisive act. The achievement of object constancy is a gradual, halting process. Mahler describes the period from twenty-four to thirty-six-plus months as a time that is "on the way" to object constancy, and she (McDevitt and Mahler 1980) suggests that the oedipal conflict is in important respects a replay of the conflict of the rapprochement period. Pursuing Mahler's suggestion about the oedipal conflict, let us propose that this conflict is indeed a replay of the conflict of the rapprochement period and, in particular, that it is a replay that has the major result of bringing the rapprochement conflict to a decisive end. The rapprochement conflict, let us propose, is finally brought to an end when the child, faced with the pressures characteristic of the oedipal triangle, is forced to undergo what psychoanalysis calls the oedipal "change of object."

The oedipal stage is a period during which the secondary caregiver, typically a male parent (henceforth "father"[4]), begins to play a decisive role in the child's life by becoming a candidate for the child's primary allegiance. Before the oedipal stage, the child's primary allegiance goes to the primary caregiver, typically a female parent (henceforth "mother"). It is, however, precisely this allegiance to the mother as love object, as we have seen, that is the child's Achilles' heel during the rapprochement period: intimacy with the Good Mother makes the child vulnerable to the Terrible Mother. The child, then, must wean itself from the mother as love object if it is to overcome splitting. This developmental requirement is posed before the oedipal period begins and might be met without oedipal incentives. The requirement in question, however, is usually not met until the child, in the oedipal period, is forced to make a fundamental choice between the mother and the father: the oedipal change of object.

Again, the child's withdrawal from radical intimacy with the mother—that is, its movement toward a commitment to primal separation and, thereby, toward the achievement of object constancy—is a gradual, halting process. It is extremely difficult for the child to relinquish the soul-satisfying nurture that goes with radical intimacy and the feeling of safety that goes with the fantasy of being lovingly protected by an all-good being. For these reasons the child yields again and again to intimate embraces with the mother and repeatedly resurrects the fantasy of the Good Mother. The need to overcome splitting, however, drives the child to make efforts to distance itself from the mother, and so the child draws back from the mother and takes refuge in the privacy of psychic space. In doing so, however, the child experiences an intensification of intimacy needs and, therefore, once again opens itself without reserve to what it hopes is the Good Mother. It does so, that is, until the oedipal father enters the scene and forces the child's hand by making the child's choice between intimacy with the mother or withdrawal from the mother at the same time a choice between primary allegiance to the mother or primary allegiance to the father.

In the oedipal situation, the father plays a dual role: he is at once an authority figure and a rival for intimacy with the mother. As authority figure, the father is a person who performs the role of disciplinarian, setting and enforcing standards of self-responsible behavior. The mother, of course, is also a disciplinarian, and the father is also a nurturer and object of love. In the traditional patriarchal family, however, it is the mother who is the primary nurturer and object of love and the father who is the primary disciplinarian. As disciplinarian or authority figure, the father, in the eyes of the child, is typically both a wrathful and a merciful being, wrathful when the child fails to meet standards and merciful—i.e., not only forgiving but encouraging and loving—when the child is contrite or otherwise strives to be a "good girl" or "good boy." The child yearns for the father's loving approval, knowing that the father's love, in contrast to the tender love of the mother, is a tough love. The child is understandably in awe of the father in his role as authority figure because the father's punishments can be severe and his approval is fervently desired.

The child is all the more in awe of the father, however, in his role as rival for intimacy with the mother, for in this role the father is not only a loving enforcer of standards but also, in the child's perception, a threat to the child's well-being. The child's intimacy with the mother is entirely unproblematic in the first years of life. As a newborn, infant, and then toddler, the child has a favored relationship with the mother as Great Mother. As the preoedipal period comes to an end, however, the child begins to have doubts about its "favorite other" status. These doubts arise because the mother not only spends less time in intimate relationship with the child but also spends more time in intimate relationship with the father and in partnership with the father as co-disciplinarian of the child. This, at any rate, is how it must seem to the child. Moreover, it sometimes happens that the father actually resents the time and affection the mother gives to the child. For these reasons the child begins to see the father as a competitor for the mother's love, a rival whose superiority in strength and developed intelligence is overwhelming. Seeing the father in this way, the child finds itself engaged in a contest with an invincible adversary. The child knows it cannot possibly win and has no choice but to submit to its superior rival.

In Freud's original interpretation, the oedipal rivalry is a contest between a boy child and the father that eventuates in the boy's capitulation to the father as rival and concomitant defensive identification with the father as exemplar of standards of responsible independence. Although Freud interpreted the oedipal rivalry in this gender-specific manner, there is no reason why it must be understood in this way; for girls, too, relate to the mother as original love object and, as time passes, begin to perceive the father as rival for the mother's love. Moreover, girl's, too, capitulate to the father and identify defensively with him. The primary difference between boys and girls is in the manner of the identification. Whereas boys identify with the father directly, as "little men," girls do so indirectly by identifying with the mother's role in relation to the father. This in any case holds true generally in traditional, patriarchally organized societies. In patriarchal societies, both boys and girls leave the world of the preoedipal mother and enter the world of the oedipal father. In doing so, however, they take different routes. Boys enter the father's world directly and as primary citizens; they seek to be like the father so that some day they can be fathers. Girls, in contrast, enter the father's world indirectly and, all too frequently, as secondary citizens; they seek to be like the mother in relation to the father so that some day they can be mothers in relation to fathers. Gender roles are changing rapidly, but these patterns continue to be deeply entrenched.[5]

Putting gender considerations aside, the point here is that the oedipal father, both in his role as authority figure and his role as rival, forces the child's hand in the rapprochement dilemma. The child enters the oedipal stage struggling with the difficulties of splitting and already taking initial steps to wean itself from radical intimacy with the mother. The child might achieve this independence from the mother on its own, but the oedipal father provides powerful additional incentives. He does so because, as authority figure, he insists that the child meet standards of self-responsible independence and because, as rival, he is perceived as a threat to the child's well-being should the child continue to pursue its "favorite other" status in relation to the mother. The child is already in the process of weaning itself from the mother when the oedipal father enters the scene. The oedipal father accelerates and finalizes the weaning process.

Once capitulation to the oedipal father as rival completes the child's shift of primary allegiance from the mother as love object to the father as authority figure, the oedipal change of object is complete. This resolution of oedipal conflict signals the consolidation of primal closing and, therefore, the end of unconditional openness to the Ground and corresponding radical intimacy with others. The Ground is now submerged, quieted, and inaccessible to the ego, except during sleep; and others are now wholly transcendent others, others with whom feelings are exchanged across a psychic distance and, typically, against some degree of defensive resistance. The child, to be sure, still experiences intimacy with others, but the intimacy experienced is no longer the radical, distanceless intimacy that the child enjoyed in the first years of life.

WHOLLY IMMANENT SELF AND
WHOLLY TRANSCENDENT OTHERS

In facilitating the achievement of object constancy, primal closing helps the child overcome abandonment anxiety and allows the child once again to feel safe in the world. In achieving object constancy, the child by no means returns to being the completely fearless adventurer that it was during the practicing subphase of the separation-individuation process. The child now knows that the primary caregiver—and guardians generally—is neither all good nor always available to respond in case of need. The caregiver, the child now understands, is an imperfect being who could be anywhere in a vast, uncharted expanse of space. This insight notwithstanding, the child who has achieved object constancy—that is to say, the latency child—is no longer seriously distressed by feelings of insecurity because it now believes, tacitly, that the caregiver, although neither all good nor always present, is at least primarily good and usually present. The child, that is, believes that the caregiver is "good enough."

As primal closing thus helps the child overcome abandonment anxiety, it—or, more precisely, primal separation—also helps the child achieve self-possession. Primal separation has this beneficial developmental consequence because it opens up within the child a private space that is exclusively the child's own and within which the child is free from outer influences. Primal separation is the means by which the child marks out a sphere of defended, wholly immanent selfhood and in doing so becomes a fully independent person. In making a final commitment to primal separation, the child trades radically intimate but incompletely differentiated relatedness with others for fully differentiated but defensively based independence from others. The pendulum swings away from complete openness to others, by no means all the way to the opposite extreme, as we explain in a moment, but nonetheless to a position of significant distance and reserve. This shift away from complete openness, although a loss of radical intimacy with others, is a net developmental advance because the achievement of independence, even if defensive independence, is a necessary step forward on the developmental path.

Latency, then, is the first stage of fully immanent selfhood and fully differentiated relationships with others, where both the immanence and the differentiation are defensively grounded, based on primal separation. The latency child experiences the world from the standpoint of private psychic space and from this standpoint relates to others in external fashion, as a private self to private others. The latency child is thus separated from others by a safe psychic distance.

This distance, we should stress, although sufficient to guard the child's fragile independence, is not so great as to close the child to real emotional exchanges. Private, externally related selves *do* open themselves and connect with others. When they do this, however, the connections made are typically bridges—or, to use an analogy suggested by the philosopher Martin Buber (1970), electrical arcs—spanning a psychic distance rather than radically intimate, distanceless confluences. They tend to be only partially open exchanges rather than fully open interfusions. Because, for the latency child, intimacy with others goes against the grain of primal separation, the kind of intimacy experienced by the latency child is typically an incomplete intimacy of closeness rather than a radical intimacy of full togetherness. As a private self relating to private others, the latency child is ambivalent about intimacy. The latency child both needs and enjoys the emotional exchanges that occur during moments of closeness with others. Held in check by primal separation, however, the latency child must overcome resistance and "let go" to achieve such exchanges.

We should stress once more that the loss of completely open relationships with others is offset by a greater developmental gain: full differentiation from others. The radical intimacy experienced by the child in the first few years of life is an intimacy of incomplete differentiation. Primal separation, in bringing this intimacy to an end, forces the child to complete its differentiation from others and thereby allows the child to begin, in a defensively limited way, to relate to others as a fully differentiated self relating to fully differentiated others. The latency child's external relationships with others, then, are developmentally superior to its original relationship with the caregiver, despite the defensive basis of the former and the radical intimacy of the latter. The first half of life is devoted to ego development, and the ego cannot continue to develop without first achieving independence. Sacrificing radical but incompletely differentiated intimacy for full even if defensive independence, therefore, counts as an essential developmental advance. It is an advance that—along with the intrapsychic calm achieved by primal repression—makes it possible for the ego to develop at an accelerated pace during the latency years.

THE OTHER AS OBJECT OF SEXUAL DESIRE AND AS TRANSITIONAL EGO IDEAL FIGURE

Corresponding to the emergence of the sexual drive in puberty is a transformation of relevant others into possible objects of sexual desire. In experiencing the awakening of sexuality, adolescents begin seeking out other people with whom they might experience intimacy, intimacy based not only on an exchange of feelings generally but also on an exchange of sexual feelings in particular. The sexual drive is inherently object related; to experience this drive is to experience the desire to be sexually intimate *with someone.*

The emergence of sexual desire indicates that the power of the Ground is astir in its instinctual organization as libido. Libido here begins to express itself as an object-seeking energy that imbues desirable others with sexual charge, thereby heightening their desirability. When two people are thus attracted to each other, this libidinal process becomes a mutually heightening interchange, a two-sided circuit of escalating desire and appeal. The power of the Ground, working thus as object-seeking libido, is an invisible power that draws people together. It is eros, the force borne by Cupid's arrow. Astir in its instinctual organization as libido, then, the power of the Ground expresses itself in the form of erotic yearnings. These yearnings are first experienced in early adolescence and take on form and focus during the teenage years, beginning with fantasies, evolving into infatuations, and sometimes culminating in falling in love.

When erotic yearnings lead to sexual involvement, a new form of love relationship emerges. Sexual activity, in stirring the sexual system, elicits intense, full-bodied feelings from deep within the psyche and activates instinctual and social programs governing mating. For this reason adolescents, when they become sexually involved, enter into an exchange that can lead to intimacy of great passion. Some adolescent sexual relationships, of course, are little more than encounters to achieve relief from sexual tension or are otherwise interpersonal in only minimal ways. Still, adolescent sexual relationships generally can be said to have the potential of becoming a new form of love relationship, a form of relationship in which the parties engage each other in a vulnerably open way and allow intense feelings to flow.

In addition to being a stage during which relevant others begin being perceived as objects of sexual desire, adolescence is a stage during which people other than parents begin being perceived as ego ideal figures. During latency, parents serve as ego ideal figures, the male parent, in the traditional family, typically serving as ego ideal figure for boys and the female parent for girls. This focus on a parent as perfect role model usually comes to an end during the teen years, during which we turn to people other than parents to meet not only intimacy but also emulation needs, people who will facilitate our push toward independence from parents and growth toward self-responsible adulthood. At the same time, then, that adolescents begin to elaborate fantasies about sexually attractive people, they also begin to elaborate fantasies about inspiring people: heroes, superstars, icons, mentors. The ego ideal figures who thus emerge during adolescence, like the romantic figures, are typically figures of passing infatuation. Adolescence is a transitional stage, and its relationships with desired and idolized others in particular have a transitional character.

THE OTHER AS PARTNER IN LIFE'S TASKS

A chief dividing line between adolescence and early adulthood is commitment to the identity project. This project, if we recall, is the endeavor by which, in entering early adulthood, we commit ourselves to making something of ourselves in the world: farmer, doctor, accountant, wife, husband, father, citizen, bohemian, gangster, femme fatale, mother, Buddhist, Jew, conservative, socialist, and so forth. Having discussed the identity project in the last chapter, we need here note only that a relationship commitment is typically one of the main components of the project. This commitment need not be a lifetime vow, nor need it be a commitment to one person only. It is, however, a commitment to another person or persons to share the responsibilities, hardships, and joys of life. It is a firm resolve to enter into partnership with another person or persons "for better or for worse, for richer or for poorer, in sickness and in health."

Such a commitment usually takes the form of a marriage between heterosexual lovers leading eventually to the parenting of children. This traditional form of commitment, however, is only one way in which people can enter into partnership. Partnerships need not be heterosexual; they need not include children; and they need not even be relationships between sexual lovers. Any long-term relationship based on cooperation, trust, and affection can be a partnership. For example, relationships among members of a commune or religious order can be partnerships in our sense of the term. The essential thing is not sexually based love, although sexuality in fact is a primary basis of most partnership relationships. Rather, the essential thing is commitment to sharing the responsibilities, hardships, and joys of life.

In partnerships—and here for the sake of convenience we speak in terms of conventional two-person partnerships—one's partner is at once one's principal love object and a person to whom an unconditional commitment is made. One's partner in this way combines the earlier roles of the preoedipal mother, who was the child's original lover, and the oedipal father, to whom an unconditional commitment was made in the oedipal change of object. The combining of these two roles in the partner teaches those in partnerships an important lesson, namely, that love is also responsibility. In partnerships, the mutuality of love is at the same time a division of labor; to love and be loved by another is at the same time to work hand in hand with another. It sometimes happens that the love side of a partnership veils the work side, allowing one or both of the partners, in being loved, to fail to meet responsibilities: "If I am loved no matter what I do, why should I do more than the minimum?" It sometimes happens, too, that the work side of a partnership exacts a toll on the love side, and a hardened, dutiful division of labor sets in, sometimes leading one or both of the partners to find love outside the partnership.

Partnerships can be destroyed when either love or work eclipses the other in these ways. People in partnerships, then, face the challenge of learning how to integrate love and work so that these two sides of partnership can enhance rather than detract from each other. To the extent that partners are able to integrate love and work, they are able to perceive each of these sides of their relationship in terms of the other. They are able to perceive love in terms of work by seeing love as a caring about and, therefore, a caring for the other, and they are able to perceive work in terms of love by seeing work as something that they want to do in behalf of the other, as a labor of love. To the extent that love and work are thus integrated, love leavens work, and work deepens love.

The integration of love and work is one of the chief lessons to be learned in the first half of life. Long-term partnerships are the primary classrooms for this lesson. They are not the only classrooms, however. People who are not in a partnership relationship are also assigned the lesson of integrating love and work, and many such people learn this lesson much better than do people with partners. Any loving relationship is also potentially a work relationship, and any work relationship is also potentially a loving relationship. To the extent that we learn to work in our love and love as we work, to that extent we have achieved not only personal but also spiritual maturity.

THE OTHER AS INAUTHENTIC ACTOR

Most people, despite occasional setbacks, continue to make satisfying progress in the identity project until the end or very near the end of their lives. Some people, however, as we know, begin to suffer an irrecoverable loss of faith in the identity project, a disillusionment that alienates them from the world and leaves them feeling not only discouraged but also disconnected, not only unmotivated but also unreal. People who experience this encroaching sense of unreality feel as though they are no longer their old selves but are, instead, only a repertoire of scripted behaviors, a mere acting out of conventional social roles. Moreover, in beginning to see themselves in this way, they also begin to see others in the same light. Unable any longer to take their own identities seriously, they cannot take the identities of other people seriously either. In seeing themselves as false façades, they see others as false façades as well.

People who suffer this type of alienation perceive others more specifically as inauthentic but nonetheless self-serious actors, as pretenders who do not know they are pretending. Seeing others in this way is at once comical and maddening. It is comical because it makes the self-seriousness of others as they act out social scripts seem utterly ridiculous. Dostoevsky's underground man, for example—who is just such an alienated person—finds bureaucrats, military officers, and people playing other professional roles ludicrous in their posturings, arrogance, and complete lack of self-insight. If, however, people suffering alienation find others comical in this way, they also find them maddening; for alienated people, oddly, envy other people. They envy others because others, despite their comical lack of self-insight, possess a sense of being and value in the world, however groundless. Alienated people, having suffered a deanimation of the self-representation, have no such sense of being and value. Dostoevsky's underground man exhibits this bitter ambivalence toward others, showing at once amused contempt and resentful desire for the sense of self and self-importance that others, in their ignorance, enjoy.

Not all alienated people are as amused or as resentful as Dostoevsky's underground man. Alienated people do, though, share the existential "insight" that worldly identity is "only" a façade or pretense. Scare quotes are used because this alienated insight is a partial truth that alienated people mistake for the whole truth. The partial truth is that worldly identity is in significant respects a dramatic performance, an enacting of socially defined roles. This partial truth, however, is not the whole truth, for worldly identity is more than a performance before an audience. In enacting social roles, we do much more than simply reproduce scripted behaviors; we *engage* roles in ways that shape and disclose our personalities. Social roles are indeed scripts for acting on the public stage, but they are also vehicles by means of which we give outer expression to our inner selves. Alienated people, then, exchange one half-truth for another: Whereas most people believe that worldly identity is the true and whole self, alienated people believe that worldly identity is a completely false self. Alienated people, disillusioned about the identity project, have awakened to the fact that worldly identity is a dramatic performance. However, in awakening to this fact, they have lost sight of the fact that, as a dramatic performance, worldly identity is also an expression of an inner self.

The alienated condition blinds one to authenticity in others. Those who suffer alienation are unable to see others as people who, in engaging social roles, give expression to themselves from the inside out. For alienated people, the world is no longer alive, and the people in it are no longer real. Everyone is an actor on a lifeless stage "playing at being" rather than truly being. Other people, still under the spell of the identity project, have not yet achieved this insight. They comically take themselves to be real agents in a real world. Only alienated people know—or, rather, believe, mistaking a half-truth for the whole truth—that "agency is only acting" and that "no one is to be taken seriously."

THE OTHER AS CHANNEL OF NUMINOUS POWER

The perception of others as only false façades comes to an end when introverted psychic energy ignites the power of the Ground in its plenipotency, for when this occurs the depth dimension of the psyche, both in oneself and others, becomes evident. Prior to awakening, the perceived depth in others is their ego-based subjectivity. Although this subjectivity in others is private and, therefore, inaccessible to us, it is a type of depth we can easily understand. The ego-based subjectivity of others, we assume, is similar to our own; it is a private psychic space in which an ego engages in conversations with itself, makes decisions, and experiences a range of familiar feelings. The inner depth of others, then, is usually familiar and readable rather than unfathomably profound—or so it seems. There are exceptions. Creative geniuses, spiritually gifted souls, and mentally disturbed people strike us as having a profound, or at least mysterious, depth. The point, though, is that these types of people are exceptions. As a rule, we perceive the inner depth of others as a depth that is private but nonetheless within the reach of understanding. The inner depth of others is only "ego deep"; it is an ego-based subjectivity similar to our own.

This perception of others as having only a "shallow depth" comes to an end when awakening occurs because people undergoing awakening, in becoming aware of the Dynamic Ground in themselves, at the same time become aware of the Dynamic Ground in others. In discovering a "deep depth" in themselves—a psychic core beneath ego-based subjectivity—they at the same time become aware of a corresponding depth in others. People undergoing awakening are aware of the Dynamic Ground in others even when the Ground in others is reduced in activity by primal repression, and they are all the more aware of the Ground in others when the Ground in others is fully awake and emanates plenipotent energy with attracting, amplifying effects. Indeed, people in the process of awakening cannot avert their attention when in the presence of others in whom the Ground is fully awake because in such meetings awakening Spirit comes under the influence of awakened Spirit and is subject to its irresistible pull and overawing intensity. People undergoing awakening for this reason experience awakened others as having not only a deep depth but also a captivating, consciousness-altering depth.

Awakened others, experienced thus, are numinous attractors and transformers. They are psychopomps, hierophants, gurus, or sages. They are channels of a powerful energy that hypnotizes and catalyzes the awakening person. The power active within these people interacts with the power that has begun to ignite within the awakening person, accelerating its combustion. Awakened people have captivating and consciousness-altering effects on all with whom they come in contact, for their plenipotent energy attracts and amplifies the energy of others irrespective of whether the energy of others is nonplenipotent psychic energy or awakening plenipotent Spirit. This fact is behind the phenomenon of *shakti-pāta* in Tantrism: the binding and kindling of the power of the Ground in a disciple by the powerful presence of the awakened guru. It is also behind many Spirit-induced (e.g., charismatic, pentecostal) phenomena in other traditions. Spiritually awakened people quicken the spiritual process in others. Their effects upon people who have not yet begun to awaken can be conspicuously evident, and their effects upon those in the process of awakening are all the more dramatic.

Let us recall that people undergoing awakening experience Spirit as numinous Spirit, as a bivalent power split into two, light and dark expressions. People undergoing awakening, then, are prone to divide awakened others in split fashion into emissaries of light and agents of darkness. Whether they experience awakened others as good or as evil, however, people undergoing awakening experience them alike as beings of captivating, consciousness-altering—indeed, entrancing, intoxicating—power. For this reason people undergoing awakening tend to feel vulnerable in the presence of awakened others, fearing that they might lose self-control. People undergoing awakening are irresistibly attracted to awakened others, but they are wary of them as well, threatened by their overawing influence and fearful that some among them may have dark, harmful intentions.

THE OTHER AS ANGELIC OR DEMONIC OTHER

The bivalence of numinous Spirit, as we know, becomes colored with instinctuality when initial awakening gives way to regression in the service of transcendence. Instinctual derepression makes the good versus evil bivalence of the numinous also an anti-instinctual versus instinctual bivalence. With regard to the ego system, we have seen that this instinctually colored bivalence is reflected in both (1) a split between an ego ideal of angelic spirituality on the one hand and an archetypal shadow representing demonic instinctuality on the other and (2) a corresponding split within the ego as it aspires to the former while feeling the countervailing tug of the latter. People undergoing regression in the service of transcendence feel as though they are being pulled in opposite directions. They want to be "pure" spiritual beings, but at the same time they feel the lure of "evils of the flesh."

In feeling the pull of demonized instincts, people undergoing regression in the service of transcendence reach out to others who they believe will be able to help them resist dark tendencies in themselves. In order to escape the clutches of their own archetypal shadow, they reach out to people who seem to embody their own ego ideal, to people they believe are saints or angelic beings. People undergoing regression in the service of transcendence are fearful not only of external agents of darkness but also of darkness within themselves, and for this reason they feel a desperate need for others who, free of such darkness, can protect them and lead them on the path to immaculate spirituality. They feel a need for spiritually perfect people who can help them overcome their "lower" selves and thus help them become spiritually perfect as well.

In idealizing some people as beings whose drives are exclusively spiritual, people undergoing regression in the service of transcendence enter into a childlike relationship with these people, a relationship in which they enjoy a sense of being protected by superhuman beings completely free of susceptibilities to evil. They relate to these ego ideal figures as spiritual parents, as flawless beings who are completely loving and protecting. This idealization of others is an exaggeration and, therefore, a falsification. It is, however, an exaggeration that serves the purpose of growth in somewhat the same way as the rapprochement child's idealization of the caregiver as a perfect Good Mother serves the purpose of growth. Similar to the rapprochement child who, confronting a suddenly enlarged and frightening physical world, fabricates the fantasy of a perfect physical protector, people undergoing regression in the service of transcendence, confronting a suddenly enlarged and frightening numinous world, fabricate the fantasy of a perfect spiritual protector.

People who are idealized as perfect spiritual protectors, of course, are only human beings. Even though they may be fully awakened in Spirit, heart, and mind, they are still instinctually grounded beings prompted by self-interest and susceptible to errors of judgment. People undergoing regression in the service of transcendence, however, do not want to see these shortcomings in their spiritual protectors; and when such imperfections are brought to their attention, they tend to explain them away in ad hoc ways. Eventually, however, the facts have to be acknowledged, and the consequence is disillusionment. People undergoing regression in the service of transcendence are for this reason likely to devalue the people whom earlier they had idealized, seeing them as evil imposters, as devils in angels' clothing. Both the idealization and devaluation symptomatic of splitting, then, are characteristic of regression in the service of transcendence. Because of their own deep vulnerability, people undergoing regression in the service of transcendence need to believe that there are perfect others who can save them. When, however, as is inevitable, they discover that presumed saviors are merely human, they feel as though they have been deceived and betrayed. The splitting that occurs here is in many respects a transpersonal variant of the rapprochement splitting occurring in preoedipal childhood.

This transpersonal splitting, however, is usually much less severe than its prepersonal forerunner. People undergoing regression in the service of transcendence test reality more effectively than do preoedipal children and, therefore, are usually able to hold splitting in check. Still, the tendency to shift between idealization and devaluation during regression in the service of transcendence should be acknowledged. Indeed, just this tendency has in fact been played out dramatically in recent years in scandals that have plagued the Catholic Church and many American Hindu, Buddhist, and other spiritual communities. Priests, swamis, roshis, and other spiritual leaders who had been idealized have subsequently been denounced as scoundrels or fiends. To be sure, some of these leaders have been guilty of serious abuses or crimes; others, however, have been denounced simply for being human after all. People undergoing regression in the service of transcendence have a difficult time acknowledging that their spiritual leaders are instinctually motivated, self-interested, fallible human beings.

THE OVERCOMING OF SPLITTING AND THE ACHIEVEMENT OF HIGHER OBJECT CONSTANCY

The tendency to idealize and devalue others is gradually outgrown as regression in the service of transcendence comes to an end and regeneration in Spirit begins. The instincts have by this time been derepressed and owned, and the ego has come to see that the influence of the power of the Ground, even when agonizingly painful, is in the ego's own interest. For these reasons the ego no longer experiences the power of the Ground as bivalent numinous Spirit and begins experiencing it instead as univalent transforming Spirit, as a power that, no longer intermixed with derepressing instincts, works redemptively within the ego as the ego's counselor, guardian, or lover. The ego, in thus beginning to perceive the power of the Ground as an undivided reality, begins to perceive people in whom the power of the Ground is awake in an undivided way as well. The ego ceases being prone to idealize such people as angels and then to devalue them as devils and begins to see that these people—like all people—are both (1) fundamentally good, that is to say, redeemably if not in fact good, and (2) limited, imperfect human beings. The unification of the power of the Ground as transforming Spirit is at the same time a unification of "spiritual object representations"; it is a new and higher form of object constancy. To use Mahler's expression, regeneration in Spirit is a stage that is "on the way to object constancy." This new form of object constancy is fully established only when regeneration in Spirit culminates in integration.

If, from the perspective of this new form of object constancy, no one is irredeemably evil, that does not mean that everyone is good enough. Many people acknowledge no good beyond self-interest; some take pleasure in doing evil things; and a few take pleasure in doing evil things because they are evil. Even these latter people, however, in serving evil, are not themselves evil in the sense of being unfree servants of an inherently evil force. They are, rather, people who have fallen prey to the dark side of the numinous without realizing that the dark power to which they have succumbed is only a stage-specific expression of a power that is not inherently dark. As we know, the dark side of the numinous comes into being as a consequence of primal repression: the denial of the Ground. This primal sin against the Ground—which, when initially committed in early childhood, is developmentally necessary and, therefore, not yet a sin—has the consequence of casting a shadow, the archetypal shadow, over the Ground. For this reason we perceive the repressed power of the Ground, the instincts, and related nonegoic potentials as primitive and menacing, as embodying all that we fear, as absolute evil.

This shadow-Ground, however, is not the Ground itself. It is only the Ground as seen by the ego repressively alienated from the Ground. The shadow darkening the Ground can, therefore, be lifted, and people who have fallen prey to the archetypal shadow can free themselves from its influence. Because the dark side of the numinous derives from primal repression, it disappears as primal repression is lifted and as derepression runs its course, that is, as regression in the service of transcendence gives way to regeneration in Spirit. People who have fallen prey to the dark side of the numinous for this reason can arrive at a point at which the shadow of evil is lifted and at which, consequently, evil loses both its grip and its ontological guise.

In approaching higher object constancy, people undergoing regeneration in Spirit understand not only that those who serve evil are not irredeemably evil but also that those who serve good are not angelically good. Unlike people undergoing regression in the service of transcendence, then, people undergoing regeneration in Spirit do not project an aura of immaculate, selfless spirituality upon spiritual leaders. They see spiritual leaders, as they see everyone else, as embodied, limited human beings. They understand, for instance, that spiritual leaders, like everyone else, experience instinctual needs; and they understand, too, that spiritual leaders are subject to motives of self-interest and mistakes of judgment. Understanding these things, people undergoing regeneration in Spirit are no longer likely to suffer disillusionment when spiritual leaders err. Sometimes they judge spiritual leaders to be unfit to continue in a leadership role, but they now rarely perceive spiritual leaders whose shortcomings have been exposed as being wholly fraudulent in their spirituality.

In sum, people undergoing regeneration in Spirit begin to see that no one is either wholly evil or perfectly good. They no longer believe in either hopeless demonic corruption or angelic impeccability. They perceive those who do evil in a less devalued manner and those who do good in a less idealized manner. Object constancy is in this way a moderating of the perception of others. Others are no longer spiritually black or white and are instead many shades of gray. This moderating, it should be stressed, is not a leveling. In being aware of many shades of gray, people undergoing regeneration in Spirit are aware that some people are much better than most and that some are much worse. Spiritual object constancy, however, is an elimination of antithetical absolutes of good and evil. It is a maturity of understanding that allows people undergoing regeneration in Spirit to see that people who are better than most are imperfect despite being graced by Spirit and that people who are worse than most never forfeit their spiritual core.

THE OTHER AS SIBLING IN SPIRIT

The perception that no one is wholly evil or perfectly good matures into the perception that everyone without exception is on the spiritual path, not only those who have experienced spiritual hunger or spiritual awakening but also those in whom, owing to primal repression, Spirit is still asleep and even those who, awakened, have given themselves to the dark side of the numinous. The pre-Socratic philosopher Heraclitus perceived others in this inclusive way. Expressing this vision, he said, "sleepers are workmen and fellow-workers in what goes on in the world" and "the road up and the road down are one and the same."[6] Sleepers, although unaware of Spirit, are at work developing their egos and are thereby preparing themselves for the spiritual journey; and those who, having given themselves to the dark side of the numinous, are traveling "the road down" are on a decending path that eventually returns to "the road up." Those who are traveling "the road down" are lost, to be sure, and the farther they pursue the downward way the more lost they become. Nevertheless, those pursuing this path are never utterly lost, for "the road down," although leading nowhere, reverts immediately to "the road up" once those lost in darkness outgrow or otherwise overcome their fascination with evil.

In seeing everyone without exception as a traveler on the same path, people who have achieved integration see all people as siblings in Spirit. In seeing others as *siblings* in Spirit, they see others as imperfect human beings, as beings who, like themselves, are never more than human; and in seeing others as siblings *in Spirit,* they see others as kin who share in a spiritual life that is at once our deepest essence, however repressed that essence might be, and our highest actualization, however far off that actualization might be. Integrated people see infants and small children as siblings in whom this shared spiritual life is powerfully active, albeit in an immature, prepersonal way. They see most older children as siblings in whom this life has become quiescent so that an ego structure can be built on the basis of which spiritual life, if later reawakened, can be expressed in a mature, transpersonal way. They see most young adults as siblings who continue to build their ego structures by performing functions in the public world, our corporate body. They see people who, awakened, have identified with the dark side of the numinous as siblings who have estranged themselves from the human community, as defiant siblings who are acting out the most destructive tendencies in themselves. Finally, they see people who, awakened, are pursuing the main path of spiritual life as siblings who, like themselves, take great joy in our shared life in Spirit.

As siblings in Spirit, we are all part of what Christians call the "mystical body of Christ" and what here shall be called the "mystical body of Spirit." Infants and small children are immature cells of this body, cells with highly permeable membranes through which nurturing infusions from other cells are received. Most older children are cells that, with less permeable boundaries, are undergoing a process of intracellular maturation. Most adults are mature cells performing particular functions in the common life of the spiritual body. Those who, awakened to Spirit, have identified with the dark side of the numinous are malignant cells releasing toxins and spreading disease within the mystical body, cells which, however, can be restored to health. Finally, those who, awakened to Spirit, are pursuing "the road up" are health-promoting cells performing restorative, integrating, and evolutionary work within the mystical body. Spirit is our deepest essence as siblings in Spirit, and mature, health-promoting participation in the mystical body of Spirit is our highest actualization. Everyone belongs to the mystical body, but few are aware of this fact. The goal of spiritual life is to awaken to our place in the mystical body and, as mature, health-promoting cells, to assist in the continuing evolution of this shared life.

The mystical body of Spirit, we should stress, is truly a body, a physical reality in this world. Our growing together in Spirit is more than a spiritual intersubjectivity; it is also a spiritual intercorporeality. As an intercorporeal reality, the mystical body of Spirit is best discussed in the next chapter, which focuses on the body.

SEVEN

THE BODY

THIS CHAPTER TRACKS the development of the experiential body from the spiral perspective. As in previous chapters, we begin with the experience of the newborn and then consider primary prepersonal, personal, and transpersonal stages of development. In tracking the transpersonal stages of the body's development, the principal point that emerges is that the awakening of the power of the Ground as Spirit is the awakening of a power that is as much a bodily power as it is a spiritual power. At first, as we shall see, the power of the Ground, as numinous Spirit, expresses itself as a power that causes a "resurrection" of the body from the deadening effects of primal repression. Then the power of the Ground, as transforming Spirit, expresses itself as a power that invites the ego to "reincarnate" itself in the awakened body. Then, finally, the power of the Ground, as transparent Spirit, expresses itself as a power that, along with the ego, has been restored to full embodiment. Spiritual awakening is thus an awakening and transformation of the body. It is a process that, as it approaches integration, makes the body once again what it was at the beginning of life, the seat of ego (the ego, reincarnated, is once again a body ego) and the "temple of Spirit" (the power of the Ground, as transparent Spirit, animates and sanctifies the body).

TABLE 7.1

DEVELOPMENTAL FORMS OF THE EXPERIENTIAL BODY

STAGE OF LIFE	BODY
Neonatal stage	Precosmic universal body
Early preoedipal stage	Body of polymorphous sensuality (oral stage)
Late preoedipal stage	Splitting of pleasures into good and bad pleasures (anal stage)
Oedipal stage	Initial phases of repressive quieting of body ("phallic" or infantile genital stage)

DEVELOPMENTAL FORMS OF THE EXPERIENTIAL BODY *(CONTINUED)*

STAGE OF LIFE	BODY
Latency	Subdued latency body; recreational body
Puberty and adolescence	Sexual awakening of body; presentational body
Early adulthood	Mature genital sexuality; instrumental body
Crossroads	Depersonalized body
Awakening	Body primed for reawakening
Regression in the service of transcendence	Derepression of instincts; "resurrection" of the body
Regeneration in Spirit	"Reincarnation" of the ego
Ego-Ground integration	"Temple of Spirit"

THE PRECOSMIC UNIVERSAL BODY

The newborn is an unbounded bodily self. Because it lacks an understanding of object permanence and, therefore, an understanding of the distinction between "baby, here" and "world out there," the newborn knows no limits to its bodily existence. Its bodily existence does not end at the skin boundary but, instead, includes all of existence. As we learned in chapter 5, the ego is here an incipient ego with a center but no circumference; and as we learned in the last chapter, all that is other to this incipient ego, including even the caregiver, for this reason exists immanently within its experience. The newborn, then, as a bodily self, is an all-encompassing bodily being. The world exists within the newborn's body. The newborn's body is a universal body.

The neonate's body, encompassing all existence, contains within itself everything that will come to be. It is, therefore, a body that is sundered when the four-or-five-month old, in beginning to understand object permanence, makes the first division of experience into separate, immanent and transcendent realms: the immanent realm of the infant's own circumscribed bodily self and the transcendent realm of an independent world beyond the child. The neonate's body can from this perspective be described as a precosmic body that is the source material for the cosmogonic process. The world comes into being by a "dismembering" of the neonate's universal body.

The idea of cosmogenesis as a sundering of a precosmic body is expressed in many of the world's mythologies. For example, in the *Rig Veda*, the most ancient source of Hindu mythology, we are told that the cosmos came into existence through the sacrificial dismembering of the giant Purusha.

> From his navel the middle realm of space arose; from his head the sky evolved. From his two feet came the earth, and the quarters of the sky from his ear. Thus they set the worlds in order. (O'Flaherty 1981, p. 31)

Similar stories are told in Norse mythology, according to which the earth and the seas were formed by carving up the dead body of the giant Ymir, and in Micronesian mythology, according to which the dead body of the god Puntan was cleaved to create the sky and the earth.

Interpreting a famous verse from the *Tao Te Ching*, the newborn's precosmic body can be said to be the "one" from which are born the "two" (the ultimate *yin* and *yang* of immanent and transcendent domains?), from which are born the "three" (the immanent and transcendent domains rejoined as dimensions of a third thing, the structured cosmos?), from which in turn are born the "ten thousand things" (the world of multiplicity as we know it?). The infant, initially a precosmic whole (the "one"), must differentiate itself from the world (the "two") before it can rejoin the world to form a structured cosmos containing both self and not-self (the "three") and, thus rejoined, begin exploring the world as a realm of objects (the "ten thousand things").

THE BODY OF POLYMORPHOUS SENSUALITY

In coming to understand that there is a transcendent world "out there," the infant also comes to understand that its own immanent existence as "baby, here" is circumscribed and, therefore, limited. More specifically, it comes to understand that, as a bodily being, its existence extends only to the skin boundary. The skin boundary now delimits the infant's existence because, as explained in chapter 5, the body within this boundary is a sensorium that is always present within the field of experience. The discovery that the sphere of immanence lies within the skin boundary ushers in the stage of the body ego. In chapter 5 we discussed the body ego from the perspective of the ego. Here we discuss it from the perspective of the body.

As a skin-bounded sensorium, the body ego experiences greatly amplified sensations, for the body ego is enlivened by the power of the Ground in its plenipotency. The flesh of the body ego, then, is intensely alive. It is highly sensitive, easily aroused, and frequently the basis of ecstatic sensations. Although the arousal capacity of the flesh, as Freud explained, is at first localized primarily in the mouth, then the anus, and then the genitals (the so-called phallic phase), it is not limited to any such zones. The three primary erotogenic zones are not the only bodily tissues in which the body ego can experience intense and even ecstatic sensations. Such sensations can arise anywhere in the body, especially when the body ego is caressed, massaged, or tickled. For the body ego, the entire body is a vehicle of powerful sensations.

Freud interpreted the arousal capacity of the body ego in terms of his theory of psychosexual development. This theory, immensely insightful and revolutionary in its time, is misleading in the stress it gives to the sexual aspect of the body ego's experience. To be sure, the sensations experienced by the body ego, especially when localized in the erotogenic zones, can be intensely, ecstatically pleasurable; nevertheless, they likely do not have a specifically sexual feeling, let alone a sexualized interpersonal focus. Genital stimulation, of course, has a sexual feeling inherently. Genital stimulation occurring in the first years of life, however, is likely not an expression of an object-related sexual drive, such as becomes active with the onset of puberty, and, therefore, is likely without significant object-related fantasy. For this reason "sensual" is a better term than "sexual" for describing the kind of arousal experienced by the body ego. Accordingly, the expression "polymorphous sensuality" is here used instead of "polymorphous sexuality" to describe the arousal capacity of the body ego.

THE SPLITTING OF PLEASURES INTO GOOD AND BAD PLEASURES

Preoedipal splitting is a splitting of the preoedipal body ego. It is the ego as body ego that splits its emerging self-representation, cleaving it into representations of two, good and bad, bodily beings: the good child and the bad child. As a sensorium, the body of the split body ego continues to experience sensual pleasures. These pleasures, however, are now divided into two opposite types: good pleasures and bad. The good pleasures are experienced by the good child, the bad pleasures by the bad child.

Good pleasures are those produced or approved by the caregivers. These pleasures include comforts associated with being embraced, delights arising from being caressed, and explosive ecstasies produced by nonmalicious intense stimulation (e.g., tickling, twirling, lifting). Good pleasures also include those associated with approved oral, anal, and genital behavior, for example, pleasures arising from sucking or swallowing hygienic or wholesome objects, pleasures arising from successful use of the toilet, and pleasures arising from permitted touching or exposing of the genitals. Pleasures arising from successful toilet training are especially gratifying to the child as good child, for this training is punctuated with triumphs, achieved when the child urinates or defecates in approved places and ways. The sensations associated with triumphs in toilet training have a particular importance because they are not only ecstatic pleasures but also self-satisfactions, feelings of pride. In sum, good pleasures are those that, in being pleasing to the child, are pleasing, or at least not displeasing, to the caregivers as well.

Bad pleasures, in contrast, are those that are displeasing to the caregivers. Primary among pleasures of this sort are those associated with prohibited oral, anal, and genital behavior, for example, pleasures arising from sucking or swallowing dirty or dangerous objects, pleasures arising from failure or refusal to use the toilet, and pleasures arising from disallowed touching or exposing of the genitals. Again, given the pressures that accompany learning how to control urination and defecation, pleasures associated with toilet training have a special importance. In the case of bad pleasures of this type—for example, urinating or defecating on the floor or out of doors—the sensations experienced are especially exciting in the knowledge that they are forbidden. They are wicked pleasures indulged by the bad child. Pleasures associated with touching or exposing the genitals are accentuated in a similar way for children who have been taught that the genitals are dirty or otherwise taboo.

The nature of splitting is such that bad pleasures, although forbidden, are not laden with shame. Shame is an experience that indicates that the child has made some progress toward an integrated self-representation, a self-representation that, in being "good enough" rather than all good, includes bad and shameful features to some extent. To experience shame the child must have an ideal of goodness (an ego ideal) that surpasses its perceived actual goodness, and the split body ego has no such ideal. The split body ego has no ego ideal because, as good child, it is already ideally good and, as bad child, it delights in being bad and does not aspire to goodness at all. The split body ego, whether the good child or the bad child, has no conscience. The good child experiences only good pleasures and, therefore, experiences no pangs of conscience; and the bad child, in experiencing bad pleasures, finds them all the more pleasurable because they are bad, that is, forbidden. The good child is a little angel, the bad child a little devil. The good child is "polymorphously innocent" in the pleasures it experiences and the bad child—to apply Freud's otherwise unfortunate expression to a case it actually fits—"polymorphously perverse."

FROM THE BODY AS EGO TO THE BODY AS EGO'S BODY

As we know, the process by which the child overcomes splitting leads to a differentiation of the ego from the body. The ego ceases *being* the body and becomes a mental ego that *has* a body. This differentiation is not a Cartesian dissociation of mind from body, for the body remains a dimension of self. The body is still part of what the ego is, but it is now an extension rather than the whole of what the ego is. The process bringing about this transformation in the status of the body, as we have seen, begins during the late preoedipal stage and is then completed in decisive fashion when the child finally undergoes the oedipal change of object, which consolidates primal closing in both its intrapsychic and interpersonal dimensions: primal repression and primal separation.

In the next section we discuss the lasting effects that primal repression has on the body, transforming it from a body of polymorphous sensuality into a subdued latency body. In this section we consider how primal separation, in internalizing the ego, has the effect of externalizing the body, transforming it from a body that is the whole of the ego into a body that is an outer extension of the ego.

The process by which the body is externalized is the outer, bodily side of the process, discussed in chapter 5, by which the ego is internalized, becoming a mental ego residing in psychic space. This process gets under way because the injurious effects of splitting—and the demands of the oedipal father, too—require that the child wean itself from the caregiver. The child, responding to this requirement, withdraws from embodied openness. It pulls back from the body and, much to its relief, discovers the safe privacy of psychic space. During the late preoedipal and the oedipal stages, this withdrawal from embodied openness into private inwardness has the character of a retreat from dangerous ground. The child retreats from embodied intimacy with the caregiver because this intimacy is precisely what exposes the child to perceived preoedipal and oedipal dangers: vulnerability to the caregiver as Terrible Mother and to the father as oedipal rival. The withdrawal from the body, then, is not only a shift of primary locus from bodily to psychic space; it is also a defensive pulling back from a vulnerable body to psychic space experienced as a refuge. In withdrawing from the body, the child finds itself in an interior realm that no one but the child can enter. The privacy of this interior realm gives the child a sense of inaccessibility and, therefore, inviolable safety.

To be sure, the child does not stay long in its inner refuge before, yearning for body-based intimacy and pleasure, it reinhabits the body. In returning to the body, however, the child again finds itself on dangerous ground and, in consequence, again withdraws into psychic space. The child's withdrawal from the body is thus a halting, retreat-and-return process indicating that the child is not happy in either physical or psychic space. In withdrawing into psychic space, the child enjoys a feeling of safety, but it also suffers from a feeling of being cut off from body-based intimacy and pleasure. In turn, in returning to physical space, the child reexperiences body-based intimacy and pleasure, but it also reexposes itself to the perceived dangers of embodied life. During the late preoedipal and the oedipal stages, then, the ego is betwixt and between bodily and psychic abodes. Although it withdraws from physical space and, therefore, is no longer merely a body ego, it is not yet at home in psychic space and, therefore, is not yet truly a mental ego. It is not until the end of the oedipal stage that the child is able to withdraw into psychic space without feeling disconnected. It is not until the end of the oedipal stage, then, that psychic space, while retaining its positive qualities, loses its negative qualities, and, in thus becoming a wholly inviting space, becomes the ego's primary dwelling place.

The transformation of psychic space into a wholly inviting space occurs because the change of object that brings the oedipal stage to an end removes the perceived dangers associated with embodiment and, in thus making it safe to return to the body, removes as well the sense of disconnection associated with psychic space. The oedipal change of object removes the perceived dangers associated with embodiment because, assuming the usual configuration of child, mother, and father, it (1) completes the child's withdrawal from the mother and thereby brings a final end to conflict with the mother as Terrible Mother (the split Good and Terrible Mothers are replaced by a single "good enough" mother); and (2) it completes the child's commitment to the father and thereby brings a final end to conflict with the father as oedipal rival. The oedipal change of object, in thus removing the perceived dangers of embodied life—and, we should add, in completing the transformation of the body into a subdued latency body (see below)—makes it safe once again for the child to return to the body in pursuit of intimacy and pleasure.

The child, in ceasing to experience embodiment as dangerous, at the same time ceases to experience withdrawal into inwardness as flight from embodiment. Psychic space remains a refuge, to be sure. It remains a citadel within which the child feels protected from threatening interpersonal contact. In remaining a refuge, however, psychic space is no longer a space in which the child feels trapped; for except when confronted by threatening people or faced with threatening situations, the child now feels safe in opening the doors of its inner citadel and reaching out to the world. Psychic space in this way ceases being a confining or disconnected space. It remains an inner space that is completely the child's own and in which the child feels safe, but it is no longer a space in which the child feels cut off from others or deprived of bodily pleasure.

This statement needs clarification because it seems to be in conflict with the view, already set forth, that the oedipal change of object consolidates primal separation, the structure that brings radical intimacy to an end by creating permanent defensive distance between the child and others. How, then, we must ask, can the oedipal change of object both (1) facilitate the child's return to embodied life and to embodied intimacy in particular and (2) distance the child from others in a way that brings an end to radical intimacy? The answer, suggested in the last chapter, is that the defensive distance created by primal separation is a bridgeable distance. The child, now a mental ego situated in psychic space, uses the body as an outer extension through which to make contact with others and as an outer connecting medium through which to experience powerful emotional exchanges with others. The child, although an inner mental ego, thus remains capable of body-based intimacy, albeit an incomplete intimacy bridging a distance rather than, as before, a radical intimacy completely without distance. The defensive distance created by primal separation, then, is not the same as disconnection.

In sum, once the child has completed the oedipal change of object, psychic space loses its negative qualities and becomes an unqualified good. It becomes not only an inner sphere of privacy into which the child can retreat but also an inner basis of operations from which the child can reach out and act in the world. It becomes not only a restricted space in the sense of being a hidden space accessible to the child alone but also an unrestricted space in the sense of being an inner theater in which the child is able to do whatever it wants without being detected by others. Psychic space becomes a completely welcoming space, a safe but not confining space that is exclusively the child's own and in which the child is completely free to be itself.

Responding to this transformation of psychic space, the child shifts its primary abode from the body to psychic space, thus completing the metamorphosis from body ego to mental ego. The child ceases being a merely bodily being and becomes primarily a mental being, a being centered in psychic space. The body remains integral to the child's self, although now as an outer extension of an inner self. The child can at any time reach out from its seat in psychic space to inhabit the body and thereby enjoy the affections of others and the pleasures of the world. The body, however, is no longer home base. Home base is now the citadel-theater of psychic space.

THE SUBDUED LATENCY BODY

The transition from the oedipal stage to the stage of latency is a *net* developmental advance. It is an overall advance based on significant sacrifice because the oedipal change of object resolves preoedipal and oedipal conflicts, thereby ushering in a long period of unimpeded ego development, only by consolidating primal closing. The transition from the oedipal stage to the stage of latency—and, correspondingly, from the body ego to the mental ego—then, is a forward developmental movement based on a loss of psychic capacities and abilities. In the last chapter we learned that, owing to primal separation, the transition from the body ego to the mental ego establishes the child as a fully differentiated, independent person only by incurring a loss of radical intimacy with others. Here we can note another developmental trade-off: owing to primal repression, the transition from the body ego to the mental ego makes possible a significant gain in egoic self-control only by incurring a loss of bodily arousal capacity. This latter loss, properly conceived in positive light as a net developmental gain, is what psychoanalytic theory refers to as latency.

Because the power of the Ground is the energy that enlivens the body, the quieting of the power of the Ground by primal repression is also a quieting of the body: the body ceases being plenipotently alive and becomes a subdued latency body. Primal repression reduces the power of the Ground in its active expression to nonplenipotent psychic energy and, in consequence, reduces the overall level of bodily excitation. The body in this way becomes not only safer ground, free of the dangers associated with preoedipal and oedipal conflicts, but also calmer ground, free of overpowering surges of feeling and sensation. This is not to say that the body becomes unfeeling or numb. The body remains acutely sensitive, even to stimuli of very subtle sorts. Still, the body of the latency child is, relatively speaking, a subdued body. Although the latency child experiences all manner of bodily pleasures, these pleasures tend not to be as intense as those experienced by the prelatency child, whose pleasures are frequently of sufficient power to dissolve the ego in ecstasy. The body of the latency child, although primarily a recreational body governed by the pleasure principle, is a body with reduced and, typically, non-ecstatic arousal capacity.

The body of the latency child is for this reason also a body that is much more compliant to the ego's will. The ego, which is now a mental ego differentiated from the body, is much less often overpowered by bodily sensations and urges and, therefore, is much better able to exercise self-control. This trade-off, again, is a net gain. Just as it is a net gain to sacrifice radical intimacy for independence, so, too, it is a net gain to sacrifice plenipotent bodily experience for improved self-control. Both of these sacrifices are developmentally warranted at this point. Both facilitate—indeed, make possible—continued ego development. As deficits on the developmental balance sheet, these sacrifices, although profound, seem slight if they are noticed at all as long as ego development continues on schedule, typically through latency, adolescence, and early adulthood. When ego development is complete, however, these deficits begin to become evident, and the ego begins to experience a need to restore what had been sacrificed.

THE SEXUALLY AWAKENING BODY

The sexual awakening of puberty profoundly changes the body. One of the most dramatic changes is that the body once again, as during the prelatency period, becomes a body capable of plenipotent arousal and ecstasy. The sexual awakening of puberty is an awakening of libido, which can be aroused to ego-dissolving, ecstatic levels in the experience of sexual orgasm. If, however, the body undergoing sexual awakening is similar to the prelatency body in being a body capable of ecstasy, it differs from the prelatency body in being a body capable of ecstasy of only one sort: genitally based sexual ecstasy. This at any rate is true generally if not always.[1] In contrast to the prelatency body, which is capable of plenipotent arousal in all of the erotogenic zones and in most other bodily areas as well, the body undergoing sexual awakening is capable of plenipotent arousal primarily if not exclusively through genital stimulation. Because puberty is a genitally organized awakening of the power of the Ground in the specific form of libido, it is an awakening that, in making the body once again an ecstatic body, localizes the area of ecstasy in the genital region.

Although the emerging capacity for plenipotent arousal is genitally localized, erotic sensation is not. During adolescence the genital organization of libido is not yet fully established, and for this reason awakening libido, although concentrated within the genital system, is not completely confined within that system. Libido "leaks" from the genital system and mixes with freely circulating psychic energy, thus giving an erotic charge to the body as a whole. The sexually awakening body, charged in this way, is primed to experience erotic sensations in being touched, caressed, or otherwise stimulated. Most of the pleasures experienced by the sexually awakening body are sensual or sensuous pleasures charged with neutral psychic energy. A good number, however, are erotic pleasures charged with sexual libido. Although the sexually awakening body is genitally organized so far as intense arousal and ecstasy are concerned, it is unrestrictedly polymorphous so far as erotic feeling is concerned. Such feeling can be subtle and fleeting or conspicuous and persistent. For the person who has just begun to awaken sexually, the experience of erotic sensations need not lead directly to genitally focused sexual arousal, let alone to the plenipotent release of sexual orgasm. It does, however, migrate in the direction of genital arousal.

The sexual awakening of the body is expressed outwardly in dramatic physiological and morphological changes. Secondary sexual characteristics appear; menstruation begins for girls and semen production and growth of the testicles and penis for boys; the shape of the body changes in conspicuous ways for both girls and boys; and the body grows at an accelerated pace. These changes are alarming, both in themselves and because (1) they bring a rapid end to the latency body, which had been the ego's outer, physical self, and (2) they signal the transformation of the body into a body that is sexually attractive or unattractive to others.

Adolescents, concerned about their bodies for these reasons, understandably feel a need to exercise control of the growth or at least appearance of their bodies so that they can help define their bodies in self-expressing, other-attracting ways. Accordingly, adolescents may commit themselves to figure-changing diets, to muscle-enhancing or form-developing workouts, or to rituals of grooming or hygiene. Efforts of these sorts are usually developmentally fitting and appropriate. Sometimes, however, the felt need to control the body can become so strong that it leads to pathologically severe regimens of diet, exercise, grooming, or hygiene or even to denial or abuse of the body in an attempt to suppress change.

Adolescents' concern about their bodies reflects a new way of relating to the body, namely, as a vehicle of self-presentation, as a medium through which one presents oneself to others as a possible object of sexual desire. To be sure, adolescents continue to relate to their bodies as recreational vehicles. Indeed, as we have seen, they relate to their bodies as vehicles not only of pleasure generally but also of erotic and sexual pleasure in particular. However, in continuing to relate to their bodies as recreational vehicles, adolescents begin as well to relate to their bodies as presentational vehicles. For adolescents, then, the body is not only a sensorium but also something to be shaped and fashioned in self-presenting, other-attracting ways.

THE SEXUALLY MATURE BODY

The mature genital organization of libido is usually achieved by the time adulthood begins. By this time the capacity for sexual ecstasy is fully developed, and the boundaries between libido and psychic energy are more clearly defined. Libido less frequently intermixes with psychic energy to produce erotic sensations in response to nonsexual stimulation and is more closely tied to explicit sexual touching or fantasy. For the young adult, erotic pleasure, although by no means only a precursor of sexual activity, is nonetheless usually a precursor of such activity. Outside of sexual situations the young adult's body tends to be libidinally quiescent. Libido, although awake in the sense of being arousable in response to sexual stimuli, is quiescent in its default state. This quiescence of libido is part of the second latency of early adulthood described by Peter Blos (1968) and discussed in previous chapters.

The young adult body is mature not only sexually but in other respects as well. As a mature body, it is no longer growing and is destined to decline. It is a body, therefore, that must be cared for if it is to continue to function well. In other words, it is an instrument requiring maintenance and repair. Adolescents, as we just saw, go to great lengths in attending to their bodies, seeking to manage their size, form, and appearance. They do so, however, not because their bodies have begun to decline but rather, in part, because their bodies are growing so rapidly. Young adults, in contrast, work on their bodies because their bodies have begun to decline and, they understand, would decline more rapidly if they ate unhealthy foods or failed to get sufficient exercise. To be sure, many young adults continue to devote effort to shaping or strengthening their bodies as vehicles of self-presentation, and many young adults quit working on their bodies altogether, "letting themselves go." These facts, however, do not contradict the point in question because those young adults who continue to work on their bodies as presentational vehicles realize that they must work extra hard to prevent decline, and those who "let themselves go" are in fact illustrations of the point in question: if one does not take good care of the adult body, it will decline.

As an instrument destined to decline, the young adult body is by no means only a "thing" requiring "work." Notwithstanding its instrumental character, the young adult body remains a recreational vehicle capable of a wide range of pleasures; and, again, it remains a presentational vehicle as well, even if the only statement being made is "I don't care how I look." What is different now is that the body, as an instrumental body, is not only a vehicle of recreation and self-presentation but also a tool for which the young adult is responsible. The young adult continues to enjoy the body and to be concerned about its attractiveness or unattractiveness to others, but the young adult also relates to the body as an indispensable instrument requiring life-long care.

The instrumental character of the body tends increasingly to predominate as years pass. After early adulthood, the primary changes occurring in the body are those related to aging. The body gradually loses its agility, shape, and strength; it requires more frequent maintenance and repair; and, especially in old age, it becomes more frequently a source of pain than a vehicle of pleasure. Because of these changes, the recreational and presentational characters of the body may begin to take a back seat, and the instrumental character may become conspicuous. As we age, we become increasingly aware of the mortality and, therefore, the irreplaceably instrumental nature of our bodies.

THE DEPERSONALIZED BODY

The body of the mental ego—whether the recreational body of the latency child, the presentational body of the adolescent, or the instrumental body of the young adult—is part of the self-system: it is an outer extension of an inner, mental self. For most people the body remains such an extension of self to the end of life. For some people, however, the body ceases being part of the self-system. In previous chapters we have learned that some people arrive at an impasse in life at which a pervasive alienation occurs. An introversion of psychic energy desiccates the world and saps the ego of motivation to pursue the identity project. The world becomes flat and dead, other people become inauthentic actors, and the ego itself, so far as its worldly identity is concerned, becomes a mere mask, not-self. This pervasive condition of alienation, we can here add, is reflected in the body as well. The body, too, is depleted of energy; the body, too, becomes not-self, a mere thing.

Because the body is part of the world, the withdrawal of energy from the world is at the same time a withdrawal of energy from the body. The body's loss of energy can be expressed in many ways: fatigue, feelings of heaviness and clumsiness, loss of interest in food, loss of desire for sex, dulling of the senses. In general, the body loses its vitality, suppleness, appetite, and capacity for pleasure. The body, depleted in these ways, quite evidently ceases being a recreational vehicle, and it ceases being a presentational vehicle as well. The body loses its presentational character because the loss of interest in the world, and in sexuality in particular, is at the same time a loss of motivation to continue working on the body in ways needed to keep it attractive to others. As one's identity in the world is deanimated, one's body, a part of that identity, is depersonalized. The body becomes a pleasureless, sexless thing. The body, to be sure, in thus losing its recreational and presentational characters, does not lose its instrumental character. Even this character, however, suffers as a consequence of energy loss, for the body, as an instrument, is now an unfeeling and unwieldy tool. The senses have lost their acuity, and the body, it seems, is heavy and difficult to set in motion.

People undergoing alienation may take desperate measures in the hope of reengaging the world, reanimating worldly identity, and reestablishing contact with others. They may also take desperate measures in the hope of reenergizing the body. Pharmacological stimulants are an obvious option. These stimulants, however, are only temporary expedients; moreover, they have the aftereffect of making the fatigue and numbness of the body all the more unbearable. People undergoing alienation may also seek to reenergize the body by intensifying bodily stimulation, for example, by subjecting the body to extremes of exercise or by exposing it to potent sensory stimuli. These measures, too, however, have only short-term results, and they, too, have the aftereffect of worsening the underlying condition. In rare cases of the most severe depersonalization, desperation may lead people undergoing alienation to attempt high-risk actions or to indulge in self-mutilation. Risk of life and injury to the body sharply accentuate the sense of being alive. They dramatically elevate the level of bodily energy. They do so, however, only briefly, for they excite surface energy without redirecting the underlying flow of energy. The process of energic introversion continues.

THE BODY ON THE THRESHOLD
OF SPIRITUAL AWAKENING

The introversion of psychic energy sometimes charges the Dynamic Ground to such a degree that the power of the Ground begins to awaken in its plenipotency. We have already seen how this awakening affects the Dynamic Ground, the energy system, and the ego system; and in the next chapter we shall see how it affects our perception of the world. Here we focus on how the awakening power of the Ground affects the body. As we shall see, it affects the body by bringing it back to life. The person on the threshold of spiritual awakening is a person who is also on the threshold of bodily awakening.

The body that is about to awaken is astir with excess energy, which can manifest itself in many ways, for example, in tingling sensations, tics, palpitations, perspiration, chills, horripilation, heightened sensitivity in erotogenic tissues, and spontaneous erotic sensations. A person might experience "pins and needles" sensations, spasmodic movements of the head, arms, or legs, a racing heart and sweaty palms, clamminess and "goose flesh," or sudden surges of strong sexual feeling. In a moment we consider why the power of the Ground, in beginning to awaken, might produce these effects. Here it suffices to list the effects and note that they are possible precursory manifestations of the awakening process.

The precursory phenomena just mentioned are not easily understood. People experiencing them, it seems likely, would view them either as an odd group of sensations of no particular significance or as expressions of relatively minor and familiar conditions. For example, perspiration, chills, and horripilation might be perceived as symptoms of influenza; tingling sensations, tics, and palpitations might be perceived as effects of stress; and erotic feelings, should they occur, might be perceived as consequences of biochemical or hormonal changes. If, however, any of the phenomena in question should persist, people experiencing them might begin to recognize their seriousness and might seek a medical diagnosis.

THE "RESURRECTION" OF THE BODY

The body in which the power of the Ground has ignited is a body that is about to awaken from the deadening effects of primal repression. It is, therefore, a body on the verge of "resurrection." Once the power of the Ground, having ignited, becomes fully active, this return to life begins. Plenipotent energy manifests itself in the body, and the body begins to undergo a profound transformation.

This resurrection of the body can be more or less dramatic depending on how suddenly the power of the Ground awakens. When the power of the Ground awakens gradually, the awakening of the body, although no doubt stressful to some degree, can be a relatively smooth process. When, however, the power of the Ground awakens suddenly, the awakening of the body can be a tumultuous—and deeply disturbing—process. We here consider what might happen in the case of especially abrupt awakening, even though such a case is the exception rather than the rule. We choose this extreme case because it allows us to see more clearly what goes on in the awakening process. In the extreme case, the features of the awakening process are writ large.

The physical phenomena accompanying spiritual awakening have been ignored or misinterpreted in the mainstream teachings of most spiritual traditions. Reports of odd somatic occurrences are usually dismissed as idiosyncratic or are considered pathological or even demonic. This disregard or suspicion of physical awakening is based on a widespread prejudice against the body, which can be found in the mainstream teachings of most major religions: Hinduism, Buddhism, Judaism, Christianity, Islam. Even religions that hold that the body is a "vehicle" or "temple" rather than "tomb" of Spirit frequently see the flesh as a snare (which predisposes us to ignorance, illusion, *māyā*) or as a weakness (which predisposes us to unspiritual concupiscence if not antispiritual sin). Regrettably, the mainstream teachings of most major religions place Spirit in opposition to the flesh, assuming that Spirit can emerge only after the flesh has been subdued.

The esoteric teachings of many religions, in contrast, have a better understanding of the role of the body in the spiritual process. In Judaism, the body's role is recognized in Kabbalah, which focuses on the emanations or spheres of the created world, on God's energy (Shekinah) as it is present in material creation, and on the awakening of this energy within the embodied soul, conceived as a microcosm within the greater macrocosm. The body's role is also recognized in the original Hermetic tradition and in later Christian and Islamic alchemy, according to which the body is the alembic in which the elixir, the sacred power implicit in nature, effects a transformation of the soul from base metal into gold, that is, from an imperfect to a spiritually perfected state. Turning to Asia, a similar alchemical view is found in religious or esoteric Taoism, according to which the body is the locus not only of alchemical transformation but also, ultimately, of immortal life. Finally, the body's role is recognized as well in Tantrism, with its notions of embodied spiritual energy, subtle material pathways and centers through which spiritual energy moves, and spiritual-somatic transformation.

Of these esoteric teachings, Tantrism is by far the best known and most widely practiced. Originally a countercultural phenomenon that challenged orthodox Brahminic Hinduism, Tantrism has since evolved over many centuries and has been assimilated within Hinduism and within Tibetan Buddhism as well. Recently, Tantrism, particularly Hindu Tantrism, has found a wide audience in the West. Many books have been written in European languages on the two major forms of Hindu Tantric practice: *hatha yoga* (the practice of physical cleansing and opening preparatory to awakening) and *kundalinī yoga* (the practice of awakening spiritual energy within the body). Because Hindu Tantrism is so well known and has been practiced widely, we shall here use it as the basis for our discussion of the body's role in the spiritual process.

Hindu Tantric yoga is the practice of preparing the body for the awakening of the sleeping serpent energy *kundalinī* so that this energy can manifest itself as the goddess Shakti, a spiritual power that transforms the body into an effective vehicle of spiritual life. In our terminology, *kundalinī* is the power of the Ground in its instinctual organization as libido, and Shakti is the power of the Ground in its awakened and free expression as Spirit. In our terminology, then, Tantric yoga is the practice of preparing the body for the awakening of "sleeping" or dormant libido so that the power of the Ground, thus awakened, can be liberated from its instinctual organization as libido and can begin manifesting itself freely, as Spirit. Tantrism is keenly aware of the intersection between the deep, bioinstinctual unconscious (the id) and spiritual life, and it is not afraid to look for the latter in the former.

Kundalinī is said to be sleeping because it is dormant in its default state. *Kundalinī*—that is to say, libido—is not completely dormant; for, following puberty, it is stirred into activity in sexual circumstances, expressing itself in erotic feelings, sexual arousal, and sexual orgasm. These are dramatic expressions of energy, to be sure, but they are intermittent and relatively brief in duration. *Kundalinī* makes its presence felt in our erotic or sexual experiences, but it reverts to quiescence when these experiences come to an end. Libidinal arousal is not our default state. For the most part *kundalinī*, or libido, is inactive, "asleep."

Although *kundalinī* is dormant in its default state, it can, according to Tantric yoga, be awakened—not just intermittently, as an instinctually organized energy, but permanently, as a spiritual energy about to break free from its instinctual organization. When such awakening occurs, *kundalinī* can affect the body in strange and distressing ways. The following list (excerpted from Collie 1995) includes commonly reported effects.[2]

- Muscle twitches, cramps or spasms
- Energy rushes or immense electricity circulating the body
- Itching, vibrating, prickling, tingling, stinging or crawling sensations
- Intense heat or cold
- Involuntary bodily movements . . .: jerking, tremors, shaking; feeling an inner force pushing one into postures or moving one's body in unusual ways . . .
- Episodes of extreme hyperactivity or . . . overwhelming fatigue . . .
- Intensified or diminished sexual desires
- Headaches, pressures within the skull
- Racing heartbeat, pains in the chest . . .
- Pains and blockages anywhere; often in the back and neck . . .
- Spontaneous vocalizations (including laughing and weeping)—are as unintentional and uncontrollable as hiccoughs

- Hearing an inner sound or sounds, classically described as a flute, drum, waterfall, birds singing, bees buzzing but which may also sound like roaring, whooshing, or thunderous noises or like ringing in the ears . . .
- Heat, strange activity, and/or blissful sensations in the head, particularly in the crown area

This list presents an odd group of phenomena, which are not well understood. The discussion that follows is for this reason offered only as a serious conjecture. With this proviso in mind, the phenomena of physical awakening can plausibly be explained as arising from one or more of the following causes: (1) surplus energy states, (2) movement of energy through blockages and body armors, (3) stimulation of the autonomic nervous system, and (4) activation of instinctual or sensorimotor systems previously disconnected from consciousness.

Itching, tingling sensations, twitches, tremors, spasms, rushes of energy, hyperactivity, and even heightened sexual desire can be understood as expressions of surplus energy states. Tissues and nerves are loaded with an excess standing charge, which causes itching, tingling sensations, restless twitching, and spasmodic contractions of small muscle groups. Excess energy also seems evident in hyperactivity, which tends to be an unfocused discharging of nervous energy. Excess energy seems evident, too, in intensified sexual desire. The awakened energy is an energy that still expresses itself primarily as libido. The power of the Ground, in awakening, is only beginning to be released from the instinctual organization created by primal repression and, therefore, is a plenipotent energy still colored with instinctual qualities and sometimes channeled toward instinctual aims. The general energy surplus for this reason often has an instinctual-erotic coloring, and sexually focused desire in particular can be amplified.

Pains corresponding to sensations of blockage, headaches involving pressure in the skull, and involuntary movements of large muscles can be understood as expressions of powerful currents of energy reopening occluded energy channels or breaking through psychosomatic "knots." The potent energy that is now circulating in the body meets with resistance along the pathways of its movement (the *nādīs* and *sushumnā* of Tantric yoga, the meridians of acupuncture?). Painful sensations of blockage may arise from obstructions in these pathways. The experience of pressure in the skull—together with associated phenomena such as tightening of the scalp, squinting of the eyes, stretching of facial and inner ear muscles—might be explained in a similar way: a knot at the base of the skull resists the influx of energy into the brain. The involuntary movements of large muscles might also be explained as resistance to the flow of energy: energy pierces blocked nerve networks or breaks through embedded body armors. Some of the effects on large muscles mimic the postures of *hatha yoga*, and others, it seems, are the result of energy breaking through psychosomatic knots specific to the individual. As a whole, this group of effects is not only dramatic but also bizarre.

Sensations of heat or cold, experiences of hyperactivity or fatigue, and reactions such as racing or slowing of the heart—along with associated phenomena such as perspiration or horripilation, fever or chill, panting or weeping—can be explained as expressions of the autonomic nervous system. Heat, fever, perspiration, fight-or-flight, panting, and racing of the heart are obviously symptomatic of activation of the sympathetic nervous system; and cold, chill, horripilation, fatigue, weeping, and slowing of the heart are symptomatic of activation of the parasympathetic nervous system. In Tantric spiritual psychology, these two branches of the autonomic nervous system are known as the *pingalā* (sympathetic) and *idā* (parasympathetic) energy channels. Before the awakening of *kundalinī,* according to Tantrism, nonplenipotent psychic energy (*prāna*) flows through these two primary channels, stimulating them at normal and, usually, unnoticeable levels. With the awakening of *kundalinī,* however, plenipotent energy may enter these channels, overstimulating them and producing the kinds of effects just described.

We would be remiss if we failed to mention that the awakening of the body can affect sexuality in more pronounced ways than by producing erotic feelings. Many people have reported experiences of spontaneous sexual arousal and even orgasm (without secretion or ejaculation of sexual fluids). Others have reported experiences of spiritual ecstasy during sexual activity, experiences of mystical transport supervening upon and transcending what began as sexual arousal. Jenny Wade (1998, 2000) has collected accounts of people whose awakening spirituality has been connected in these ways with sexual arousal or activity. The awakened power of the Ground is here in the process of being liberated from its instinctual organization as libido, and for this reason it expresses itself not only in sexual ways but also in ways that, although still tied to the sexual system, are at the same time to some degree free of the sexual system. Sexuality and spirituality are at this point intimately interrelated and frequently intermixed. The awakening power of the Ground, in being released from its instinctual organization as libido, expresses itself as "libido on the way to being Spirit." Tantric, Taoist, and other practices of sacred sexuality may for this reason be especially powerful—and, perhaps, dangerous—disciplines at this stage of development.

THE "REINCARNATION" OF THE EGO

The resurrection of the body, owing to its bizarreness, may be a cause of anxiety for the person undergoing the process. Such anxiety, however, tends to subside as the resurrection process unfolds and its long-term opening, cleansing, and revitalizing effects become apparent. As these effects are revealed, the transformation of the body becomes less frightening and more inviting, and the ego's relation to the body undergoes a fundamental shift. The ego ceases being a frightened witness to the body's resurrection and becomes a willing participant in its own "reincarnation." This reembodiment of the ego is a dimension of the more general process of regeneration in Spirit. In being healingly transformed by Spirit, the ego is also returned to awakened embodied life. The ego is not completely reembodied until the regeneration process is complete. Some degree of disequilibrium between the ego and the body—a steadily diminishing degree—exists until integration is achieved.

During regeneration in Spirit, the body is charged with plenipotent energy and is, therefore, superabundantly alive. It is a vehicle of intense and mostly pleasurable sensations, which cause the ego to swoon with delight. Plenipotent energy, no longer limited to an instinctual organization, is now able to express itself freely, that is, polymorphously, in any tissue or area. The most dramatic expressions of plenipotent energy at work in the body, to be sure, occur earlier, during the period of the body's resurrection, which coincides with regression in the service of transcendence. During this period, as we have seen, the awakened power of the Ground is in the process of opening the body by breaking through psychosomatic blockages, obstructions which, when dissolved, release accumulated energy in explosive bursts, triggering experiences like those described in the preceding section. If, however, the most dramatic expressions of plenipotent energy are characteristic of early stages of bodily awakening, that does not mean that the body is any less alive in later stages, after blockages have been removed. The contrary is true. Although there are fewer explosive discharges of energy, energy still pulses or surges through the body in ways that are "too much" for the ego. The ego during regeneration in Spirit is not yet fully adapted to plenipotent energy and, therefore, is still prone to be overpowered—typically in pleasurable, ecstatic ways—by its embodied expression.

The body of the person undergoing regeneration in Spirit is a mature body that has been restored to full vitality. Resurrected from the "death" of primal repression, it is a body that is open, clean, and intensely alive. Blockages and body armors have been dissolved; plenipotent Spirit rather than nonplenipotent psychic energy flows through energy pathways; and the body in general is free of impediments and purged of toxins. The plenipotent power of the Ground may not be an elixir of immortality, as some adepts of alchemy and Taoism have maintained. It is, however, an energy that dramatically reenlivens the body and keeps it, relative to the natural aging process, in good health. The body of the person undergoing regeneration in Spirit is a body that, for its age, is energetic and hale.

In yielding to reincarnation, the ego becomes once again a body ego, an ego whose seat is in the body rather than the mind, in public rather than private space. In becoming once again a body ego, however, the ego becomes a body ego of a new sort, a transpersonal body ego. Unlike the body ego of early childhood, which, unaware of psychic space, lives only in physical space, the body ego that emerges during regeneration in Spirit lives in both psychic and physical space. The differentiated sphere of psychic space does not collapse; it remains an inner realm of privacy. Psychic space, however, as an inner realm of privacy, is no longer a walled citadel, for the ego no longer needs to protect itself from others and can, therefore, open the doors of psychic space and begin once again living unguardedly in the public sphere. The reincarnated ego remains a mental ego in the sense that it can, and frequently does, step back from the public, bodily realm to enjoy the solitude of inwardness. It ceases, however, being a mental ego in the sense of relating to psychic space as defensive retreat and primary abode.

The return to full embodiment is also a return to full—undefended, radical—intimacy with others. The ego, in returning to the body, relinquishes its prior stance of inwardness and the defensive distance and sense of hiddenness that went with it. The ego steps out from behind the veil of privacy and places itself in unshielded view and immediate, unprotected contact with others. In initial phases of reincarnation, this undefended openness may make the ego feel as if it were naked and vulnerable. As the ego begins to feel more at home in the body, however, it also begins to feel more comfortable living without defenses. It begins to feel more comfortable "being seen" and "being touched."

As feelings of nakedness and vulnerability subside, undefended openness to others increasingly becomes uninhibited intimacy with others. Feelings of nakedness become feelings of transparency, and feelings of vulnerability become feelings of healing reconnection. People undergoing regeneration in Spirit, no longer held back in a stance of inwardness, experience intimacy with others without needing to reach out across a psychic distance. This distance-less intimacy is similar in many ways to the radical intimacy experienced in early childhood. It differs from the intimacy of childhood, however, in the following crucial respect: it is a transpersonal intimacy of true joining with others rather than a prepersonal intimacy of not yet being fully differentiated from others. It is a radical intimacy without sacrifice of independence. The reincarnation of the ego, then, in thus reestablishing radical intimacy, leads to a higher form of embodied relationship.

In entering this higher form of relationship, we join together as embodied beings in the profoundest intimacy of Spirit. We return, on a transpersonal level, not only to awakened corporeality but also to awakened intercorporeality. We become conscious members of the mystical body and begin to see that our individual bodies are cells of this larger body of Spirit. We discussed the mystical body as a spiritual body, a spiritual life to which we all belong, in the last chapter. Our point here is that this body is indeed a body in very much a literal sense of the term. It is an organic reality of which we are the component cells.

THE BODY AS "TEMPLE OF SPIRIT"

Once the power of the Ground is reawakened, the distinction between active psychic energy and "absent" or "sleeping" Spirit disappears. The awakening of the power of the Ground means that the energy active in the body is no longer ordinary psychic energy and is instead Spirit itself in its plenipotency. During the resurrection of the body, corresponding to regression in the service of transcendence, Spirit is perceived as numinous Spirit, a power that is wholly and dauntingly other. For this reason, as we have seen, the resurrection of the body is perceived, to some degree, as an alien and frightening affair. During the reincarnation of the ego, corresponding to regeneration in Spirit, Spirit is perceived as transforming Spirit, a power that, although still other rather than self, is other in a way that is closely related and beneficial to the self. For this reason the ego experiences reincarnation as a salutary even if—should the ego feel naked and vulnerable—a difficult process. Finally, once the reincarnation of the ego is complete and the stage of integration is attained, Spirit is perceived as transparent Spirit, as Spirit in its fully manifest form, as the ego's higher Self. For this reason the stage of integration is the stage in which the spiritual nature of the energy at work within the body is fully disclosed.

Once the body's energy has thus been revealed to be Spirit, it becomes evident, in looking back, that the awakening of the body was at the same time Spirit's awakening in the body and that the ego's return to the body was at the same time Spirit's return. It becomes evident, that is, that the stages of regression in the service of transcendence and regeneration in Spirit were stages leading to a rejoining of the ego and Spirit as a "married couple" in the tabernacle of awakened flesh. From the perspective of integration, the body is the dwelling place of both the ego and Spirit. The ego that has been integrated with Spirit is a body ego that has been wedded to embodied Spirit. It is an ego that has been married to Spirit in the "temple of Spirit," the human body.

We are inherently corporeal beings, and our corporeality is inherently a spiritual corporeality. It follows from this that bodily life, rather than being an obstacle to or enemy of Spirit, is the vehicle of Spirit. We have seen in this chapter that Spirit reveals itself most truly, as transparent Spirit, as Spirit fully incarnate in the flesh. In the next chapter we shall see that it reveals itself as well as Spirit fully present in the world.

EIGHT

THE WORLD

THE WORLD WE live in is not a completely objective state of affairs; rather, it is a *life-world*, a world as comprehended by the human mind and colored by human desires and feelings. As a life-world, our world is a product of subjectivity as well as objectivity and is, therefore, something that changes during the course of human development. In this chapter we trace the principal forms of the life-world from the spiral perspective and propose that the spiral path returns us—on a higher, transpersonal level—to our original "home." We plot our journey through the life-world as we depart from our original home in early childhood, as we enjoy ourselves on the playground of youth, as we prepare for adult life on the rehearsal stage of adolescence, as we enter the arena of responsible action in early adulthood, as we lose our way at the crossroads of midlife, as we are transported into numinous realms in the early stages of spiritual transformation, and as we begin to find our way back home as we spiritually mature.

The discussion of developmental forms of the life-world presented in this chapter has an inner or subjective focus. For we are here describing the different lenses through which the world is perceived at different stages of development. This inner focus, however, gives primary attention to only one side of the life-world, which is a joint product of inner and outer sources, of subjective projection and objective manifestation.[1] As Harold Coward (1996) explains in a discussion of Jung, the life-world, properly understood, is a balance of intrapsychic and extrapsychic contributions, of archetype and eliciting object. The inner construing lens does not create the objects perceived through the lens; rather, it seeks or is drawn to them. The saying "When the student is ready, the teacher appears" gives expression to this interactive balance of subjectivity and objectivity. The perceiving subject finds or is found by the kinds of objects that it is able to perceive. This fact should be kept in mind in reading the ensuing text, which includes a brief discussion of the objective side of the life-world in each section but still gives primary consideration to the subjective side. The primary focus is on intrapsychic (i.e., depth-psychological, energic, ego-psychological) factors governing life-world formation and life-world change.

TABLE 8.1

DEVELOPMENTAL FORMS OF THE LIFE-WORLD

STAGE OF LIFE	WORLD
Neonatal stage	Ouroboric sphere
Early preoedipal stage	Garden of delight
Late preoedipal stage	Split enchanted-haunted world
Oedipal stage	Transition from plenipotently charged world to natural world
Latency	Natural world I: playground of youth
Puberty and adolescence	Natural world II: rehearsal stage for adult life
Early adulthood	Natural world III: arena of responsible action
Crossroads	Natural world denaturalized: existential desert
Awakening	On the threshold of the supernatural
Regression in the service of transcendence	Denaturalized world supernaturalized: realm of numinous powers
Regeneration in Spirit	Supernatural becomes natural: world of transforming Spirit
Ego-Ground integration	Native, hallowed ground; "home": world of transparent Spirit

THE OUROBORIC SPHERE

The fact that the newborn has not yet understood that objects continue to exist when not perceived means that the newborn does not yet know of any world beyond its immediate experience. The newborn's experience is, therefore, all-inclusive. In the last chapter we described this all-inclusiveness of the newborn's experience as the newborn's precosmic body, the all-inclusive matter from which the structured world is carved once the infant begins to distinguish between its skin-bounded self and the independent external world. Here we can note that this precosmic body, as the child's original world, is an *ouroboric sphere*.

The ouroboros is the ancient Egyptian and Greek symbol of the world-encircling snake that devours its own tail. This symbol conveys the three principal ideas of (1) *centeredness:* the snake's head and eyes represent the center from which all is experienced; (2) *boundlessness:* the fact that the snake swallows its own tail means that there is no boundary indicating where the snake ends and a world beyond the snake begins; and (3) *all-inclusiveness:* the snake, in encircling the world, represents an unbroken wholeness beyond which nothing exists. In conveying these three ideas, the ouroboros nicely represents the world of the newborn, whose incipient ego occupies the center of experience, whose experience is without a boundary dividing this center from a larger realm of objective existence, and whose experience, therefore, is all-inclusive.

The all-inclusiveness of the ouroboric sphere means that the newborn has not yet marked off an innermost region of immanence, a region of subjectivity, from an external realm of transcendence, a realm of objectivity. Subjectivity and objectivity, the two sides of the life-world, are not yet differentiated. By default, then, everything exists within an unbounded sphere of immanence; everything is self, nothing other. The newborn lives in a world that is a joint product of subjective and objective factors but has no inkling that this is so. So far as the newborn knows, all of existence is part of the newborn's limitless body. All of existence is part of the newborn's primordial, undifferentiated self.

The all-inclusive nature of the ouroboric sphere is reflected in the worldview of many archaic peoples, who believe that the cosmos is a geocentric sphere containing all possible existence. The modern mind understands how a cosmic sphere might contain all that exists *as a matter of fact.* The modern mind, however, does not understand how a cosmic sphere could contain all *possible* existence. Substituting the idea of mathematical infinity for the arcahic idea of the boundless, the modern mind asks, "What lies beyond the sphere?" In asking this question, the modern mind implicitly (and illicitly) imputes a boundary where none exists in the archaic understanding. In the archaic worldview, there is no cosmic boundary marking off what lies within and what beyond the cosmic sphere. All of existence must necessarily be contained within the sphere. The archaic geocentric sphere is like the newborn's ouroboric sphere in excluding the possibility of transcendent realms of existence.

The modern notion of mathematical infinity, we should note, was already present in early premodern times. Indeed, the tension between the modern concept of infinity and the archaic idea of the unlimited was already evident in pre-Socratic Greece, in views that emerged in response to the philosopher Parmenides (early fifth century B.C.E.). Whereas the philosopher Anaximander (sixth century B.C.E.) held that the cosmos is a boundless, unlimited whole (*apeiron*), Parmenides insisted that "what is" must be limited, must have shaping or defining boundaries, if it is to be conceivable at all. Parmenides for this reason concluded that the cosmos is a "well-rounded sphere," a sphere which, he said, "mighty Necessity holds in the bonds of a limit, which pens it in all round" (McKirahan 1994, p. 154).

Although Parmenides thus insisted on cosmic boundaries, he continued, in the archaic mindset, to assume that nothing in principle could exist beyond the cosmos. Parmenides, in thus combining a brilliant new idea with a traditional assumption, arrived at the bizarre conclusion that the cosmos is both bounded and all-inclusive. Others challenged this conclusion immediately, asserting what was now evident for the first time, namely, that if the cosmos is "penned in all round," it must be penned in *by something.* Generalizing on this insight, Parmenides' contemporaries realized that any boundary requires something beyond it—even if only empty space—just in order to be a boundary. Parmenides' bizarre conclusion thus led to an understanding of infinite extension, to an understanding that all boundaries have a far side and, therefore, can be exceeded in thought, ad infinitum.

Parmenides' younger associate, Zeno of Elea, was the first to explore this newly discovered notion of mathematical infinity, which he used exclusively for critical purposes, to refute Parmenides' opponents. He argued in ingenious ways that mathematical infinity, whether of extension or division, whether of space or time, is a self-contradictory notion, and therefore that Parmenides was correct in holding that the cosmos is limited. Zeno's arguments, however, novel and brilliant though they were, were unable to suppress the powerful emerging notion of mathematical infinity. Accordingly, Melissus, a pre-Socratic philosopher who argued in favor of many of Parmenides' ideas, held that "what is" must be infinite rather than finite in magnitude. Soon thereafter the atomists, Leucippus and Democritus, argued that "what is" consists of tiny atoms moving about in the infinite void of space. Although the notion that the cosmos might be spatially infinite inevitably emerged in this way, it remained a minority view until the modern period, and even then it became generally accepted only after considerable resistance. The primary premodern notion of the cosmos continued to bear traces of the ouroboric sphere.

THE GARDEN OF DELIGHT

Once the child begins to understand object permanence—at about four or five months of age—a new world is revealed to the child: the external world lying beyond the limits of immediate experience. As this new world takes form in the child's awareness, the child draws the first dividing line between immanent subjectivity and transcendent objectivity, between self and not-self. This line, as we have learned, is the surface of the child's body. The child, then, here ceases being a limitless precosmic body and becomes the limited body of the flesh. Correspondingly, the world ceases being a realm of all-inclusive immanence, an ouroboric sphere, and becomes a transcendent realm existing beyond the child's bodily self.

Let us recall that a primary difference between the child's body and the rest of the world is that the child's body is always present to experience, whereas everything else is sometimes absent. This present-absent difference, now understood in terms of object permanence, becomes the immanent-transcendent difference. At four or five months of age, then, the child begins to understand that objects absent from experience remain in existence in a domain beyond, transcendent to, the child. In achieving this understanding, the child becomes a body ego in the proper sense of the term; and the world, correspondingly, becomes an external world in the proper sense of the term. The child becomes an ego-centered region of corporeal immanence, and the world becomes a realm of material transcendence.

The transcendent world that is revealed to the child at this point is a paradisiacal *garden of delight*. We are not falling prey to mythological thinking or to naive romanticism in describing the world of the early preoedipal stage in this way, as some would argue. We are not saying that the early preoedipal child never suffers and is always perfectly loved and protected. Rather, our point is that under normal conditions the world of the early preoedipal child possesses at least the following four ideal qualities: (1) it is a world in which the child's needs are immediately met, without effort on the child's part; (2) it is a world that is centered in the child, who is an object of love; (3) it is a world that is rendered appealing, resplendent, and wondrous by the plenipotent power of the Dynamic Ground; and (4) it is utterly native ground, "home."

These paradisiacal qualities, to be sure, are based in part on false assumptions. They are based not only on the caregiver's loving attentions and on the child's openness to the Ground but also on cognitive limitations that allow the child falsely to assume that the transcendent world is a small, friendly realm and that the caregiver is always close by and ready to help when the child is in need. If, however, the paradisiacal qualities of the garden of delight are based in part on false assumptions, that does not mean that these qualities are any less real as aspects of the child's lived experience. The child's assumptions, even when false, guide the child as it brings into focus a world that, as a lifeworld, is entirely real.

Most children in the early preoedipal stage—from four or five to sixteen or eighteen months of age—have their needs met by the caregiver with nothing expected of them in return. This, tragically, is only a general truth, for many toddlers and even infants suffer from deprivation, neglect, or abuse. Still, it remains true both (1) that most children in the early preoedipal stage are cared for in at least a "good enough" way and (2) that the protection and nurture given them are provided unconditionally, without behavioral expectations. In the early preoedipal stage, the caregiver seeks to anticipate the child's needs, which, consequently, frequently are not experienced as needs. When needs do importune, they are usually quickly allayed. When the child is hungry, it is fed; when it is tired, it sleeps; when it is distressed, it is held and embraced. Moreover, the child is the center of the adoring attention not only of the caregiver and other members of the child's immediate family but also of grandparents, aunts, uncles, friends of the family, and others. The child for these reasons assumes that the world is a caring world, a world that is devoted to meeting the child's needs and fostering its well-being.

The child in the early preoedipal stage also assumes that the world is free of danger. In first awakening to the transcendent character of the caregiver, the child experiences anxiety, as is evident in fear of strangers. This anxiety, however, lasts for only a brief period, corresponding to the differentiation subphase of the separation-individuation process. The child is soon relieved of anxiety because the child's cognitive limitations allow the child to assume that the caregiver, even when absent, is close by and available to attend to the child's needs. Although the child understands object permanence and, therefore, object transcendence, it does not yet understand the full independence of transcendent objects. As explained in chapter 5, the child assumes that objects exist at nearby locations. The child understands that objects exist beyond the range of perception, but it assumes that objects beyond the range of perception remain within the range of accessibility. It does not take long, then, for the child, having experienced initial anxiety, to begin taking comfort in the belief that the caregiver, even when not perceived, is close by and ready to rescue or otherwise care for the child. The child in this way soon comes to believe that there is nothing in the world to fear.

Indeed, the child soon becomes a fearless explorer of the world, taking delight in it as a radically new field of experience. The child, developmentally ready for the challenges it now faces, cathects its new world with plenipotent energy, the attracting, amplifying, and dissolvent powers of which have dramatic effects. When the child awakens to the existence of the transcendent world, the power of the Dynamic Ground ceases being pooled as an inner reservoir and flows out from its source to the world. Thus charged with plenipotent energy, the world becomes irresistibly attractive. It stirs in the child an experiential greediness, an insatiable desire to inspect, feel, taste, and otherwise test everything it encounters. The child, now in the practicing subphase of the separation-individuation process, is passionately interested in its new world. The world is fascinating in its myriad treasures and marvels. Moreover, the world is extravagent in its perceptual qualities, for the power of the Ground, as an amplifying energy, embellishes the world with arresting colors, powerful aromas, luxuriant textures, and a radiant atmosphere. The world, perceptually enhanced in these ways, is resplendently beautiful.

The world of the early preoedipal stage is charged not only with attracting and amplifying energy but also with dissolvent energy. The power of the Ground in its plenipotency is frequently more than the child can withstand. The child's ego, consequently, is frequently dissolved, either cathectically, by yielding to trances, or infusively, by being inflated to the point of rapture. The child is spellbound or transported as it beholds the wonders of the world. Invested with dissolvent potency, the world possesses magical power, power that has hypnotic and ecstatic effects upon the child. The plenipotency of the power of the Ground, then, renders the child's world not only irresistibly inviting and resplendently beautiful but also pleasurably overawing. Charged with plenipotent energy, objects in the child's world captivate the child in wonderment or burst the child's budding ego in experiences of uncontainable delight.

Finally, the world of the early preoedipal child is "home." It is native ground not only because it is the world into which the child is born but also because it is a world in which the child is the primary being, a being who resides at the center and is beloved by all. To be sure, as a realm of transcendently existing objects, the world of the early preoedipal child, unlike the ouroboric sphere of the newborn, is larger than the child. Although larger than the child, however, this world remains small, for everything in this world, and in particular the all-providing caregiver, the Great Mother, is located within range of accessibility. Despite being a realm of transcendent existence, then, the world of the early preoedipal child remains an inherently local world in which the child is the center of loving attention. It is a world in which the child is served and adored as a little divine being.

Lest it seem that the world of the early preoedipal child is only a reflection of the child's cognitive limitations and projections, we should remember that the garden of delight, like all forms of the life-world, is an interplay of subjective and objective factors. The garden of delight is indeed the world as experienced by the child, but it is not for that reason a mere appearance, a merely subjective phenomenon. On the contrary, it is the world itself as it presents itself to the child, setting challenges for the child and eliciting from within the child cognitive, cathectic, and other responses that both give expression to and further develop the child's capabilities. The garden of delight, then, is as much a world that shapes the child as it is a world that is shaped by the child. It is a world that, protectively overseen by the Great Mother and full of secrets to be unlocked or laid bare, draws the child out of itself and motivates it to develop sensorimotor skills. It is a world that stirs the child's curiosity and reveals its unending wonders to the child.

We should note that the garden of delight would not be irresistibly appealing were it not magnetized by plenipotent attracting energy. This magnetic charging of the world, however, is a response to an appeal inherent to the world, which, as a transcendent domain, has just revealed itself to the child as a virgin frontier awaiting exploration. We should note, too, that the garden of delight would not be experienced in such rich variety and vivid detail were it not magnified by plenipotent amplifying energy. This magnification of the world, however, is a magnification of variety and detail that actually exist. It is a magnification of the child's power of vision: the greater the level of magnification provided by the subject, the more the world discloses itself to the subject. The garden of delight, then, is not a subjectively spawned illusion; it is the world in its objectivity as it comes into focus for a child who, having just awakened to the world's transcendence, is developmentally ready to enter the world and to begin exploring it.

THE SPLITTING OF THE WORLD INTO ENCHANTED AND HAUNTED WORLDS

Splitting brings an end to the preoedipal garden of delight. The cause of splitting, as we know, is the insight, occurring sometime after the middle of the

second year of life, that unperceived objects are not tied to the child's experience. The child here comes to understand not only object permanence but also
full object independence. This understanding greatly enlarges the region of
transcendent existence. Unperceived objects need no longer exist in nearby
locations and can now exist anywhere in a vastly expanded space. In awakening to this fact, the child is disabused of its former sense of being the center
of a small, caring, and safe world. The child now understands that absent
objects can be far away and inaccessible and, therefore, that objects upon
which the child depends, most importantly the caregiver, can, in exiting the
field of experience, never be found again. For this reason the child begins to
experience severe anxiety, which most fundamentally is an abandonment anxiety focused on the caregiver.

The discovery of the full independence of objects triggers a negative
restructuring of the world. The small, caring, and safe world of the early
preoedipal stage is undermined as the child begins to experience frightening
glimpses of the vastness of the world. When the caregiver is present, the
child is usually able to suppress these unwelcome insights. When the caregiver is absent, however, the child is frequently assailed by thoughts of vulnerability in relation to a world that is suddenly seen as huge, hostile, and
dangerous. This kind of shift occurs most dramatically when the child goes
to bed at night. When the caregiver turns out the light and leaves the room,
the child is left defenseless in an enormous black world full of terrifying
specters. The next morning, when the light and the caregiver return, the
child is greatly relieved. The world shrinks in size and seems small, caring,
and safe again. The child thus returns to paradise, or so it seems. In fact, the
child never again fully returns to paradise, for the assumptions underlying
the perception of the world as small, caring, and safe are now compromised.
The paradise to which the child returns is no longer a completely real life-
world. It is a world that has begun to fade, a "paradise lost" to which the
child clings. The paradise to which the child returns is increasingly a world
of make-believe.

The child undergoing splitting has not yet closed itself to the Dynamic
Ground, and for this reason the split world in which the child lives is charged
with plenipotent attracting, amplifying, and dissolvent energy. Once splitting
occurs, then, not only the garden of delight but also the terrifying realm that
is its negative counterpart—let us call it "anti-Eden"—is accentuated by
plenipotent energy. Anti-Eden is for this reason similar to the garden of
delight in being a world that is irresistibly fascinating, magnified in its perceptual qualities, and dissolvent in its effect upon the child. Unlike the garden of
delight, however, this dystopian realm is fascinating, magnified, and dissolvent
in negative ways.

The child wants desperately to avoid thinking about what lurks beneath
the bed or in the closet or down the hallway, but the child's attention is
ineluctably—indeed, obsessively—drawn to monsters that, the child believes,

are lying in wait in these hiding places. The child is fixated on invisible ghostly presences and dark, dangerous recesses and crevasses. The child tries to avert its attention and to focus on things that might bring comfort, for example, the favorite blanket or stuffed animal that the child takes to bed. These efforts, however, are not entirely successful, for the child is caught in the grip not only of its own fears but also of an irresistible power, the plenipotent power of the Ground acting as a dark attracting energy.

As the child is thus riveted on malevolent creatures and perilous possibilities, it is also unnerved by exaggerated perceptual qualities. The power of the Ground, acting as a dark amplifying energy, magnifies the features of objects in disturbing ways, distorting them and making them appear repugnant or menacing. Deep shadings and lurid colorings prevail. Objects seem either cloaked and hidden or garish and enormous, and in either case they pulsate with dark power. Moreover, the overall atmosphere of the world is charged with a sinister electricity, an electricity that keeps the child on edge, braced for a sudden epiphany of a denizen of darkness. In these and other ways, the plenipotent power of the Ground, acting as a dark amplifying energy, ominously enlarges the child's world.

The power of the Ground sometimes energizes objects to such a degree that they have dissolvent effects upon the child, inducing dreadful absorptions or triggering disintegrative fear. Like the garden of delight, anti-Eden is alive with a magical, mind-dissolving energy, but in anti-Eden this energy is a dark energy that engulfs or discomposes the child, causing morbid trances or flights of panic. In succumbing to morbid trances, the child experiences goose flesh, clamminess, and feelings of eeriness or creepiness. The child senses that it is in the presence of something ghastly or ghostly and cannot pull itself away. In turn, in succumbing to flights of panic, the child experiences racing heart, feverishness, and runaway fear. The child is terrified that some evil presence is about to leap out of its hiding place and eat or otherwise harm the child. Such trances and panics typically occur at night, when the child is alone in the dark. Nothing can calm the child except the embrace of the caregiver. The child's ego is thus prone to being dissolved, either dreadfully captivated or terrifyingly scattered.

Anti-Eden is the complete opposite of the garden of delight. Whereas the garden of delight is a small, safe, wondrous paradise, anti-Eden is a vast, dangerous, horrific realm. Whereas the garden of delight is native ground on which the child is the center of loving attentions, anti-Eden is alien ground on which the child is lost and defenseless in the midst of invisible predators and bogeymen. Both worlds are saturated with plenipotent attracting, amplifying, and dissolvent energy, but whereas the garden of delight is saturated in ways that heighten the appeal, beauty, and delight of the world, anti-Eden is saturated in ways that heighten the repugnance, monstrousness, and frightfulness of the world. In general, whereas the garden of delight is an *enchanted* world, anti-Eden is a *haunted* world.

The onset of splitting is the beginning of the child's banishment from paradise. The child cannot entirely suppress its emerging understanding of object independence, and it therefore continues to experience some degree of anxiety even when the caregiver is present and attending to the child's needs. The child is no longer able to take the caregiver for granted, as is apparent in such behaviors as clinging to the caregiver and demanding the caregiver's attentions. The child, consequently, is no longer able to act in the world with the same abandon it enjoyed during the early preoedipal stage. The child's repeated attempts to return to Eden are, then, just that: attempts. They are attempts based on pushing to the background an insight the child cannot suppress and on clinging to a caregiver whom the child can no longer take for granted. Deep inside, the child now knows that it lives in a large and dangerous world.

Quite evidently, much of the world as seen through the lens of preoedipal splitting is exaggeration or mere imagining. For instance, the child (1) one-sidedly cathects—thus magnetizing and amplifying—either exclusively beautiful, pleasing, and reassuring aspects of the world (the fading garden of delight) or exclusively ugly, repugnant, and frightening aspects (anti-Eden); (2) splits and exaggerates its perception of the caregiver, seeing the caregiver as either the all-good Good Mother (who here replaces the Great Mother) or the all-bad Terrible Mother (the ogress of anti-Eden); and (3) projectively populates the world with imaginary beings of both good and evil sorts, for example, good fairies and horrific monsters. The child's fear of the larger and more dangerous world in which it now lives stimulates the child's imagination, which runs wild in creating all-good and all-bad phantasms and scenarios. Much of the child's world is a fabrication based either on reassuring make-believe or on obsessing about evil beings and possible dangers. Much of the world seen through the lens of preoedipal splitting, then, is distortion or false projection.

Not all of the world seen through this lens, however, is subjective error of these sorts. We have already explained how the garden of delight is a world the appeal, rich variety, and vivid detail of which are due as much to objective as to subjective factors. We can now add that the same is true of anti-Eden, for the vast, dark, and dangerous world that the child now perceives is by no means a completely false world. The world *is* vast and mostly hidden from view; it *is* dark and unperceivable in many places and at frequent times; and it *does* contain many dangers. To be sure, in the child's perception, these aspects of the world are greatly exaggerated. Still, these aspects are now perceived by the child for the first time. If, as garden of delight, the world reveals its treasures and wonders to the child, then, as anti-Eden, it reveals those of its dimensions that are threatening to life. In becoming aware of these dimensions, the child is overwhelmed. The discovery of the vastness, darkness, and dangerousness of the world is a learning experience that eventually advances the child's development. It is, however, a learning experience that initially is traumatic for the child.

THE NATURAL WORLD I: THE PLAYGROUND OF YOUTH

The child must eventually learn that the world, although larger and more dangerous than previously realized, is not for that reason a hostile environment; and in fact the child, in overcoming splitting, achieves this understanding. Just as the child, in overcoming splitting, learns that the caregiver is a good enough provider and protector, so, too, the child, in overcoming splitting, learns that the world is a safe enough world. The child is thus eventually able to accept its new circumstances and to begin adjusting to its new world. It is able to leave behind the enchanted and haunted worlds of prelatency stages and to enter what, as a life-world, can be called the *natural world*.

The natural world—emerging in latency and restructured in adolescence and early adulthood—is neither enchanted nor haunted because, owing to primal repression, it is animated by the power of the Ground in its diminished expression as psychic energy rather than in its original plenipotency. The natural world is charged with energy and, therefore, is a world that is inviting and alive. The natural world, however, in being charged with nonplenipotent psychic energy, usually is not charged to such a degree that, in attracting the child, it takes possession of the child or that, in amplifying objects, it renders them resplendent or monstrous. Moreover, the natural world usually is not charged to such a degree as to affect the child dissolvently, either by entrancing the child or by inwardly energizing the child beyond the limits of self-cohesion. The natural world is alive with energy, but not with the plenipotent, magical energy that animated the world in prelatency stages. The world has been divested of its "supernatural" character and has become the natural world as we know it.

The natural world in which the child now lives is the natural world in its first developmental form: the playground of youth.[2] The natural world in this initial form is a world of pleasure and play, and in this respect it resembles the garden of delight of the early preoedipal stage. Many developmental theorists of psychoanalytic orientation have observed that the stage of latency is similar to the practicing subphase of the preoedipal separation-individuation process, noting that in both the child enjoys the world in a sensuously immediate way and acts on the assumption that it will be cared for in case of need. This observation is accurate, but the following two qualifications should be added: (1) the pleasures experienced by the latency child typically are not plenipotent, ego-dissolving pleasures; and (2) the assumption about being cared for in case of need is, during latency, a qualified assumption, to wit, the assumption that parents or guardians are available in a good enough rather than a perfect way. The playground of youth is similar to the preoedipal garden of delight in being a world of pleasure and presumed safety. These similarities, however, are at the same time differences, for the pleasures are less intense pleasures and the safety is known to be without guarantee.

The pleasures are less intense pleasures because, again, the world is now charged with nonplenipotent psychic energy rather than with the power of the

Ground in its plenipotency. The latency child has a passion for the world, to be sure. This passion, however, typically does not lead to ego-dissolution. Because psychic energy is nonplenipotent in intensity, the pleasures experienced by the latency child rarely completely entrance or enrapture the child. It is rare for the latency child to be drawn out of itself to the point of complete absorption or inwardly inflated to the point of unbounded ecstasy. The world of the latency stage is full of breathtaking sights, sounds, and textures and of tantalizing unknowns to explore. As the playground of youth, it is a realm of powerful, body-based pleasures. Still, it usually is not, as was the garden of delight, a realm of plenipotent, ego-dissolving pleasures.

Nor is it a realm in which the child can play with complete abandon. Unlike the preoedipal child in the garden of delight, the latency child in the playground of youth knows full well that the world is a large and dangerous place and that parents or guardians are sometimes unavailable when needs arise. The latency child is not terrified by this inescapable insecurity, however, because the latency child has overcome separation anxiety and has learned that parents or guardians, although by no means perfect, are good enough. Moreover, the latency child has already learned a good deal about the world and, in particular, about what kinds of activities and places are safe and what kinds are not. The latency child indeed plays with a high degree of abandon. It usually does so, however, only in ways and in places that it knows are safe.

Similar to the body of the latency child, which is a depotentiated, subdued body, the world of the latency child is a depotentiated, "merely" natural world. It is a world that, charged with psychic energy, is inviting and alive but that, divested of plenipotent energy, is neither enchanted nor haunted. The body of the latency child remains fundamentally a recreational body, and the world of the latency child remains fundamentally a recreational world. The child is still a pleasure-seeking being, and the world is the child's playground. As a rule, however, the child's pleasures are no longer ego-dissolving pleasures, and the world is no longer a "supernatural" world.

Shifting focus from the subjective to the objective side of the life-world, the following question arises: "In perceiving the world as a depotentiated natural world, does the latency child thereby perceive the world more or less objectively, that is, more or less clearly or accurately?" In considering this question, one might think that the reduction of energy from plenipotent to nonplenipotent intensity would by itself bring the world more clearly into view. This is not so, however. Such a reduction, by itself, means only that the world is perceived at a lower level of magnification (amplification) and, therefore, in less variety and detail. The depotentiation of the world occurring in the transition to latency, then, considered by itself, causes the child to perceive the world less clearly in the sense of less fully. The latency world is less differentiated, brilliant, and deep in its qualities than are the worlds of prelatency stages. We should stress the relative character of this statement, however, because the latency world, in being charged with psychic energy, if not with the power of the Ground in its plenipotency, is by no means a completely decathected, denaturalized, dead world—as is the "existential desert" of the stage of alienation (see below). It is a world that discloses countless treasures to the latency child. It is, however, a world that, relative to the worlds of prelatency stages, is experienced at a lower level of magnification.

If, however, the natural world of latency is perceived less fully than were the "supernatural" worlds of prelatency stages, it nonetheless is a world that is perceived more accurately overall. It is perceived more accurately because the depotentiation of the world that occurs in the transition to latency allows the child to make dramatic advances in reality testing. In particular, the reduction in energy helps the child (1) to bring an end to splitting and, therefore, to the misperceptions associated with splitting and (2) to achieve self-possession and, therefore, to maintain control of the reality-testing process. Whereas the child in the late preoedipal and oedipal stages, suffering from splitting, is prone to see the world in extremes of black and white and to populate the world with corresponding evil and good imaginary creatures, the latency child, free of splitting, is able to perceive the world without such defensive distortions and fabrications. Moreover, whereas the child in prelatency stages is frequently overpowered by plenipotent energy, thus "losing its head," the latency child is empowered by nonplenipotent energy and is for this reason able to explore the world without suffering breaks in the thread of ongoing experience. Whereas, for example, the prelatency child is easily entranced, enraptured, or otherwise dissolved by plenipotently energized objects or situations, the latency child, undisturbed by the supercharging effects of plenipotent energy, is able to remain gathered and focused and, therefore, to maintain a course of investigation. The latency child's reality testing is for this reason more disciplined and systematic in nature. On balance, then, the latency child perceives the world more accurately than did the prelatency child. Although the latency child perceives the world less fully, it perceives the world with fewer distortions and disruptions to cognitive processing.

THE NATURAL WORLD II: THE REHEARSAL STAGE FOR ADULT LIFE

In becoming adolescents, we cease any longer being interested in child's play. The world, accordingly, ceases any longer being the playground of youth. It remains the natural world as we know it, a world that is inviting and alive but not enchanted or haunted. In remaining the natural world, however, the world otherwise changes in fundamental character: it is transformed from a playground into a rehearsal stage. Adolescents do still play, but what they do most earnestly is play*act*, and the world is the stage on which adolescents perform. For adolescents, the world is the rehearsal stage for adult life.

Performing before an audience is inherent to adolescence as a developmental stage. Adolescents must act because they face a vast repertoire of adult roles that must be selectively tested before adult role commitments can be made. As actors, adolescents differ from theater performers in the following way: unlike theater performers, who try to lose themselves in the roles they play, adolescents try to find themselves in the roles they play. Adolescent acting is in this way like trying on new clothes to see how well they fit so that, eventually, the clothes can serve as an outer expression of the inner person. Adolescents test outer, social scripts so that scripts that are fitting can be owned and internalized as vehicles for the expression of inner tendencies and talents. Undeniably, much in adolescence is mere pretense; the heart of adolescence, however, is an attempt to find ways in which the inner self can be effectively engaged and expressed through the role-scripts of the social world.

The audience before which adolescents perform is the peer group. This audience is difficult to please because adolescent insecurities and the pressure to conform predispose adolescents to be critical of each other. Adolescents are acutely aware of pretense in themselves, and for this reason they tend to be suspicious of pretense in their peers. If, however, the peer group tends to be a critical audience for these reasons, adults are much more accepting. Adults give adolescents room to behave in all manner of ways, knowing that they are "going through a stage." This special allowance given to adolescents is what psychoanalyst Erik Erikson called a "psychosocial moratorium," a reserving of judgment until after adolescent rehearsals are over and the real performance of adult life begins.

Adolescents on the rehearsal stage for adult life suffer from stage fright. This performance anxiety is understandable, for adolescents, in stepping forth on stage, abandon prior ego supports and become first-time actors performing unfamiliar roles before an audience of skeptical peers. The stage fright experienced can be severe, but it rarely derails development. Adolescents, although frightened by the prospect of performing before peers, are nonetheless driven to perform. The adolescent rehearsal stage, as a form of the natural world, is alive with attracting, amplifying psychic energy; it is "where the action is." Most adolescents for this reason work through their stage fright. Their desire to begin testing adult roles and identity possibilities exceeds their fear of failure. Adolescents are strongly motivated to put themselves to the test so that they can discover how and where they will fit, and who they will be, in the larger world of adult society.

The transformation of the life-world from a playground into a rehearsal stage is quite evidently a consequence of stage transition: teenagers, in undergoing rapid physical and psychosexual maturation, lose interest in child's play and begin to pay attention to adult social realities. This transformation, however, if primarily a result of subject-side maturation, is by no means exclusively a result of inner change, for teenagers begin to focus on adult social realities in part because they are called forth and called to action by those realities. Adolescents find themselves in new social circumstances. Parents and adults generally begin placing adult expectations on adolescents, and so, too, do adolescents' peers, whose so-called peer pressure, with its cool-uncool, ingroup-outgroup divisions, is an expression of the expectation that adolescents behave in mature ways. What counts as mature behavior according to adolescent peer pressure is frequently only a caricature of true adult behavior. This fact notwithstanding, adolescent peer pressure plays a key role in facilitating departure from the playground of youth and entrance upon the rehearsal stage for adult life. Adolescents, then, not only outgrow previous interests but also grow into new circumstances, circumstances that motivate and guide their development. As in all stages of development, both subjective and objective factors contribute to the formation of the life-world.

THE NATURAL WORLD III: THE ARENA OF RESPONSIBLE ACTION

The rehearsal for adult life is over all too quickly. Adolescence soon comes to an end, and one begins to feel pressure to make, or at least earnestly prepare for, the primary commitments of the identity project of early adulthood. Among these commitments, as we know, are commitments to an occupational role and, usually, a relationship with a significant other. In making these and other commitments of the identity project, one exits the rehearsal stage of adolescence and enters a new world: the arena of responsible action.

The arena of responsible action is also a stage. Not a rehearsal stage, it is the stage of life's actual performance, the stage—or, in fact, stages—on which one performs the roles to which one has committed oneself in the identity project. One performs roles such as those of worker, citizen, partner, and parent in order to *be* a worker, citizen, partner, and parent, indeed to be a *good*— or at least a good enough—worker, citizen, partner, and parent. Let us recall that in the identity project one seeks to achieve not only a socially recognized sense of being but also a sense of justification, a sense that one is at least good enough in what one does and, therefore, worthy in who one is. Young adults, in pursuing the identity project, pursue both being and value, and the point here is that they pursue both of these goals by performing roles on the stage of adult life. Young adults seek to earn a sense of being and value by performing roles such as worker, citizen, partner, and parent sufficiently well to meet with the acceptance of the people before whom they perform.

Young adults perform on many stages rather than only one. Principal among these stages are those of professional life, private life, and civic life. In acting on these stages, young adults perform before different audiences with different interests and standards of judgment. When performing on the stage of professional life, young adults perform before co-workers and are judged by the requirements of the workplace. When acting on the stage of private life, they perform before significant others and are judged by how well they fulfill the responsibilities of partner, parent, guardian, or friend. In turn, when acting on the stage of civic life, they perform before members of social groups, political organizations, or churches and are judged by how well they accomplish the tasks or meet the obligations of civic roles.

Like adolescents about to step forth on the rehearsal stage for adult life, young adults about to enter the arena of responsible action experience performance anxiety. Most young adults, however, like most adolescents, work through their fears; for the arena to which young adults are called, like the rehearsal stage to which adolescents are called, is usually more inviting than daunting. Most young adults, therefore, find the courage to make the commitments and follow through on the responsibilities of adult life. Moreover, most young adults find that performance anxiety subsides as they become more accomplished in their chosen roles and, therefore, more solid in their social self. As they become more accomplished in their chosen roles, performing these roles becomes less a matter of unsure imitation and more a matter of confident self-expression. Most young adults become less anxious about critical reviews of their acting and more secure in their established identity and sense of earned value. Performance anxiety, of course, never disappears entirely, but for most people it abates significantly.

As a life-world, the arena of responsible action is an interweaving of subjectivity and objectivity. The primary subjective factor in play is the need to rebuild the ego system. The ego system, having been dismantled during adolescence, must be rebuilt in early adulthood. The identity project, as we know, is the vehicle for this reconstruction. The identity project provides the ego with ideal goals toward which to aspire (ego ideal), self-discipline with which to persevere in striving toward these goals (superego), and an increasingly solid sense of being and earned value (identity, self-representation). The arena of responsible action, then, as the life-world in which the identity project is pursued, is a life-world in which fundamental ego needs are met.

It is also a life-world in which deeper, species needs are met, needs relating to sustenance and the reproduction of the species. The need for sustenance expresses itself as the need to perform some physical, mental, or cultural work that will help feed the body, mind, or soul; and the need to reproduce expresses itself as the need for intimacy and family. In contemporary society, the primary way in which the need for work is met is by making a commitment to a job or career, and the primary way in which the need for intimacy and family is met is by making a commitment to a long-term, exclusive relationship with a significant other. For most people, identifications with such work and relationship commitments are central components of the identity project. In general, the arena of responsible action is a life-world in which we seek to fulfill what Freud described as the two fundamental needs for a healthy, meaningful life: work and love. These needs become developmentally imperative in early adulthood and are primary subjective factors contributing to the formation of the arena of responsible action as a life-world.

The objective factors contributing to the arena of responsible action mirror the subjective. The needs for work and love are not only inner drives but also outer, social expectations. We are expected to be contributing members of society, and the two primary contributions expected are to work in the public domain and to care for children within the sphere of the family. Historically, people have been expected to contribute to society primarily in one or the other of these ways: men have been expected to work in the public domain and women have been expected to be responsible primarily for the care of children. This one-sided distribution of the two primary social expectations is now disappearing in the West, but the expectations themselves are not. They remain as objective factors contributing to the formation of the arena of responsible action as a life-world.

The arena of responsible action remains the life-world for most people for the rest of their lives. Even people who suffer a midlife loss of faith in the identity project are usually able to find ways to restore their faith in the project and, thereby, to reanimate the arena of responsible action as a life-world. Our goals change as we age, and we sometimes have to lose our way before we can reset our sights and begin life anew. This is especially true not only at midlife but also later in life, when most people, in retiring from a job and no longer having growing children to raise, leave behind parts of life that had made up a good deal of their identity and earned value. Most people, however, are able to meet these challenges and to find new, satisfying roles to perform, roles that allow them to continue to make meaningful contributions to society and, thereby, to continue to participate in the arena of responsible action.

THE NATURAL WORLD DENATURALIZED: THE EXISTENTIAL DESERT

Some people suffer a loss of faith in the identity project that is so profound that they are unable to redefine the project in a way that allows them to reengage the world. For these people, as we know, withdrawal from the world evolves into serious existential alienation, depression into despair. For these people, the world ceases being an arena of responsible action; indeed, it ceases being an inviting, living natural world of any sort. The world loses its appeal and vibrancy; it is denaturalized and reduced to an existential desert.

We learned in chapter 4 that a major cause of the denaturalization of the world is the ebb tide of psychic energy that occurs during the alienation process. Psychic energy recedes from the world and flows back to its source in the Dynamic Ground. The world in this way ceases being charged with the attracting, amplifying energy that had made it an inviting, living natural world. The world becomes remote, arid, flat, and unreal. It becomes a desert. Everything is dead; nothing stands out as urgent or important or even noteworthy. The alienated person is cut off from the world, and the world for this reason appears remote and unreal to the alienated person.

It will be worthwhile to give separate consideration to each of the four features of the existential desert just mentioned: remoteness, aridity, flatness, and unreality. The existential desert is remote because the alienated person's withdrawal from the world is at the same time, it seems, a withdrawal of the world from the alienated person. As the alienated person is pulled inward by receding psychic energy, it appears to the alienated person as though the world were receding from consciousness. The alienated person is thus separated from the world by an ever-widening gulf, a gulf that makes it increasingly difficult to reengage the world effectively. For the alienated person, the world becomes increasingly distant and out of reach.

The existential desert is arid because it has been drained of psychic energy. Psychic energy, as an attracting and amplifying energy, had made the world appealing and alive. The removal of psychic energy from the world therefore takes away the world's appeal and aliveness. The removal of psychic energy makes the world dull and barren, incapable of stirring interest; and it desiccates the world, leaving it dry and dead. No longer imbued with attracting or amplifying energy, the world ceases being inviting and vibrant and becomes an arid wasteland, a desolate landscape in which nothing sparks curiosity or shows any sign of life.

The existential desert is flat because, in being devoid of appeal and life, everything is equal, equally uninteresting, equally unimportant. Nothing is more prominent than anything else. The world has no peaks or valleys, challenges or disappointments, profundities or banalities, heroes or fools. All differences of value have been leveled. Horizons have disappeared, and the world has collapsed into a two-dimensional setting, a stage without figure or ground. The world of the alienated person is one in which nothing stands out and in which there are no rankings of importance. It is a world in which everything is shallow, neutral, uniform, gray.

Finally, the existential desert is unreal because it is pervasively odd and devoid of meaning. The alienated person knows full well what things are, that oak trees are oak trees, that one's house is where one lives. This fact notwithstanding, the alienated person finds things uncannily different, for things have lost the familiarity and functional significance they had when experienced within the context of engaged activity. Consider what it is like to focus on a word outside the flow of communicative speech or writing. The word is thrown into relief as an incoherent sound or scribble on a piece of paper. Similarly, everything in the existential desert has an obtrusive, pointless character. As Jean-Paul Sartre put it, objects in the alienated world are *de trop:* needless, in the way, "just there," without reason for being. Rather than being implicit instruments of worldly actions or background elements of worldly situations, they are things that, lacking meaning or purpose, stick out and get in the way.

Cinema offers a useful analogy for understanding the existential desert. Consider what it is like to lose interest while watching a film. The world of the film suddenly goes flat and dead. What were real people engaged in serious actions are reduced to decontextualized images emitting meaningless sounds. What was a real-life drama becomes only a plot or story line. One is no longer "into" the film, and in consequence the film seems remote and unreal. The world as experienced by the alienated person is similar to such a cinematic world except that the alienated person's world, the existential desert, is not a world of fantasy but is rather the world of physical and social reality. The alienated person is disconnected from the world, and the world, correspondingly, seems distant and defunct. As a life-world, it is a dead world. It is nothing more than a succession of pointless sights and sounds.

The existential desert is the absurd world described by the existentialists, the spiritual wasteland described by writers on contemplation, and the derealized world described in works on clinical diagnostics. It is a remote world in which everything is out of reach, an arid world in which everything is barren and dead, a flat world in which everything is gray, and an unreal world in which everything is ripped from the fabric of ongoing life. The alienated person is condemned to being a mere spectator or stranger in this lifeless, meaningless land, in which there is no place to go, nothing to do, and no reason for being.

The denaturalization of the world is quite evidently due primarily to subjective factors: loss of faith in the identity project and corresponding introversion of psychic energy. Objective factors do not play a major role. The world seems to be undergoing a pervasive transformation, but this apparent transformation of the world is only a reflection of a change occurring within the subject. Still, because the change in question so dramatically affects how the world appears, we should consider again the question posed earlier: "Does the depotentiation of the world bring the world into focus more or less clearly or accurately?" Here the answer, emphatically, is that depotentiation brings the world into focus less clearly and accurately. This emphatic negative answer is required because the depotentiation that occurs as a consequence of alienation has no immediate developmental benefits. Unlike the depotentiation of the world occurring in the transition to latency, which facilitates reality testing by freeing the ego from preoedipal splitting and by helping the ego gain self-control—and which, moreover, leaves the world charged with nonplenipotent psychic energy—the depotentiation occurring as a consequence of alienation leads only to an impoverishment of perception. The world ceases being animated even by psychic energy. It loses all energic charge and, therefore, all amplification. The level of magnification through which the world is experienced is reduced to zero, and consequently the world goes flat and gray, losing variety and detail.

Denaturalization of the world can occur during any developmental stage. Psychic energy can in principle reverse its normal outward flow at any time. It is not, then, only the adult arena of responsible action that can be drained of energy and thereby lose its appeal and aliveness as a natural world. The latency child's playground and the adolescent's rehearsal stage can also suffer such desiccation. Instances of denaturalization occurring in childhood and adolescence, however, are rare and are usually cases of pathological derealization. Indeed, instances of denaturalization occurring in adulthood are rare and are frequently symptomatic of psychological dysfunction. Some instances, however, are stage-appropriate expressions of a midlife transition moving in the direction of spiritual awakening. For some adults, the denaturalization of the world is a proper prelude to its supernaturalization.

THE DENATURALIZED WORLD SUPERNATURALIZED: THE REALM OF NUMINOUS POWERS

The ebb tide of psychic energy sometimes regathers sufficient energy in the Ground to awaken the power of the Ground in its plenipotency. This awakening of the power of the Ground, as we know, is an awakening of numinous Spirit, the *mysterium tremendum et fascinans*. Numinous Spirit, an immense, compelling, bivalent, otherworldly power, begins to manifest itself, and the life-world is profoundly transformed.

At first, during initial awakening, the presence of this otherworldly power is evident only vaguely, intermittently, and in localized epiphanies. It may seem as though the atmosphere is charged with a strange, awesome energy or that "the gods are near." The body, as discussed in the last chapter, may begin to show the first signs of "resurrection": perspiration, shivers, horripilation, tingling sensations, erotic feelings. Correspondingly, the world may begin to show the first signs of a "rupture of planes": supernatural forces may begin manifesting themselves in particular places (e.g., haunted or hallowed grounds, eerie or sacred openings or enclosures), objects (e.g., precious gems and metals, scriptures, relics), and events, (e.g., archetypal actions and rituals, awesome natural occurrences). In the face of such manifestations of numinous Spirit, one may experience goose flesh, hair standing on end, and arrested breath.

These initial signs of numinous Spirit are precursors of an outpouring of the awakened power of the Ground that, not limited to particular places, objects, and events, charges the entire world with numinous energy. If and when this flowing forth begins—corresponding to the onset of regression in the service of transcendence—the world becomes a realm of numinous powers, that is to say, a realm teeming with starkly bivalent—dark and light, lower and higher, infernal and celestial—supernatural forces. Dark powers break loose from a nether world and begin to hold sway on the surface of the earth, and celestial radiance descends from above, creating safe spaces bathed in redeeming light. The world, as a realm of numinous powers, is in this way a realm of opposed supernatural forces.

Two metaphors that convey the supernatural and bivalent aspects of the realm of numinous powers are those of the shrouded forest and the lighted clearing. These metaphors have been used throughout history to convey the presence, respectively, of dark and light supernatural powers. The shrouded forest in particular has been used to convey the idea of a dark place in which one is exposed to invisible dangers. One can wander into such a wood without forewarning. In Dante's *Comedy,* for example, the pilgrim Dante, halfway through life, awakens to find himself in a dark wood from which escape is blocked. Stranded in this wood, Dante is enveloped in dreadful darkness (negative numinous energy) and is exposed to unseen, lurking dangers. In such a forest there is no way out; wherever one goes, one remains in darkness. The darkness is inescapable because the person undergoing regression in the service of transcendence projects negative numinous energy upon the world. In thus painting the world in dark, sinister tones, the person undergoing regression in the service of transcendence experiences every place in the world as a dark, sinister place, a forest.

Closely related to the metaphor of the forest is the metaphor of the lighted clearing. These two metaphors form a complementary pair, for there are places within the forest that are clear of vaulting trees and, therefore, that are open to light descending from above. These clearings represent moments in the experience of the person undergoing regression in the service of transcendence when the positive, light side of numinous energy breaks through and becomes manifest. Numinous energy manifesting itself in this way has a markedly otherworldly, liberating quality. It is a radiance from a higher world that penetrates the dark shroud of the forest and lifts the spirits of the person who had been enveloped in darkness. Forest clearings represent the prospect of salvation that is present within the darkness of regression in the service of transcendence, especially during its darkest, initial phases.

The foremost writer on the phenomenon of the clearing is the philosopher Martin Heidegger, who in his later work spoke of a need to move toward a new way of thinking. This new way of thinking is a meditative thinking that, rather than imposing conceptual structures upon things, allows things to disclose themselves in their uniqueness and fullness. Such a "releasing" way of thinking (*Gelassenheit*), Heidegger believed, would prepare a clearing (*Lichtung*) for the disclosure of Being itself. Heidegger lived in Germany's Black Forest and appreciated the special qualities of shafts of light piercing the forest canopy. Such light has the appearance of being heaven sent to save us from the dangers of the forest and to uplift our vision to the source of redeeming light.

Another image frequently used to convey the idea of otherworldly radiance is that of celestial light shining through overcast skies. Here the shafts of redeeming light penetrate tempestuous clouds rather than a forest canopy. This difference is significant because tempestuous clouds convey the turbulence of regression in the service of transcendence, which is a stage not only of numinous awakening but also of instinctual derepression. The world during this stage is astir with a plenipotent energy that expresses itself both as daunting numinous energy and, intermittently, as violent instinctual energy, energy that suggests an agitated, stormy atmosphere. The image of ethereal light shining through overcast skies, then, conveys redeeming light not only as a liberating radiance that illuminates a clearing in a region of darkness but also as a calming radiance that pacifies turbulent forces.

The reawakening of the power of the Ground in its plenipotency dramatically animates the world with bivalent energy. The world of regression in the service of transcendence is one in which forces of darkness arising from an infernal "below" are driven off by forces of light descending from a heavenly "above." Rays of celestial light touch the earth and thus establish a connection between heaven and earth. This connection, however, is a connection from afar because the rays of light that touch the earth derive from a celestial source that remains separate from the earth. The sun is hidden above a vault of forest trees or above a covering of storm clouds, shining through only in clearings in the forest or openings in the clouds. Moreover, as heaven in its radiance is thus hidden from the earth, the earth, except where light breaks through, is enveloped in darkness. The earth is charged with turbulent, menacing energy and is full of terrifying specters.

Having thus far focused on subjective factors—the reawakening of the power of the Ground, the animation of the world with numinous energy—let us now shift focus to objective factors. Two points are noteworthy: (1) the reawakening of the power of the Ground is an interactive, psyche-world process rather than exclusively an affair occurring within the psyche, and (2) both the plenipotency of the reawakened power of the Ground and the splitting characteristic of numinous awakening interfere with reality testing and, therefore, with the accuracy of perception.

The reawakening of the power of the Ground is an interactive process because the world in its objectivity plays a role in eliciting the power of the Ground. Particular types of objects function as numinous attractors, that is, as objects that tap and channel the numinous energy awakening within the psyche. Caves and openings to underground depths, dark spaces and hidden recesses, lighted clearings and mountaintops, protective enclosures and shrines, vaulted cathedrals and stained glass windows, and sparkling gems and metals are examples of such numinous attractors. It is not arbitrary that the person undergoing regression in the service of transcendence invests such objects with energy and, therefore, finds them gripping, awesome, and otherwise numinously potent, for these objects symbolically embody aspects of regression in the service of transcendence. The person undergoing regression in the service of transcendence is both captivated and energized by objects functioning as numinous attractors, dreadfully by those that symbolically embody the dark side of the numinous and reverentially by those that embody the light side. These objects attract, quicken, and give thematized focus to the plenipotent energy awakening within the psyche.

Not only objects but also people—that is to say, awakened people—are numinous attractors. We have already discussed the extraordinary influence that awakened people have upon people in initial stages of awakening. People undergoing numinous awakening are irresistibly drawn to awakened others, whose active plenipotent energy has entrancing and stimulating effects. The well-known wisdom saying "When the student is ready, the teacher appears" reflects the fact that teachers, always in our midst, begin being perceived as teachers once we are developmentally ready for them. Likewise, spiritually oriented groups come into view when we are developmentally ready to benefit from their teachings and practices. In these and other ways the life-world of the person undergoing numinous awakening is a product of an interactive, psyche-world process, a process of subjective awakening seeking its appropriate objects and persons and of these objects and persons in turn facilitating awakening.

The person in whom numinous energy has awakened is thus able to bring into focus spiritually significant objects and persons hitherto unrecognized as such. Moreover, this person perceives the world at a higher, plenipotent level of magnification, which means that the world, correspondingly, manifests itself to this person in richer variety and more vivid detail. Given these particular improvements in perception, the question arises whether, all things considered, the person in whom numinous energy has awakened perceives the world more clearly or accurately. The answer is no, for the plenipotency of numinous energy here interferes with reality testing, as, too, does the splitting characteristic of numinous awakening.

The ego undergoing initial awakening and regression in the service of transcendence is not accustomed to plenipotent energy and is thus more often overpowered than empowered by it, falling prey to trances, intoxications, and dislocations. These conditions immobilize or derange mental faculties and, therefore, disrupt reality testing. The result is that the world, although brought into focus in new ways and magnified in rich, vivid detail, is not perceived by a gathered, clear mind. The new focus and higher level of magnification are offset by a loss of self-possession and lucidity.

Furthermore, the world as it is brought into focus by numinous awakening is exaggerated by splitting and, occasionally, simply fabricated by an overactive imagination driven by fear of the dark side of the numinous or by reaching out to the light side. The person caught in the splitting characteristic of numinous awakening is similar in these regards to the child caught in preoedipal splitting. Both see the world in extremes of black and white. Both find themselves in worlds with haunted and enchanted realms: the shrouded forest and the lighted clearing, anti-Eden and the garden of delight. Moreover, both are vulnerable to populating their worlds with creatures of imagination: demons and angels, monsters and good fairies. Both the person undergoing numinous awakening and the child in the late preoedipal stage have lost their bearings. To be sure, they are sensitive to new kinds of objects and persons, and they see the world at a plenipotent level of magnification. They also, however, are prone to distortions, and they see, or believe they see, things that are not there. For both, reality testing has been significantly impaired.

THE SUPERNATURAL BECOMES NATURAL:
THE WORLD OF TRANSFORMING SPIRIT

The transition from regression in the service of transcendence to regeneration in Spirit is reflected in the world in a progressive integration of the dark and light sides of numinous bivalence, the dark, earthly side losing its darkness and the light, heavenly side losing its otherworldly character. Some degree of conflict between darkness and light remains throughout regeneration in Spirit. The conflict that remains, however, is conflict (1) that is no longer perceived as a confrontation between evil and good—for the dark side of the numinous has by this point been transvalued and redeemed; and (2) that eventually disappears as regeneration in Spirit unfolds toward integration. Metaphorically, the dark and dangerous forest of regression in the service of transcendence gradually thins until it becomes a beautiful glade open to light. The violent weather abates and the sky brightens, as radiance from above now begins to pour through scattering clouds. The world in this way gradually loses its darkness, storminess, and heaven-earth separation and becomes a world of clearing skies, calming atmosphere, and increasing openness to the heavens above. The numinous thus becomes the sacred; the supernatural becomes natural—not all at once but in unfolding, progressive fashion. This world on the way to the integration of heaven and earth is the world of transforming Spirit.

The removal of darkness from the world gives expression to the fact that the earth has been redeemed. The removal of darkness, we should note, is not a removal of anything in fact. Nothing passes from existence to nonexistence, for the removal of darkness is a transvaluative rather than an ontological process. It is a process that reflects a change in the perceiver, not in the world. Specifically, the lifting of darkness reflects that the perceiver—the person undergoing regeneration in Spirit—no longer experiences the world, in its plenipotency, as having a dangerous, threatening side. It reflects, then, that the perceiver has overcome fear of experiencing the world in its fullness. The earth, which along with the instincts had been cloaked in menacing darkness, is thus progressively relieved of darkness and bathed in radiant light. Light increasingly shines through from above to illuminate the world, revealing its superabundant richness and intrinsic value.

The lifting of darkness opens the earth to heaven. Heaven is no longer a remote celestial realm separated from the earth. The thinning of the forest and parting of the clouds allow the light of heaven to reach the earth. The brilliant upper sky is no longer a far-removed realm to which we would aspire for an otherworldly salvation and is, now, the upper sky of the earth. Heaven and earth are thus joined, and they are increasingly integrated as dimensions of a single world as the person undergoing regeneration in Spirit nears the edge of the forest and the full light of day. The supernatural in this way becomes natural. Heaven ceases being removed from the earth and becomes, increasingly, "heaven on earth."

Whereas regression in the service of transcendence is a stage during which the world is more dark than light, regeneration in Spirit is a stage during which the world is more light than dark—and increasingly more light than dark as regeneration in Spirit approaches integration. Regeneration in Spirit, like all stages of development, is multidimensional in character. If we recall, it is a stage during which the Ground becomes a source of renewing life, the power of the Ground expresses itself as transforming Spirit, and the ego is regenerated by Spirit and "reincarnated" in the body. Regeneration in Spirit is a stage during which the night of numinous Spirit gives way to the dawn of transforming Spirit and during which the violence of resurgent instincts gives way to an increasingly harmonious expression of instinctual life. Correspondingly, regeneration in Spirit is a stage during which the world gradually ceases being dark and turbulent and becomes increasingly radiant and serene.

Regeneration in Spirit is also a stage during which the ego gradually regains its bearings and begins once again to test reality effectively. The ego, having been overpowered by plenipotent energy, is now increasingly adjusted to this energy and, consequently, is able increasingly to remain gathered and clear-headed as it navigates experience. Moreover, the disappearance of the dark side of the numinous is at the same time a surmounting of the splitting that had afflicted earlier stages of awakening. During regeneration in Spirit, then, the ego is no longer subject to the exaggerations and fabrications that had plagued the ego during regression in the service of transcendence and, to a lesser extent, initial awakening. The ego, thus empowered rather than overpowered by plenipotent energy and free of the misperceptions caused by splitting, is now able to experience the world at a high level of magnification without loss of clarity or accuracy. That is, the ego is increasingly able to experience the world in this way as regeneration in Spirit unfolds in the direction of integration.

RETURNING HOME: THE WORLD OF TRANSPARENT SPIRIT

The joining of heaven and earth that begins in regeneration in Spirit is not complete until integration is achieved. It is only when, intrapsychically, the ego and the Dynamic Ground are fully one that, extrapsychically, heaven and earth become fully one. During regeneration in Spirit, some degree of darkness—a steadily diminishing degree—remains. It is only with the achievement of integration that the world loses all traces of darkness and that the unqualified sacredness of the world is revealed in a wholly transparent way. It is only with the achievement of integration, then, that the world ceases being the world of transforming Spirit and becomes the world of transparent Spirit. This world of transparent Spirit, this completely integrated world of heaven on earth, represents the end of the spiral path.

If the integrated world represents the end of the spiral path, it also represents a return on a higher level to the ground from which the spiral path began. The integrated world, in other words, is in important respects similar to the preoedipal garden of delight (the first life-world with differentiated, immanent and transcendent spheres). The integrated world, of course, differs from the garden of delight in important respects. The integrated world, for instance, is not a world free of work; nor is it a small, inherently local world; nor is it a world in which any given person is the center of loving attention. The integrated world is a world in which needs are met only by the sweat of the brow; it is a world of vast expanse and remote places; and it is a world that is centered in the human community and the larger community of life on earth rather than in any particular person. These differences notwithstanding, the integrated world at the end of the spiral path is similar to the garden of delight at the beginning of the spiral path in being a world of exquisite beauty, sacred value, and native ground.

The integrated world is a world of exquisite beauty because, like the garden of delight, it is charged with a plenipotent energy that, as an attracting energy, renders the world irresistibly inviting and that, as an amplifying energy, intensifies perceptual qualities in pleasing ways. This plenipotent energy is no longer to any degree a bivalent energy, as we have explained. It is an energy, therefore, that renders the world appealing without also rendering it daunting and that intensifies perceptual qualities in pleasing ways without also intensifying them in repugnant ways. The energy that enlivens the integrated world is a radiant and soothing energy, an energy that makes the world gleam with sparkling, gentle light. The integrated world is resplendent through and through. It is a glorified world.

The world thus seen in its glory, we should stress, is the "real" world. It is not a world that has been fabricated or that has been given a false sheen by the experiencing subject. The world of transparent Spirit, to be sure, is glorious in part because it is charged with plenipotent attracting and amplifying energy. Such energy, however, does not alter the world; rather, it facilitates perception of the world by intensifying interest in the world and by increasing the power of perception. Plenipotent energy, as an attracting energy, quickens the desire to experience the world; and plenipotent energy, as an amplifying energy, brings the world into focus at a higher level of magnification, in richer variety and more vivid detail. Moreover, because the plenipotent energy that animates the integrated world, transparent Spirit, is an energy that is no longer to any degree divided by splitting and that no longer, in its plenipotency, overpowers the ego, it is an energy that animates the world without causing perceptual errors or disruption to cognitive faculties. The world as perceived by the integrated ego, then, is a real world perceived by an ego that tests reality effectively. If this world is charged with plenipotent energy, it is so without any loss of objectivity.

The integrated world is a world of sacred value because it is a world animated by transparent Spirit. Transparent Spirit accentuates not only the beauty but also the preciousness of the world. The world as experienced by the integrated person cannot be taken for granted, for it elicits wonder, appreciation, and affirmation. Like the preoedipal child in the garden of delight, the integrated person is in love with the world. Friedrich Nietzsche gave voice to this perspective in *Thus Spoke Zarathustra*, in which Zarathustra proclaims his love of the earth, extolling its beauty, majesty, and profusion of life; its fragility, finitude, and contingency; its perfection—just as it is. A principal aim of Nietzsche's work was to combat the otherworldly perspective of much of religion and philosophy, the perspective that posits a higher world of eternity and perfection in contrast to which this world is devalued, reduced to a realm of imperfection, corruptibility, and evil. In combating this otherworldly perspective, Nietzsche sought to restore our appreciation of the earth and to help us understand how fortunate we are to live here, even if for only a fleeting moment of cosmic time.

Finally, the integrated world is a world of native ground because the earth is where we dwell. Dwelling, as Heidegger explained in "Building Dwelling Thinking," is a way of living that calls forth a "gathering of the fourfold" (*das Gaviert*): earth, sky, mortals, and gods. Earth, sky, mortals, and gods are intimately interrelated when living is dwelling. To dwell upon the earth is to know that the earth is alive and that we are part of the life of the earth. It is to have reverence for the earth and for all that grows and lives upon it. It is to care for the earth as our home. To dwell upon the earth, as Heidegger says, is to want to spare the earth from harm, especially the harm posed by technology. Furthermore, to dwell upon the earth is to look up to a clear sky and to be fed spiritually by the light that pours down from the sky. Earth and heaven are now joined. We are at once rooted in the soil and bathed in warmth by the sun.

Thus nurtured by both earth and heaven, we are mortals rather than immortals, part of the growing, flourishing, and dying life of the earth. We are natives of the earth who live for a short time on this planet rather than immortal souls temporarily assigned here as a test for an otherworldly destiny. As mortals, we are grateful for our earthly existence, for every precious minute of our finite "being-toward-death." We do not aspire to immortality; and because we value our mortal existence, we live in the intimate company of "immortals." The gods live among us rather than on mountain tops or in remote celestial regions. Heidegger is fond of quoting Heraclitus, who, in warming himself by the fire, said "Here too are gods." The life of dwelling upon the earth is, in our terms, a life lived in the company of transparent Spirit. The divine is not hidden; it lives with us here on earth. Both mortals and immortals, both humans and the divine are at home on the earth as native ground.

Moving from West to East, the gathering of the fourfold, the seamless unity of heaven, earth, the divine, and the human, is what Nagarjuna, the second-century Buddhist philosopher, described as the unity of *nirvāna* and *samsāra*.

> There is not the slightest difference
> Between cyclic existence [*samsāra*] and nirvana
> There is not the slightest difference
> Between nirvana and cyclic existence.
> Whatever is the limit of nirvana,
> That is the limit of cyclic existence.
> There is not even the slightest difference between them,
> Or even the subtlest thing.[3]

Nirvāna is not a transcendent realm beyond *samsāra,* the conditioned world in which we now live and may, according to Buddhism, yet live again (cyclic existence). *Nirvāna* is not a place or a state other than *samsāra;* rather, it is a way of living in *samsāra*. In particular, it is a way of living that does not grasp after anything ultimate or eternal, a way of living, therefore, that unconditionally accepts this world and our lives in it as "dependently arisen" and "impermanent." *Nirvāna,* that is, is a way of living in this world that affirms this world and our lives in it as the locus of sacred value. *Nirvāna* is the end of suffering because it is the end of grasping after an impossible transcendent reality and immortal existence and a full acceptance of the here and now. In following Buddhism's Eightfold Noble Path, then, we finally "arrive" at *nirvāna* and, in spiral fashion, realize that we have been in *nirvāna* all along.

In arriving at the end of the spiral path, then, we return home. The home to which we return, however, is transformed. We who return are different, and therefore the home to which we return is different as well. The home to which we return is similar to the home from which we set out in being a native dwelling place that is enlivened, hallowed, and made resplendent by the plenipotent power of the Dynamic Ground. The home to which we return, however, differs from the home from which we set out in being a vast world in which we must work to survive and in which no individual person is the center of loving attention. It differs as well in being a world that to a significant extent has been grasped by the mind and brought under the control of the will. The home to which we return is not an uncharted, virgin paradise, as was the garden of delight, but is instead a large world that has been extensively mapped, studied, and transformed. The home to which we return has to a significant extent yielded to human science and technology.

This world that has yielded to science and technology, however, is also a world of exquisite beauty, sacred value, and native ground. As our home, it is a world that we hold dear and, therefore, that we desire to protect from the very technical prowess that has in so many ways benefited us. Caring for the earth is not inconsistent with technology, as Heidegger sometimes suggests. The simplistic setting of technology in opposition to nature is an error of naive romanticism. Caring for the earth, however, *is* inconsistent with the use of technology in ways that would irreparably harm the living space in which we dwell. Technology must be constrained by care.

This need for a caring constraint of technology is already pressing urgently upon us and will press more urgently in the years immediately ahead. The world is fast becoming a global community, and we are increasingly aware that ideological, national, and economic competitions are endangering the planet. We have already corrupted natural resources sufficiently to foresee the possibility of ecological disaster, and for this reason we are beginning to awaken, by necessity, to both the fragility and the preciousness of the earth. As the world shrinks in the information age, we are moving toward a truly integrated, planetary perspective. This perspective, however, is only beginning to emerge.

NOTES

CHAPTER ONE
THE SPIRAL PATH: HISTORY
AND CRITICISM OF THE IDEA

1. These terms, well established in the vocabulary of transpersonal psychology, are not entirely satisfactory. The terms *preegoic, egoic,* and *transegoic* are problematic, both because the ego is present from the outset of life and because the expression *transcendence of the ego* has been so much discussed and so little understood. The terms *prepersonal, personal,* and *transpersonal* are problematic as well, for similar reasons; but they are less misleading and, therefore, to be preferred.

2. See Lovejoy (1948) for an historical account of the paradox of the fortunate fall from early patristic writings through Milton's *Paradise Lost.*

3. Although Wilber has been a highly vocal critic of traditional spiral theories of development, he has recently affiliated himself with Don Beck and Christopher Cowan (1996)—whose ideas are based on the work of Clare W. Graves—and has begun using the term *spiral* as they use it in their theory (spiral dynamics) to describe his own theory. This adoption by Wilber of the term *spiral* has understandably led to confusion because it obscures the fundamentally hierarchical character of his perspective and suggests that he is endorsing an idea of which he has been a fierce critic.

4. The scope of Wilber's work has grown dramatically in the last ten years. His current work, in addition to stressing developmental lines or waves, also emphasizes what he calls an "all-quadrant, all-level" (AQAL) perspective. A truly integral perspective, he believes, must study development or evolution from four inclusive, jointly comprehensive dimensions: (1) *the interior–individual (subjective or "I") dimension,* which examines the developmental emergence of lines or waves of individual consciousness as they unfold through the hierarchy of levels of basic structures; (2) *the external–individual (objective or "it") dimension,* which looks at the hierarchy of evolved organic and neurological structures correlated with the levels of basic structures of individual consciousness; (3) *the interior–collective (cultural or "we") dimension,* which considers the forms of cultural consciousness correlated with the levels of basic structures; and (4) *the external–collective (social or "its") dimension,* which

examines corresponding levels of social organization. Although Wilber's work has thus become much wider in scope, it is still based on his original conception of the hierarchy of levels of basic structures of individual consciousness (corresponding to the interior-individual quadrant of the AQAL perspective). The ensuing discussion focuses on that conception, as updated and revised in his recent works.

5. For *nonegoic potentials, autosymoblic process,* and other terms, see the glossary.

CHAPTER TWO
THE SPIRAL PATH: A STAGE VIEW

1. This term is here transplanted from politics (where it means full authority or sovereign power) to psychology. See the glossary entry for the term.

2. Although, historically, the primary love object has been the female parent and the primary authority figure the male parent, there is no reason why the roles of love object and authority figure have to be divided in this gender-exclusive manner or even why they have to be performed by different people. The fact is, however, that most societies have kept these roles not only separate but also divided by gender, with the consequence that the child's oedipal change of object has been a rite of passage from a female-centered preoedipal universe into patriarchal society. For a discussion of these issues, see the author's *Transpersonal Psychology in Psychoanalytic Perspective,* chapter 3.

3. *Primal separation* here replaces *primal alienation,* used in early publications (1994, 1995), to describe the child's withdrawal from the caregiver. See the glossary entry on *primal repression* for background on Freud's use of the expression.

4. Freud used *libido* to refer to sexual or erotic energy, and in his later work he distinguished between libido and aggressive energy as two basic forms of instinctual energy. In this book *libido* is used in a more general way to refer to all energy that is instinctually organized or expressed, whatever the specific instinctual channel might be. This use does not assume that energy channeled in an instinctual manner must itself be inherently instinctual in character. See the glossary entries for *power of the Ground, libido,* and *psychic energy.*

5. D. W. Winnicott's expression *good enough mother* is here shifted in application from infancy to the end of preoedipal childhood (when the child, as Mahler says, is "on the way to object constancy") and to the oedipal stage (during which the achievement of object constancy is brought to completion). Winnicott focused on the caregiver of the early preoedipal stage who, as good enough mother, provides sufficient nurturing acceptance of the infant's true, spontaneous self to foster healthy growth. The focus here, in contrast, is on the caregiver who emerges as splitting is overcome and object constancy achieved. This caregiver is good enough in the sense of being neither perfectly good nor wholly bad but sufficiently good to be trusted to take care of the child's basic needs.

6. *Bivalent* is not Otto's term. The idea, however, plays an essential role in his discussion of the numinous. See the glossary for background on the term and its usage in this book.

CHAPTER THREE
THE DYNAMIC GROUND

1. Andrew Meltzoff and his associates have performed experiments demonstrating the multimodal character of the infant's experience. Meltzoff has demonstrated that infants are able to imitate the caregiver's facial expressions and, therefore, are able directly to translate visual impressions into corresponding motoric expressions (Meltzoff and Moore 1977, 1983, 1989). Infants are also able to match speech sounds with corresponding visual impressions (Kuhl and Meltzoff 1982) and tactile sensations with corresponding visual impressions (Meltzoff and Borton 1979). This intermodal translation and cross-modal matching of sensory data suggests that the infant's imagination, in producing inner likenesses of perceptual materials, does so in a way that is inherently intermodal and, therefore, multimodal in character. It suggests that the earliest imagination is not exclusively a visual imagination producing inner images but is instead an imagination that produces complex groupings of images, inner sensations, and motoric promptings corresponding to multiple sense modalities and to innate and learned action schemes.

2. See the entries "Axis Mundi" (Sullivan 1987) and "Trees" (Frese and Gray 1987) in *The Encyclopedia of Religion,* Mircea Eliade, editor (New York: Collier Macmillan, 1987).

3. See the glossary for definitions of *Spirit, transparent Spirit,* and related terms.

CHAPTER FOUR
ENERGY

1. Freud originally posited only a single instinctual drive, sexuality, and corresponding drive energy, libido or sexual energy. In 1923, however, he introduced a two-drive theory, positing two fundamental instinctual drives, sexuality and aggression, and two corresponding drive energies, libido and aggressive energy.

2. *Enstasy* is a term coined by Mircea Eliade (1969) to describe meditative absorption achieved by means of yoga.

3. It has long been well established that infants in the first months of life are capable of "recognition memory." Infants can recognize patterns that they have experienced earlier (see Rovee-Colier et al. 1980).

4. The initial understanding of object permanence may occur as early as four or five months of age and may at first trigger a fear response. Four or five months of age is the beginning of the differentiation subphase of the separation-individuation process (Mahler et al. 1975), a brief period during which the child suffers from stranger anxiety (Spitz 1965) and clings to the caregiver. This insecure period is soon over. By the time the child is a toddler, typically, it has lost all fear and, entering the practicing subphase of the separation-individuation process, begins exploring the newly discovered world with reckless abandon and delight. The differentiation and practicing subphases of the separation-individuation process are discussed more fully in chapter 6.

5. As noted earlier, *libido* refers to the power of the Ground insofar as it is channeled through or contained in an instinctual system, be it sexuality or some other instinctual system.

6. See Feuerstein (1992) and Wade (1998, 2000) for discussions of the phenomenon of sacred sexuality.

7. These distinctions do not coincide because both bound and free energy as defined in psychoanalysis are forms of channeled energy in the meaning of the term used here. According to psychoanalysis, bound energy is energy channeled in a relatively fixed way by the secondary process and related conscious systems, whereas free energy is energy channeled in a relatively unrestricted way by the primary process and related unconscious systems. In contrast to both of these forms of energy, free energy in the sense used here is energy that is not channeled through any psychic process or system, egoic or nonegoic, conscious or unconscious. It is energy that is experienced by the ego directly, without being mobilized by psychic systems or invested cathectically in the objects of psychic systems.

8. Three major forms of Spirit are distinguished in this book: (1) numinous Spirit, which, in addition to being plenipotent and free, is "wholly other" (mysterious, foreign, not-self) and bivalent (light-dark, good-evil) in perceived character; (2) transforming Spirit, which is kindred (rather than wholly other) and univalently redemptive (rather than bivalent) in perceived character but still violent or overpowering in the ways it affects the ego; and (3) transparent Spirit, which, no longer to any degree other in relation to the ego, is the ego's higher Self and, no longer violent, is almost always empowering rather than overpowering in its plenipotent effects.

9. Otto does not use this term. The term, however, effectively conveys a major theme in Otto's account of the numinous. See the glossary for background on the term and the way it is used in this book.

10. This misperception may be only a strong developmental tendency. Although one cannot avoid experiencing the newly awakened power of the Ground as other, immense, and irresistible, one might be able to avoid experiencing it as inherently bivalent. If one has a solid personality structure and a proper understanding of the psychodynamics of spiritual awakening, it is possible that one can resist the tendency to misconstrue subjective ambivalence as objective bivalence. If one has a strong ego and is well counseled in advance that awakening Spirit, in its plenipotency, can seem a menacing, negative force, one might be able to avoid attributing dark or evil aspects to awakening Spirit. This possibility acknowledged, it remains true that people undergoing initial awakening are predisposed to project bivalence upon the power of the Ground.

11. See Blais (1997) for a discussion of such seeming pathology in the mystical experience of St. Teresa of Avila.

12. As is true of the phenomenon of bivalence generally (see note 10), this instinctualization of bivalence may be only a developmental tendency. Still, the ego during regression in the service of transcendence is predisposed to perceive numinous Spirit as a power that is split not only along dark and light but also along instinctual and anti-instinctual lines.

CHAPTER FIVE
THE EGO

1. Again (see chapter 2, note 5), we are shifting the application of D. W. Winnicott's expression "good enough" to later stages of development. Winnicott focused on the caregiver of the early preoedipal stage who, as good enough mother, provides sufficient nurturing acceptance of the infant's true, spontaneous self to foster healthy growth. The focus here, in contrast, is on the good enough caregiver who emerges when preoedipal splitting is overcome and, in this context, on the good enough child who emerges at this point as well.

2. One might think that the depotentiation of experience from plenipotent to nonplenipotent intensity would by itself improve reality testing. This is not the case, however, as we explain in chapter 8. The effectiveness of reality testing depends not only on the degree to which experience is charged with energy but also on whether the ego is empowered or overpowered by energy of a particular intensity. The developing ego of the young child is weak and consequently tends to be overpowered by plenipotent energy. The reduction of energy from plenipotent to nonplenipotent intensity in the transition to latency for this reason empowers the child and improves reality testing.

3. In his account of the dark night, St. John of the Cross distinguishes between the night of the senses and the night of spirit. The former is the period of alienation, aridity, and despair that we have just described. The latter is a period occurring after spiritual awakening has begun. The night of spirit is a period during which one, after coming into direct contact with spiritual power, feels unworthy and forsaken by the divine. In terms used here, the night of the senses is the period of alienation that precedes and leads the way to the awakening of the power of the Dynamic Ground; and the night of Spirit is the period of regression in the service of transcendence, the period, following the awakening of the power of the Ground, of descent to the Ground and instinctual recrudescence.

4. Jung believed that the archetypal shadow, or evil itself, is inherent to the psyche. He believed that such evil is a co-equal member of a psychically based quaternity: good, evil, male, female. The account presented here departs from Jung's view in suggesting that demonic evil is not inherent to the psyche but is instead a phenomenon that derives from a specific developmental organization of the nonegoic bases of life, an organization that can be transcended.

5. It is worth noting that other stages of development have not only a superego but also an anti-superego. This is especially true of stages, such as adolescence and the crossroads of midlife, during which the personal, worldly shadow is derepressed. These, too, are stages during which we have not only an angel on one shoulder but also a devil on the other, each arguing against the other for the allegiance of the will. This kind of conflict between superego and anti-superego, however, is especially dramatic and disturbing during regression in the service of transcendence.

CHAPTER SIX
THE OTHER

1. This object is the Great *Mother* because over the course of human evolution females have performed the role of primary caregiver. The connection between infant care and female mothering has deep roots in the psyche.

2. For example, virtually from birth babies exhibit visual preference for the human face (Fantz 1963; Haaf and Bell 1967; Sherrod 1981) and are attuned to the rhythmic movements of human speech (Hutt et al. 1968; Demany, McKenzie, and Vurpillot 1977; Condon and Sander 1974). Moreover, as parents have always known, infants are social creatures innately preadapted for distinctively human interactions (see Brazelton, Koslowski, and Main 1974; Stern 1974; Trevarthen 1977, 1979; Bower 1979; Kaye 1982; Schaffer 1984). This social character of the infant is expressed not only in the differential perception of the human face and voice but also in subtle interactional synchronies and in turn-taking imitation exchanges between the infant and caregiver.

3. We should remember that the Dynamic Ground, as the psychoid unconscious, is inherently unfathomable in its depths. Primal repression submerges and quiets the Ground, making it not only the psychoid unconscious but also the deepest level of the repressed unconscious.

4. The oedipal relationships between the child and the primary caregiver on the one hand and the child and the secondary caregiver on the other need not be conceived in gendered terms. Both women and men can perform the roles of love provider (the primary caregiver's role: "tender love") and disciplinarian (the secondary caregiver's role: "tough love"). Any gender arrangement, therefore, is possible so far as these roles are concerned. Two or more same-sex parents or members of an extended family can divide the two roles, and a single parent or guardian can perform both of the roles. These possibilities acknowledged, the fact is that the roles in question have a long gender-divided history. Given this history, in the ensuing discussion "mother" is used in the place of "primary caregiver" and "father" in the place of "secondary caregiver." The reader should follow the discussion with this usage in mind, understanding that the roles of primary and secondary caregiver need not be assigned to a single gender or even a single person.

5. See *Transpersonal Psychology in Psychoanalytic Perspective,* chapter 3, for an extended discussion of this topic.

6. The Greek is translated by Richard D. McKirahan (1994).

CHAPTER SEVEN
THE BODY

1. Erotogenic zones other than the genitals—the anus, in particular, given its proximity to the genitals—can also be vehicles of ecstasy if they should somehow become charged with activated libido.

2. The physical manifestations of *kundalinī* awakening, long well known in India and Tibet, are becoming better known in Europe and the Americas. Gopi Krishna (1971), whose experience was far from representative, was the first to bring *kundalinī*

awakening to the attention of a wide group of Western readers. Many books devoted to *kundalinī* awakening were published in the 1980s and 1990s, and in recent years several excellent Internet sites on the *kundalinī* phenomenon have appeared.

CHAPTER EIGHT
THE WORLD

1. The author is indebted to an anonymous reader for the State University of New York Press for pointing out the need for a more balanced discussion of subjective and objective factors.

2. The natural world corresponds to personal stages of development and assumes three primary forms: (1) the playground of youth (latency), (2) the rehearsal stage for adult life (adolescence), and (3) the arena of responsible action (early adulthood). In all of these forms of the natural world, the outer environment is charged with non-plenipotent rather than plenipotent energy.

3. The quotation is from Nagarjuna's *Mūlamadhyamakakārikā,* translated by Garfield (1995, p. 75).

GLOSSARY

Absorption. A state of unself-conscious envelopment or immersion. See *cathexis, ecstasy, enstasy, infusion.*

Alienation. A pervasive sense of being disconnected from the world. Primary expressions of alienation are deanimation of the self-representation, depersonalization of the body, and derealization of the world. Alienation is frequently associated with midlife transition. See *deanimation, depersonalization, derealization.*

Apperception. See *unity of apperception.*

Archetypal shadow. See *shadow.*

Archetype. C. G. Jung's term for inherited patterns of imaginal projection. In this book Jung's theory of archetypes is adopted generally but applied sparingly. Only a few archetypes are discussed, for instance, the Great Mother and the shadow. In applying Jung's theory of the archetypes sparingly, this book focuses more on the autosymbolic process or creative imagination—one of the nonegoic potentials of the Dynamic Ground—than on particular archetypal patterns. See *autosymbolic process, Dynamic Ground, Great Mother, nonegoic potentials, shadow.*

Autosymbolic process. Term introduced by Herbert Silberer (1909) to describe the creative imagination as it is active in dreams and the hypnagogic state. This imagination, according Silberer, spontaneously forges symbolic images giving concrete expression to emerging meanings before the meanings have been explicitly conceptualized. In psychoanalysis, the autosymbolic process is the primary process, which gives symbolic expression to instinctual demands and their derivatives. In Jungian psychology, the autosymbolic process is the archetypal imagination, which produces symbols giving expression to archetypal meanings. The autosymbolic process or creative, symbol-producing imagination is one of the nonegoic potentials of the Dynamic Ground. See *nonegoic potentials.*

Bivalence. Originally a chemical term, *valence* has by extension become a psychological term used to describe the positive or negative charge of emotions or of objects eliciting emotions. The term is used in this book to describe the positive or negative charge of objects eliciting emotions. *Bivalence,* accordingly, describes objects possessing (alternately) both positive and negative charges. An object becomes bivalent when, as a consequence of splitting, it is divided into alternating positive and negative manifestations. For example, the preoedipal child, as a consequence of splitting, perceives the caregiver alternately as a good object and a bad object or, in the Jungian terms used in this book, as a Good Mother and a Terrible Mother. Corresponding to the bivalence of an object is the ambivalence of the subject toward the object. See *Great Mother, splitting.*

Body ego. The body-identified ego of the preoedipal child who has not yet discovered private psychic space (prepersonal body ego) and the "reincarnated" ego of the person who, in undergoing regeneration in Spirit, has returned to fully embodied life (transpersonal body ego). The body ego is to be distinguished from the mental ego. See *mental ego, regeneration in Spirit, reincarnation of the ego.*

Cathexis. English translation of *Besetzung,* Freud's term for the investment of psychic energy in an object (idea, image, etc.). A cathexis, in charging an object with energy, makes the object a salient if not compelling attractor of consciousness. In this book a distinction is made between object and energy cathexes: whereas an object cathexis is an investment of consciousness-attracting energy in an object, an energy cathexis is a concentration (a massing or pooling) of consciousness-attracting energy without a targeted object. Both object and energy cathexes attract consciousness and can absorb the ego. See *absorption, countercathexis, ecstasy, enstasy, infusion.*

Change of object. In psychoanalytic theory the change of object is the shift of primary allegiance from the mother to the father that resolves the oedipus complex. In this book the change of object is interpreted in a gender-neutral way as a shift of primary allegiance from the preoedipal caregiver (whether a woman or a man) as love object to the oedipal disciplinarian-rival (whether a man or a woman) as authority figure.

Collective unconscious. C. G. Jung's term for the deepest level of the unconscious, lying beneath the personal level. The collective unconscious is inherited rather than biographical, universal rather than specific to any person. In this book *collective unconscious* (or *deep unconscious*) refers to the Dynamic Ground, both as psychoid unconscious and as the deepest level of the repressed unconscious. See *Dynamic Ground, psychoid unconscious, unconscious.*

Core of psyche. See *psychic core.*

Countercathexis. A mobilization of energy against an object (e.g., feeling, idea, psychic potential) aimed at suppressing or repressing the object. See *cathexis, repression.*

Deanimation. The loss of the sense of lived, authentic selfhood. Deanimation can occur during any developmental stage but is most characteristic of transitional stages, such as adolescence and midlife transition. During adolescence the latency self-representation is outgrown and, therefore, deanimated, becoming a merely childish former self rather that the adolescent's "real" or "true" self. Similarly, during midlife transition the loss of faith in the identity project can lead to a deanimation of the self-representation forged during early adulthood. When this happens, the self-representation forged during early adulthood "dies" and is seen as only a false mask. See *alienation, depersonalization, derealization, identity project, self-representation.*

Deep psyche. Term used to refer to the Dynamic Ground as psychic core, the seat of nonegoic potentials and the deepest level of the unconscious. See *collective unconscious, Dynamic Ground, psychic core, unconscious.*

Deep unconscious. See *deep psyche.*

Depersonalization. The sense of being alienated from one's experience. In this book *depersonalization* is used primarily to describe the sense of being alienated from one's body and the corresponding perception of the body as a mere thing. Depersonalization—along with deanimation and derealization—belongs to a group of existential difficulties that can emerge at midlife. See *alienation, deanimation, derealization.*

Derealization. The sense that the world is remote and unreal. A derealized world seems dead and flat, arid and devoid of positive and negative values. Derealization—along with deanimation and depersonalization—belongs to a group of existential difficulties that can emerge at midlife. See *alienation, deanimation, depersonalization, life-world.*

Derepression. The lifting of repression and ensuing resurgence of materials that had been repressed. The key to the notion as used in this book is that the lifting of repression reawakens materials that had been quieted rather than releases materials that had been contained under pressure. This conception of derepression assumes that repression, rather than having a hydraulic character, is a barrier that subdues or deactivates what it contains. See *primal repression, repression.*

Dimensional view. The perspective that focuses on a single dimension of human development, following it through stages of the spiral path. In this book the dimensions thus considered are the Dynamic Ground, the power of the Ground, the ego, the perceived other, the experiential body, and the life-world. The dimensional view is to be contrasted with the stage view, which focuses on the major stages of the spiral path and shows how different dimensions of development are interrelated during these stages See *spiral path of development, stage view.*

Dynamic Ground. Frequently shortened to *Ground,* this term designates the deep core of the psyche and seat of nonegoic psychic potentials. The Dynamic Ground is to be distinguished from the ego, the center of consciousness and executor of ego functions. The Dynamic Ground undergoes many restructurings during the course of human development, the primary organizations being these: primordial source of life, intrapsychic dimension of the Great Mother, id, dark gravitational attractor, numinous core of psyche, psychic underworld or sea, source of renewing life, and fertile-sacred void. See *ego, ego functions, nonegoic potentials, psychic core, psychoid unconscious, unconscious.*

Ecstasy. State of euphoric infusive dissolution: rapture, transport. See *enstasy, infusion.*

Ego. The ego—also called the *nuclear ego*—is the proprietary center of consciousness (unity of apperception) and executor of ego functions. The ego is the basis of the larger ego system. It is the ego, as nuclear ego, that "has" a self-representation, ego ideal, and superego. The ego is to be distinguished from the Dynamic Ground, the deep core of the psyche and seat of nonegoic potentials. See *body ego, ego functions, ego system, mental ego, unity of apperception.*

Ego functions. The primary functions carried out by the nuclear ego, included among which are synthesis (of competing or disconnected elements of experience), reality testing, discursive cognition (e.g., data organization, conceptual mapping, hypothetico-deductive reasoning), impulse control, and intentional action. Ego functions are to be distinguished from the nonegoic potentials of the Dynamic Ground. See *Dynamic Ground, ego, ego system, nonegoic potentials.*

Ego ideal. The ideal goal or goals toward which the ego strives. The ego ideal emerges as preoedipal splitting is overcome and the child, realizing that it is not perfect, ceases identifying with the former good-child representation and instead posits this representation as an inspiring ideal goal. The first ego ideal, established at the beginning of the latency period, is an internalization of the parents' idea of a perfect child. This ego ideal is disowned during adolescence, and a new, self-chosen ego ideal is formulated in early adulthood as part of the identity project. The ego ideal is restructured again in transpersonal stages of development. During regression in the service of transcendence, an ego ideal emerges that is the contrary opposite of the archetypal shadow, an ego ideal representing disembodied angelic goodness. This one-sided ego ideal is dispelled in the transition from regression in the service of transcendence to regeneration in Spirit, when embodied life ceases being demonized and instinctual motivation, correspondingly, ceases being perceived as antithetical to spirituality. During regeneration in Spirit, the ego projects a more realistically human ego ideal, which is fashioned in response to Spirit acting as counselor. As regeneration in Spirit approaches integration, the ego ceases needing to project an ego ideal that is in any sense independent of the action of Spirit, for the counsel of Spirit at this point becomes the ego's own spiritual vision. See *ego, ego system, shadow, transforming Spirit, transparent Spirit.*

Ego system. The ego system at first consists only of the nuclear ego, the proprietary, executive center of consciousness. The larger ego system, including the nuclear ego, self-representation, ego ideal, and superego, is gradually formed during the preoedipal and oedipal stages and is consolidated in the transition to latency. The personal shadow is inherently tied to the ego system as the unconscious underside of the system. It consists of those tendencies and traits that are repressed because they are incompatible with the self-representation. The ego system undergoes many restructurings during the course of development. The initial ego system of the latency period is disavowed during adolescence, and a new ego system is then forged during early adulthood on the basis of the identity project. The ego system undergoes several more restructurings during transpersonal stages of development. During regression in the service of transcendence, the ego system is split into competing subsystems reflecting a perceived opposition between spiritual and instinctual life and, therefore, between higher (immaculately spiritual) and lower (instinctual, demonic) possible selves. This splitting is overcome in the transition to regeneration in Spirit, when the perceived opposition between spiritual and instinctual life disappears and the ego system begins to be brought into unity with the Dynamic Ground. In arriving at the stage of integration, the ego system is completely unified with the Dynamic Ground, and the ego is "wedded" to the power of the Ground as transparent Spirit. See *Dynamic Ground, ego, ego ideal, identity project, sacred marriage, self-representation, shadow, superego, transparent Spirit, unity of apperception.*

Energy. See *power of the Dynamic Ground.*

Energy cathexis. See *cathexis.*

Enstasy. Term coined by Mircea Eliade (1969) to describe meditative absorption (*samādhi*) and used in this book to describe absorption generally. *Enstasy,* meaning "to stand in," well describes states of subjectless envelopment or immersion, such as trance states and meditative absorption, and should be contrasted with *ecstasy,* meaning "to put outside," which describes states of subjectless euphoric infusion, such as rapture and transport. See *absorption, infusion.*

Garden of delight. The idyllic world of the child in the early preoedipal stage, before splitting occurs. The garden of delight is a small, safe, resplendent paradise. It is a world in which the child, provided for by the archetypal Great Mother, is free of danger and need; and it is a world that, embellished by the plenipotent power of the Dynamic Ground, is glorious and wondrous. The preoedipal child in the garden of delight is the practicing toddler, who fearlessly explores and greedily enjoys the world. See *Great Mother, life-world.*

Good Mother. See *Great Mother.*

Great Mother. The preoedipal child's primary object representation: the archetypal caregiver. The Great Mother is the caregiver amplified and otherwise embellished by plenipotently charged nonegoic potentials of the Dynamic Ground. Once preodipal splitting occurs, the Great Mother is divided into two contrary opposites, a good object and a bad object: the Good Mother, who loves the child unconditionally and provides for the child perfectly, and the Terrible Mother, who is cruel, neglectful, and smothering. See *nonegoic potentials, splitting.*

Id. Freud's term for the deep, inherited unconscious, the seat of instinctual drives and the prerational primary process. Freud's view seems to have been that the id is originally and inherently unconscious, although he is not completely clear on this point. In this book *id* is used to refer to a stage-specific organization of the Dynamic Ground, namely, the organization, consolidated in the transition to the stage of latency, imposed by primal repression. The Dynamic Ground, organized thus, is similar in most respects to the id as described by Freud. As a stage-specific organization of the Dynamic Ground, the id is a structure that can be developmentally superseded. Formed by primal repression, the id comes to an end if and when primal repression gives way. See *Dynamic Ground, latency, primal repression, unconscious.*

Identity project. The project, begun in early adulthood, that restructures the ego system by establishing a self-chosen identity. The identity project is based on commitments—such as those to occupation, relationship, group membership, religion—that define (1) who one is as a social being (self-representation), (2) standards of "good enough" behavior or achievement (superego), and (3) an ideal of perfect behavior or achievement (ego ideal). The self-representation forged on the basis of the identity project is similar to what C. G. Jung called the "persona." This self-representation, however, is not a mere outer mask, even if it sometimes appears as such during periods of existential challenge (e.g., midlife transition). Rather, it is an outer vehicle for the expression and development of the inner personality. See *ego system.*

Immanent. Meaning "within," this term is used to designate the ego's inner world of experience as opposed to the outer world of transcendent, independent objects. The boundary marking off the immanence of the self from the transcendence of the world changes during early childhood. No such boundary exists for the newborn, whose experience, therefore, is all-inclusive, wholly immanent. The surface of the skin is the boundary separating immanence from transcendence for the preoedipal body ego, and the dividing line between private psychic space and public physical space is the boundary separating immanence from transcendence for the mental ego. See *body ego, mental ego, object permanence, ouroboros, transcendent.*

Infusion. The movement of the power of the Ground within the ego, which energizes and inflates the ego, sometimes beyond limits of self-cohesion (rapture or rupture, ecstasy or dispersion). The infusive movement of the power of the Ground is to be distinguished from its cathectic movement, which concentrates the power of the Ground outside the ego, usually in objects, attracting the ego to and sometimes absorbing the ego in objects. See *absorption, cathexis, ecstasy, enstasy, power of the Ground.*

Integration. The final stage of the spiral path, integration is a higher unification of the ego system and the Dynamic Ground. Integration is also a "marriage" of the ego to transparent Spirit, of self to Self. See *Dynamic Ground, ego, ego system, sacred marriage, self, transparent Spirit.*

Latency. According to Freud, latency is a stage of development during which instinctual drives are quiet. In this book latency is conceived more broadly as a stage during which nonegoic potentials generally are quiet, having been submerged and subdued by primal repression. Latency extends from approximately five and a half years of age to puberty. See *id, nonegoic potentials, primal repression.*

Libido. In this book *libido* is used to designate the power of the Ground insofar as it is channeled through an instinctual system or restricted to an instinctual organization. Conceived thus, libido is instinctual energy generally rather than, as Freud held, sexual energy exclusively. Moreover, it is energy that, although instinctually channeled or organized, is not instinctual in inherent nature. Under conditions of primal repression, libido is the plenipotent power of the Ground restricted to an instinctual organization as the potential energy of the id. Libido is one of three principal expressions of the power of Ground, the other two being psychic energy and Spirit. See *id, plenipotent, power of the Ground, psychic energy, Spirit.*

Life-world. The distinctive way in which the world is experienced at a particular stage of development. Principal forms of the life-world are (1) the ouroboric sphere (neonatal stage), (2) the garden of delight (early preoedipal stage), (3) the split, enchanted-haunted world (late preoedipal and oedipal stages), (4) the playground of youth (latency), (5) the rehearsal stage for adult life (adolescence), (6) the arena of responsible action (early adulthood), (7) the existential desert (midlife transition), (8) the realm of numinous powers (initial awakening and regression in the service of transcendence), (9) the world of transforming Spirit (regeneration in Spirit), and (10) the world of transparent Spirit (integration). See *garden of delight, natural world, ouroboros.*

Mental ego. The ego whose primary identification is with the private inner realm of psychic space rather than with the body. The mental ego emerges in the late preoedipal and oedipal stages and is consolidated in the transition to latency. The ego remains primarily a mental ego until primal repression is lifted and the power of the Ground is reawakened. The body is "resurrected" during regression in the service of transcendence, and the ego is then "reincarnated" during regeneration in Spirit, becoming once again a body ego. See *body ego, ego, reincarnation of the ego, resurrection of the body.*

Natural world. Forms of the life-world corresponding to personal stages of development: the playground of youth (latency), the rehearsal stage for adult life (adolescence), and the arena of responsible action (early adulthood). Natural forms of the life-world are charged with nonplenipotent psychic energy and, therefore, are to be distinguished from forms of the life-world that are either (1) charged with the power of the Ground in its plenipotency (the ouroboric sphere, the garden of delight, and the split, enchanted-haunted world of prepersonal stages and the realm of numinous powers, the world of transforming Spirit, and the world of transparent Spirit of transpersonal stages) or (2) divested altogether of the power of the Ground (the existential desert of midlife transition). See *garden of delight, life-world, numinous, personal stage, plenipotent, power of the Ground, prepersonal stage, transpersonal stage.*

Nonegoic potentials. Sources of experience situated in the deep core of the psyche, the Dynamic Ground: energy (the power of the Ground), instincts, sources of affective response, and the creative imagination (autosymbolic process). Primal repression submerges and quiets nonegoic potentials at an early stage of development, confining them to a prepersonal organization as the primitive potentials of the unconscious id. The lifting of primal repression and the reactivation of nonegoic potentials later in life mark the beginning of spiritual transformation. Nonegoic potentials, situated in the deep psyche, are to be distinguished from ego functions, which are exercised by the ego, the organizing agency of consciousness. See *autosymbolic process, Dynamic Ground, ego, ego functions, id, psyche.*

Nuclear ego. See *ego, ego functions, ego system, unity of apperception.*

Numinous. Rudolf Otto's (1917) term to designate the experience of the sacred or holy. Otto described the numinous as the *mysterium tremendum et fascinans,* a compelling and mysterious energy of prodigious magnitude. In this book the numinous—referred to as *numinous Spirit*—is interpreted developmentally as a stage-specific expression of the power of the Dynamic Ground, namely, the expression that emerges when the power of the Ground is first reawakened in its plenipotency and manifests itself to the ego as an immense, daunting power, a power that seems "wholly other." Numinous Spirit corresponds to the stages of initial awakening and regression in the service of transcendence. See *plenipotent, power of the Ground, regression in the service of transcendence, Spirit.*

Numinous Spirit. See *numinous.*

Object cathexis. See *cathexis.*

Object constancy. The reunification of an object representation that had been split along all-good and all-bad lines. In early childhood the representation of the primary caregiver is split into representations of an all-good caregiver (the Good Mother) and an all-bad caregiver (the Terrible Mother). This splitting is finally overcome in the transition to latency, when the representation of the caregiver is reunified as a single representation of a person who is neither perfectly good nor utterly bad but is good enough to meet the child's needs. Object representations are split once again later in life when the person undergoing regression in the service of transcendence becomes prone to perceive others as either saints or sinners, angels or demons. This splitting is overcome and a higher, transpersonal form of object constancy emerges during regeneration in Spirit, during which it becomes evident that no one is spiritually perfect or wholly evil. See *Great Mother, regeneration in Spirit, regression in the service of transcendence, self-representation, splitting.*

Object permanence. In Piagetian psychology this term refers to the fact that objects continue to exist after they have exited the field of perception. Piaget believed that understanding of object permanence is first achieved around eight months of age. More recent research, however, indicates that understanding of object permanence is achieved earlier, perhaps as early as four or five months. The discussion of object permanence in this book stresses the following points: (1) understanding of object permanence is what first brings the external world into focus as a transcendent realm, that is, as a realm of objects existing beyond consciousness; (2) the initial understanding of object permanence is not yet an understanding of the full independence of objects and in particular is not yet an understanding that objects, including the caregiver, need not be located in accessible proximity to the child but can be located anywhere in a vast region of space; (3) the initial understanding of object permanence, therefore, allows the child to believe that it is living in a world that, although transcendent to the child, is still small and safe; (4) this comforting illusion is dashed sometime around the second half of the second year, when the child achieves understanding of the full independence of objects; and (5) the dashing of the illusion of living in a small, safe world triggers preoedipal splitting. See *immanent, life-world, splitting, transcendent.*

Ouroboros. The ancient Egyptian and Greek symbol of a world-encircling snake that swallows its own tail. The ouroboros symbolically represents the world of the newborn, which is an all-inclusive, wholly immanent sphere. See *immanent, life-world, transcendent.*

Personal shadow. See *shadow.*

Persona. C. G. Jung's term for a person's outer social identity. See *identity project.*

Personal stage. Also called the egoic stage, the personal stage is one of three stages—or, rather, groups of stages—recognized by transpersonal theory, the other two being the prepersonal (or preegoic) and the transpersonal (or transegoic) stages. For many people the personal stage, beginning in the transition to the stage of latency, is virtually coextensive with life itself. For other people, however, the personal stage comes to an end—typically at the turning point of midlife—and the transpersonal stage begins. See *prepersonal stage, transpersonal stage.*

Plenipotent (plenipotency). Used to refer to the nonegoic potentials of the Dynamic Ground—and to the power of the Ground in particular—when experienced in undiminished, full intensity. The nonegoic potentials of the Ground are plenipotently active in early childhood, before primal repression quiets the Ground; and they are reactivated in their plenipotency later in life if and when primal repression is lifted and the Ground is reawakened. The power of the Ground in its plenipotency is to be distinguished from the power of the Ground in the repressed and diminished form of psychic energy. See *Dynamic Ground, nonegoic potentials, power of the Ground, primal repression, psychic energy.*

Power of the Ground. The energy of the Dynamic Ground, which influences the ego in the following prinicipal ways: (1) *by amplifiying the ego's experience:* the power of the Ground intensifies thought and feeling and magnifies perceptual stimuli; (2) *by attracting the ego:* the power of the Ground, concentrated in the form of cathexes, attracts the ego's attention; (3) *by infusing the ego:* the power of the Ground inwardly energizes and inflates the ego; and (4) *by dissolving the ego:* the power of the Ground, if present at a sufficiently high level of intensity, dissolves the ego, either by drawing it into absorptions or by infusing it beyond limits of self-cohesion. The three principal expressions of the power of the Ground are libido, psychic energy, and Spirit. See *absorption, cathexis, infusion, libido, psychic energy, Spirit.*

Prepersonal stage. Also called the preegoic stage, the prepersonal stage is one of three stages—or, rather, groups of stages—recognized by transpersonal theory, the other two being the personal (or egoic) and transpersonal (or transegoic) stages. The prepersonal stage extends from birth to the beginning of the stage of latency and includes the following major substages: the neonatal stage, the early preoedipal stage, the late preoedipal stage, and the oedipal stage. See *personal stage, transpersonal stage.*

Pre-trans fallacy. The fallacy, identified by Ken Wilber (1980), of inferring that prepersonal and transpersonal forms of experience, in being alike nonpersonal, are fundamentally the same in nature. Employing the notion of the pre-trans fallacy, Wilber argues (1) that many transpersonal theorists have mistaken prepersonal forms of experience for transpersonal forms, with naively romantic and regressive consequences, and (2) that many critics of the transpersonal perspective have mistaken transpersonal forms of experience for prepersonal forms, with antispiritual and repressive consequences. See *personal stage, prepersonal stage, spiral path of development, transpersonal stage.*

Primal closing. The two-sided "act" by which the child surmounts preoedipal splitting. The inner or intrapsychic side of primal closing is primal repression, the submerging and quieting of the nonegoic potentials of the Dynamic Ground. The outer or intersubjective side of primal closing is primal separation, the withdrawal by the child from fully embodied intimacy with the caregiver to the protected privacy of psychic space. Primal closing begins in the late preoedipal stage and, typically, is consolidated as a psychic structure in the transition from the oedipal stage to the stage of latency, when the child commits itself to the oedipal change of object. See *change of object, primal repression, primal separation, splitting.*

Primal repression. Freud's term for the first and deepest layer of repression. Freud maintained as early as *The Interpretation of Dreams* (1900) that the secondary process cannot accommodate primary-process materials and, therefore, that a repressive elimination of these materials from awareness occurs as soon as the system of consciousness is formed. Freud later (1911b) termed this initial form of repression *primal repression.* After 1923, Freud explained primal repression in terms of the ego's emergence from the id. Instinctual impulses of the id, Freud explained (1926, 1933), overwhelm the fledgling ego, triggering severe anxiety. The immature ego is unable to deal with these impulses in any way other than by repressing them and thereby keeping them contained within the id. Freud held that this original and basic repression likely occurs before the end of the oedipal stage. In this book primal repression is conceived as a principal means by which the ego brings preoedipal splitting to an end. Primal repression submerges the nonegoic potentials of the Dynamic Ground, thus reorganizing the Ground as the id. Primal repression is the intrapsychic side of primal closing, the outer or intersubjective side of which is primal separation. Primal repression, in submerging nonegoic potentials, does not work in hydraulic fashion; rather, it is a countercathexis that quiets—without completely deactivating—nonegoic potentials. Although primal repression disconnects the ego from the Dynamic Ground, it is developmentally warranted because, in quieting nonegoic potentials, it provides the ego with a calm inner atmosphere that facilitates reality testing, self-control, and continued growth. Once ego development is complete, primal repression loses its warrant and becomes an impediment to spiritual awakening. See *countercathexis, derepression, primal closing, primal separation, repression.*

Primal separation. The outer or intersubjective side of primal closing, primal separation is the act by which the child withdraws from radical (i.e., undefended, fully embodied) intimacy with the caregiver to the safe privacy of psychic space. Although primal separation brings an end to radical intimacy with the caregiver, it is developmentally warranted because, in providing the ego with safe distance from others, it helps the ego establish self-possession and autonomy. Once ego development is complete, primal separation loses its warrant and becomes an impediment to spiritual awakening. See *primal closing, primal repression.*

Psyche. Subjectivity as a whole, including both the ego and the Dynamic Ground, both consciousness and the unconscious. According to the view set forth in this book, the psyche is fundamentally bipolar, having both a center of agency in consciousness (the ego) and a deep core (the Dynamic Ground). See *deep psyche, Dynamic Ground, ego, ego system, psychic core, unconscious.*

Psychic core. The underlying base of the psyche, here conceived as the Dynamic Ground, the seat of nonegoic psychic potentials. The Dynamic Ground, as psychic core, is to be distinguished from the ego, the center of consciousness. See *deep psyche, Dynamic Ground, ego, ego functions, nonegoic potentials.*

Psychic energy. One of the three principal expressions of the power of the Dynamic Ground, psychic energy is the "fuel" that powers psychomental processes under the limiting conditions of primal repression. Primal repression divides the power of the Ground into two organizations, one active and one latent: psychic energy (active) and libido (latent). As a consequence of primal repression, the power of the Ground in its plenipotency is restricted to an instinctual organization and quieted, becoming latent libido, the potential energy of the Dynamic Ground organized as the id. Thus deactivated as a plenipotent energy, the power of the Ground remains active only as a nonplenipotent energy. This nonplenipotent energy is psychic energy, the neutral, or noninstinctual, energy of conscious life. Psychic energy ceases to exist as an organization of the power of the Ground once the power of the Ground is reawakened in its plenipotency and liberated, as Spirit, from its prior restrictive association with instinctual life. See *id, libido, plenipotent, primal repression, Spirit.*

Psychoid unconscious. C. G. Jung's term for the deepest roots of the psyche, which reach into nonpsychic, neurological strata. In this book the term refers to the neurological bases of the Dynamic Ground. The psychoid unconscious, underlying the psyche proper, is unfathomable and, therefore, inherently unconscious. Although psychic expressions of the Dynamic Ground are available to consciousness if the Ground is not repressed, the psychoid bases of the Dynamic Ground are not. See *Dynamic Ground*.

Regeneration in Spirit. Following regression in the service of transcendence and preceding integration, regeneration in Spirit is the stage during which the power of the Ground, as transforming Spirit, ceases being wholly other, or numinous, and becomes the ego's counselor, guardian, or lover. Regeneration in Spirit is also the stage during which the perceived opposition between spiritual and instinctual life, which had plagued the ego during regression in the service of transcendence, comes to an end and the ego is "reincarnated" in the body, becoming once again a body ego. See *body ego, reincarnation of the ego, transforming Spirit*.

Regression in the service of transcendence. Following initial awakening and preceding regeneration in Spirit, regression in the service of transcendence is the stage during which the Dynamic Ground opens as a psychic underworld or turbulent sea, the body undergoes a disconcerting "resurrection," and instinctual derepression occurs in seeming opposition to spiritual life. Regression in the service of transcendence is also the stage during which the ego system is split into all-good and all-bad potential selves. Inspired by an angelic ego ideal, the ego aspires to be a purely spiritual self; and "tempted" by the archetypal shadow, the ego fears that it will become a wholly evil, antispiritual self. See *Dynamic Ground, numinous, resurrection of the body, shadow, splitting*.

Reincarnation of the ego. The ego's return to the body during regeneration in Spirit. As the perceived opposition between spiritual and instinctual life disappears, the ego ceases feeling threatened by the body's "resurrection" and begins returning to fully embodied life. The ego thus once again becomes a body ego, an ego living primarily in the body rather than in inner psychic space. See *body ego, mental ego, regeneration in Spirit, resurrection of the body*.

Repression. A negative mobilization of energy, or countercathexis, aimed at excluding psychic materials from consciousness. According to Freud, the first and most basic repression is *primal repression,* which in this book is conceived as a structure that, consolidated in the transition to the stage of latency, submerges the nonegoic potentials of the Dynamic Ground. In contrast to Freud's hydraulic account of repression, according to which repression is a countercathexis that contains targeted materials under pressure, the account presented in this book explains repression as a countercathexis that quiets or subdues targeted materials. Repression, conceived in this manner, need not lock the psyche in a chronic state of tension. See *countercathexis, derepression, primal repression*.

Resurrection of the body. The enlivening of the body that accompanies the reawakening of the power of the Ground in adulthood. Nonplenipotent psychic energy here gives way to the power of the Ground in its plenipotency, and the body, thus charged with high-intensity energy, returns dramatically to life. Initial signs of the body's awakening occur before regression in the service of transcendence and may include such indications as tingling sensations, palpitations, perspiration, chills, horripilation, heightened sensitivity in erotogenic tissues, and spontaneous erotic feelings. More dramatic expressions of the body's awakening occur after regression in the service of transcendence—and, with it, instinctual derepression—has begun, for example, sensations of energy movement, dismantling of body armors, involuntary bodily movements and postures, vocalizations, and strong sexual feelings. See *plenipotent, regression in the service of transcendence, reincarnation of the ego.*

Sacred marriage (*hieros gamos*). The integration of male and female principles, indicating spiritual fulfillment. In this book the sacred marriage is conceived as the integration of the ego and the Dynamic Ground or, more precisely, as the joining of the ego as lesser self to transparent Spirit as greater Self. See *self, transparent Spirit.*

Self. With a lowercase *s*, this term is used to designate the ego's understanding of itself as defined by the self-representation. With an uppercase *S*, the term is used to designate the power of the Ground in its highest expression as transparent Spirit. This usage of *Self* differs from C. G. Jung's, according to which the Self is an archetype rather than a power or energy, namely, the archetype governing the general course of development, guiding it toward the telos of wholeness. See *integration, self-representation, transparent Spirit.*

Self-representation. A component of the ego system, the self-representation is the ego's implicit conception of itself. In the account given in this book, the self-representation emerges in the middle of the second year and, in this first form, has the fate of being a split self-representation. Prior to preoedipal splitting, the child, immediately aware of its bodily self, has no need of a self-representation. Once the situation leading to splitting emerges, however, the child is forced to begin thinking about itself because it now desperately wants to believe that it is a perfectly good child worthy of the caregiver's affection. The child, of course, is not a perfectly good child, and it therefore thinks of itself as being in effect two children, one all good and the other all bad. This split in the first self-representation is mended during the late preoedipal and oedipal stages, and then, in the transition to latency, a unified "good enough" self-representation emerges. Much of the earlier good-child self-representation is now projected as the ego ideal, and much of the earlier bad-child self-representation is now repressed as the personal shadow. The self-representation of the latency period is disavowed during adolescence, and adult identity possibilities are explored. A new self-representation is then forged during early adulthood on the basis of the identity project. This self-representation is revised as years pass and is for most people the final self-representation. For those who enter transpersonal stages, however, the self-representation undergoes new restructurings. During regression in the service of transcendence, the self-representation is split once again, this time into higher and lower potential selves. Inspired by an angelic ego ideal, the ego struggles against the instincts and aspires to be a purely spiritual self; and preyed upon by the archetypal shadow, the ego fears that it will succumb to temptations of the flesh and become an instinctually depraved, antispiritual self. This split in the self-representation is mended in the transition to regeneration in Spirit, and a self-representation that integrates spiritual and instinctual sides of life emerges. As regeneration in Spirit approaches integration, the self-representation is increasingly united with the Dynamic Ground and with the power of the Ground as Spirit in particular. Once integration is achieved, the self-representation becomes a self-Self representation, a representation of the ego, as lesser self, completely integrated with Spirit, as greater Self. See *ego ideal, ego system, identity project, sacred marriage, self, shadow, splitting, superego, transparent Spirit.*

Separation anxiety. The fear of losing or being abandoned by the caregiver. In this book separation anxiety is explained as arising from an understanding of the full independence of objects, an understanding achieved sometime near the middle of the second year of life. In coming to understand the full independence of objects, it dawns upon the child that not only objects generally but also the caregiver in particular can exist inaccessibly in a vast region of space. The child, in achieving this insight, is struck by its own smallness and vulnerability and feels a need to be a perfectly good child so that the caregiver will not abandon it. This felt need to be a perfectly good child is the cause of preoedipal splitting. See *object permanence, splitting.*

Shadow. The shadow, a Jungian concept, consists of the traits, tendencies, and psychic potentials that, in being incompatible with the self-representation, are repressed and hidden from consciousness. The personal shadow consists of the traits, tendencies, and potentials that are incompatible with the self-representation as it is first forged during early childhood and then later restructured during early adulthood. The archetypal shadow consists of the traits, tendencies, and potentials that, in bearing the stigma of absolute evil, are most deeply repressed. Derepression of the personal shadow occurs during adolescence and can occur again at midlife. Derepression of the archetypal shadow occurs during regression in the service of transcendence. See *derepression.*

Spiral path of development. The general course of human development as conceived in this book. According to the spiral view, development in the first half of life leaves behind essential sources of life, sources to which we must return later in life if we are to achieve higher, transpersonal wholeness. The spiral view can be found in spiritual and religious literatures around the world. In the West the spiral view has biblical sources in the idea of our fall from grace and eventual higher redemption. As an account of human development, the spiral view must avoid the pitfalls of naive romanticism and related pre-trans fallacies. See *personal stage, prepersonal stage, pre-trans fallacy, transpersonal stage.*

Spirit. With an uppercase *S*, this term is used to designate the power of the Ground in its plenipotent, free (i.e., unchanneled) expression. The three major forms of Spirit are numinous Spirit (associated with initial awakening and regression in the service of transcendence), transforming Spirit (associated with regeneration in Spirit), and transparent Spirit (associated with the stage of integration). See *numinous, power of the Ground, transforming Spirit, transparent Spirit.*

Splitting. Splitting is a defense mechanism that allows the ego to avoid acknowledging unacceptable aspects of itself without having to repress those aspects. The first form of splitting occurs in preoedipal childhood, during the rapprochement subphase of the separation-individuation process, and is a response to separation anxiety. The child suffering from separation anxiety cannot accept aspects of itself that meet with the caregiver's disapproval and for this reason groups these aspects together as making up a bad child who is separate from, and therefore not compromising of, the child as good child. Corresponding to this splitting of the child's self-representation is a splitting of its principal object representation, the representation of the caregiver, which is divided into opposing good (Good Mother) and bad (Terrible Mother) representations. Preoedipal splitting is overcome and object constancy achieved in the transition to latency, when the self-representation is mended as a single good enough self-representation and the caregiver is perceived as a single good enough caregiver. Splitting occurs once more as part of normal development during regression in the service of transcendence, when the self-representation is split into higher, purely spiritual and lower, instinctual-demonic potential selves. People undergoing regression in the service of transcendence, in thus splitting the self-representation, are able to hold on to the belief that that they are potentially all-good spiritual selves even though they are tempted by demonized instincts. Corresponding to this transpersonal splitting of the self-representation is a splitting of object representations: people undergoing regression in the service of transcendence are prone to perceive others as either saints or sinners, angels or demons. Transpersonal splitting is overcome and a new, higher object constancy is achieved in the transition from regression in the service of transcendence to regeneration in Spirit. See *object constancy, object permanence, regeneration in Spirit, regression in the service of transcendence, self-representation, separation anxiety.*

Stage view. The perspective that focuses on the major stages of the spiral path of development and shows how principal dimensions of development are interrelated during these stages. The stage view is to be contrasted with the dimensional view, which isolates a single dimension of development and tracks its unfolding along the stages of the spiral path. See *dimensional view, spiral path of development.*

Superego. A component of the ego system, the superego is the inner agency that regulates behavior. Antecedents of the superego can be found in the split good-child self-representation of the late preoedipal stage: the child, as good child, seeks to regulate its behavior by trying to be a perfectly good child. This attempt to be a perfectly good child is, of course, an attempt to do something impossible, which is the reason the good child alternates again and again with the bad child. The superego proper is established in the transition to the stage of latency in the consolidation of the first true ego system (nuclear ego, self-representation, ego ideal, superego). The latency superego is essentially the internalized voice of the parents, which exhorts the child to be at least a "good enough" child. The superego breaks free from parental standards during adolescence, and the will is asserted as an exercise of independence. The identity project of early adulthood reharnesses the superego by tying it to the long-term commitments of that project. Young adults discipline themselves in striving to meet occupational, interpersonal, and other social and private commitments in at least a good enough way. For people who enter transpersonal stages, the superego undergoes new restructurings. During regression in the service of transcendence, the superego is split into a good superego, which commands the ego to stay on course in aspiring toward immaculate spirituality, and an evil anti-superego, which dares the ego to yield to the temptations of the archetypal shadow. This split in the superego is mended in the transition to regeneration in Spirit, during which the superego is progressively integrated with transforming Spirit's guardian function. Once integration is achieved, the superego and Spirit are completely unified. The ego no longer needs to command itself to follow the promptings of Spirit, for under integrated conditions the higher will of transparent Spirit is the ego's own will. See *ego, ego ideal, ego system, identity project, shadow, transforming Spirit, transparent Spirit.*

Terrible Mother. See *Great Mother.*

Transcendent. Meaning "beyond," this term is used to describe the world understood as a realm of objects existing beyond consciousness. The transcendence of the world is to be contrasted with the immanence of the self. The child achieves an initial, incomplete understanding of the transcendence of the world when, in the first year of life, it begins to understand object permanence; and it achieves a more complete understanding when, in the second year of life, it begins to understand the full independence of objects. See *immanent, life-world, object permanence*.

Transcendental unity of apperception.   See *unity of apperception*.

Transforming Spirit.   The awakened power of the Ground once it ceases being wholly other, or numinous, and becomes the ego's superior ally, the ego's counselor, guardian, or lover. Transforming Spirit corresponds to the stage of regeneration in Spirit. See *power of the Ground, regeneration in Spirit*.

Transparent Spirit.   The awakened power of the Ground once it ceases being to any degree other in relation to the ego and becomes the ego's higher Self: the ego's higher will, wisdom, and love of others. Transparent Spirit corresponds to the stage of integration. See *integration, power of the Ground, Self*.

Transpersonal stage.   Also called the transegoic stage, the transpersonal stage is one of three stages—or, rather, groups of stages—recognized by transpersonal theory, the other two being the prepersonal (or preegoic) and personal (or egoic) stages. The major substages of the transpersonal stage are initial awakening, regression in the service of transcendence, regeneration in Spirit, and integration. See *integration, personal stage, prepersonal stage, regeneration in Spirit, regression in the service of transcendence*.

Unconscious.   Divided most basically into personal (i.e., biographical, person-specific) and inherited (i.e., collective, universal) levels, the unconscious is the part of the psyche that is inaccessible to consciousness. This book focuses primarily on the inherited level of the unconscious, conceived as the Dynamic Ground. Because the Dynamic Ground has roots that reach into neurological strata, it is unfathomable in its depths. The depths of the Dynamic Ground, therefore, constitute an original and inherent unconscious, which, employing C. G. Jung's term, is in this book called the *psychoid unconscious*. Despite being unfathomable, the Dynamic Ground is by no means completely hidden from consciousness because expressions of the Ground, which arise from its psychoid depths, manifest themselves in consciousness. That is to say, expressions of the Ground manifest themselves in consciousness until primal repression submerges and quiets the Ground, making the Ground not only the psychoid unconscious but also the deepest level of the repressed unconscious. Primal repression, occurring early in life, restricts the Ground to an exclusively instinctual, prerational organization, which psychoanalysis calls the id. The awakening of the sexual drive during puberty stirs the Ground, as id, which is then restabilized in early adulthood when mature genital sexuality is achieved. This restabilized id is for most people the final developmental form assumed by the Dynamic Ground. For people who enter transpersonal stages, however, the Dynamic Ground is derepressed and reawakened, and its expressions once again begin to manifest themselves in consciousness. During regression in the service of transcendence, the Dynamic Ground opens, and the ego becomes aware of it as a dark and ominous underworld or sea. The darkness of the Dynamic Ground disappears as derepression runs its course, and then, in the transition to regeneration in Spirit, the Dynamic Ground begins to express itself as a source of renewing life. Finally, once integration is achieved, the Dynamic Ground becomes the ego's own

Ground and is experienced by the ego as a bottomless dynamic field from which life and thought spontaneously arise: the fertile-sacred void. See *Dynamic Ground, id, nonegoic potentials, primal repression, psychoid unconscious.*

Unity of apperception. An expression introduced by the eighteenth-century philosopher Immanuel Kant to designate the abiding reference point in relation to which temporally unfolding consciousness is at once *one* consciousness and *someone's* consciousness. The unity of apperception is the ego understood in the minimal sense as proprietary center of consciousness. See *ego.*

Univalent. The antonym of *bivalent,* this term is used to designate an object that is either wholly positive or wholly negative—rather than both positive and negative (bivalent)—in charge and effect upon the ego. See *bivalence.*

REFERENCES

Abrams, M. H. 1971. *Natural Supernaturalism: Tradition and Revolution in Romantic Literature*. New York: Norton.

Adler, Gerald. 1985. *Borderline Psychopathology and Its Treatment*. New York: Jason Aronson.

Akhtar, Salman. 1995. "Aggression: Theories Regarding Its Nature and Origins." In *Psychoanalysis: The Major Concepts*, ed. B. E. Moore and B. D. Fine, pp. 364–80. New Haven: Yale University Press.

Arieti, Silvano. 1967. *Creativity: The Magic Synthesis*. New York: Basic Books.

Assagioli, Roberto. 1971. *Psychosynthesis: A Manual of Principles and Techniques*. New York: Viking Press.

Baillargeon, Renée. 1987. "Object Permanence in 3½ and 4½-Month-Old Infants." *Developmental Psychology* 23:655–64.

Beck, Don, and Christopher C. Cowan. 1996. *Spiral Dynamics: Mastering Values, Leadership, and Change: Exploring the New Science of Memetics*. Cambridge, Mass.: Blackwell Business.

Blais, Donald. 1997. *Passion and Pathology in Teresa of Avila's Mystical Transformation*. Toronto: Th.D. diss., Toronto School of Theology and the University of Toronto.

Blos, Peter. 1962. *On Adolescence: A Psychoanalytic Interpretation*. New York: Free Press.

———. 1967. "The Second Individuation Process of Adolescence." In *The Adolescent Passage: Developmental Issues*, pp. 141–70. New York: International Universities Press, 1979.

———. 1968. "Character Formation in Adolescence." In *The Adolescent Passage: Developmental Issues*, pp. 171–91. New York: International Universities Press, 1979.

———. 1972. "The Function of the Ego Ideal in Adolescence." *Psychoanalytic Study of the Child* 27:93–97.

———. 1974. "The Genealogy of the Ego Ideal." In *The Adolescent Passage: Developmental Issues*, pp. 319–69. New York: International Universities Press, 1979.

Bower, T. G. R. 1979. *Human Development*. San Francisco: W. H. Freeman.

_____. 1982. *Development in Infancy*. 2nd ed. San Francisco: W. H. Freeman.

_____. 1989. *The Rational Infant: Learning in Infancy*. New York: W. H. Freeman.

Brazelton, T. Berry, Barbara Koslowski, and Mary Main. 1974. "The Origins of Reciprocity: The Early Mother-Infant Interaction." In *The Effect of the Infant on Its Caregiver*, ed. M. Lewis and L. A. Rosenblum, pp. 49–76. New York: Wiley.

Broughton, John. 1978. "Development of Concepts of Self, Mind, Reality, and Knowledge." In *New Directions for Child Development: Social Cognition*, ed. W. Damon, pp. 75–100. San Francisco: Jossey-Bass.

_____. 1980. "Genetic Metaphysics: The Developmental Psychology of Mind-Body Concepts." In *Body and Mind: Past, Present, and Future*, ed. R. W. Rieber, pp. 177–221. New York: Academic Press.

_____. 1982. "Genetic Logic and the Developmental Psychology of Philosophical Concepts." In *The Cognitive Developmental Psychology of James Mark Baldwin*, ed. J. M. Broughton and D. J. Freeman-Moir, pp. 219–76. Norwood, New Jersey: Ablex.

Buber, Martin. 1970. *I and Thou*. Trans. W. Kaufmann. New York: Charles Scribner's.

Campbell, Joseph. 1949. *The Hero with a Thousand Faces*. New York: Pantheon.

Collie, El. 1995. "Kundalini Signs and Symptoms." Accessed 20 April 2003. <http://www.elcollie.com/st/symptoms.html>.

Condon, William S., and Louis W. Sander. 1974. "Neonate Movement is Synchronized with Adult Speech: Interactional Participation and Language Acquisition." *Science* 183:99–101.

Coward, Harold. 1996. "Taoism and Jung: Synchronicity and the Self." *Philosophy East and West* 46:477–96.

Demany, Laurent, Beryl McKenzie, and Elaine Vurpillot. 1977. "Rhythm Perception in Early Infancy." *Nature* 266:718–19.

Eliade, Mircea. 1969. *Yoga: Immortality and Freedom*. Princeton: Princeton University Press.

Erikson, Erik H. 1950. "Growth and Crises of the Healthy Personality." In *Identity and the Life Cycle*, pp. 50–100. Published in *Psychological Issues*, Monograph 1, 1959.

_____. 1956. "The Problem of Ego Identity." In *Identity and the Life Cycle*, pp. 101–64. Published in *Psychological Issues*, Monograph 1, 1959.

Fantz, Robert L. 1963. "Pattern Vision in Newborn Infants." *Science* 140:296–97.

Feuerstein, Georg. 1992. *Sacred Sexuality: Living the Vision of the Erotic Spirit*. New York: Jeremy P. Tarcher.

Fraiberg, Selma. 1969. "Libidinal Object Constancy and Mental Representation." *The Psychoanalytic Study of the Child* 24:9–47.

Frese, Pamela R., and S. J. M. Gray. 1987. "Trees." In *Encyclopedia of Religion*, vol. 15, ed. M. Eliade, pp. 26–33. New York: Collier Macmillan.

Freud, Anna. 1946. *The Ego and the Mechanisms of Defense*. New York: International Universities Press.

_____. 1958. "Adolescence." *The Psychoanalytic Study of the Child* 13:255–78.

Freud, Sigmund. 1900. *The Interpretation of Dreams*. In *The Standard Edition of the Complete Psychological Works of Sigmund Freud*. Vols. 4 and 5. London: Hogarth Press, 1953.

_____. 1911a. "Formulations on the Two Principles of Mental Functioning." In *Standard Edition*. Vol. 12, pp. 213–26. London: Hogarth Press, 1958.

_____. 1911b. "Psychoanalytic Notes on an Autobiographical Account of a Case of Paranoia (Dementia Paranoides)." In *Standard Edition*. Vol. 12., pp. 9–82. London: Hogarth Press, 1958.

_____. 1923. *The Ego and the Id*. In *Standard Edition*. Vol. 19, pp. 12–66. London: Hogarth Press, 1961.

_____. 1926. "Inhibitions, Symptoms and Anxiety." In *Standard Edition*. Vol. 20, pp. 87–175. London: Hogarth Press, 1959.

_____. 1933. *New Introductory Lectures on Psycho-Analysis*. In *Standard Edition*. Vol. 22, pp. 5–182. London: Hogarth Press, 1964.

Frobenius, Leo. 1904. *Das Zeitalter des Sonnengotes*. Berlin: Reimer.

Garfield, Jay L. 1995. *The Fundamental Wisdom of the Middle Way* (translation and commentary on Nagarjuna's *Mūlamadhyamakakārikā*. New York: Oxford University Press.

Gopnik, Alison, and Andrew N. Meltzoff. 1997. *Words, Thoughts, and Theories*. Cambridge: MIT Press.

Gray, Deborah. 1995. "My Experience with Depression." Accessed 20 April 2003. <http://www.wingofmadness.com/articles/mystory.htm>.

Haaf, Robert A., and Richard Q. Bell. 1967. "A Facial Dimension in Visual Discrimination by Human Infants." *Child Development* 38:893–99.

Heidegger, Martin. 1954. "Bauen Wohnen Denken." In *Vortrage und Aufsatze*, pp. 145–62. Pfulligen: Gunther Neske Verlag, 1954.

Hutt, S. J., Corinne Hutt, H. G. Lenard, H. V. Bernuth, and W. J. Muntjewerff. 1968. "Auditory Responsivity in the Human Neonate." *Nature* 218:888–90.

Isaacs, Susan. 1943. "The Nature and Function of Phantasy." In *Developments in Psychoanalysis*, ed. M. Klein, P. Heimann, S. Isaacs, and J. Riviere, pp. 67–121. London: Karnac, 1989.

John of the Cross, Saint. 1991. *The Dark Night*. In *The Collected Works of Saint John of the Cross*, rev. ed., trans. K. Kavanaugh and O. Rodriguez, pp. 359–457. Washington, D.C.: ICS.

Jung, Carl G. 1912. *Symbols of Transformation*. In *Collected Works of C. G. Jung*. Vol. 5. New York: Pantheon, 1956.

_____. 1928. "On Psychic Energy." In *Collected Works*, vol. 8, pp. 3–66. 2nd ed. New York: Pantheon, 1960.

Kagan, Jerome. 1989. *Unstable Ideas: Temperament, Cognition, and Self*. Cambridge: Harvard University Press.

Kaye, Kenneth. 1982. *The Mental and Social Life of Babies: How Parents Create Persons*. Chicago: University of Chicago Press.

Kernberg, Otto. 1976. *Object-Relations Theory and Clinical Psychoanalysis.* New York: Jason Aronson.

_____. 1987. "The Dynamic Unconscious and the Self." In *Theories of the Unconscious and Theories of the Self*, ed. R. Stern, pp. 3–25. Hillsdale, New Jersey: Analytic Press.

Kierkegaard, Søren. 1849. *The Sickness unto Death: A Christian Psychological Exposition for Upbuilding and Awakening.* Trans. H. G. Hong and E. H. Hong. Princeton: Princeton University Press, 1980.

Kirschner, Suzanne R. 1996. *The Religious and Romantic Origins of Psychoanalysis.* New York: Cambridge University Press, 1980.

Krishna, Gopi. 1971. *Kundalini: The Evolutionary Energy in Man.* Boston: Shambhala.

Kroll, Jerome. 1988. *The Challenge of the Borderline Patient: Competency in Diagnosis and Treatment.* New York: Norton.

Kuhl, P. K., and A. N. Meltzoff. 1982. "The Bimodal Perception of Speech in Infancy." *Science* 218:1138–41.

Lampl-de Groot, Jeanne. 1962. "Ego Ideal and Superego." *Psychoanalytic Study of the Child* 17:94–106.

Long, Phillip W. 1998. "Surviving Depression: 'Foundations Once Destroyed'." Statement written by "Louise," a patient of Dr. Phillip W. Long for Internet Mental Health. Accessed 20 April 2003. <http://www.mentalhealth.com/story/p52-dps7.html>.

Lovejoy, Arthur O. 1948. "Milton and the Paradox of the Fortunate Fall." In *Essays in the History of Ideas*, pp. 277–95. Baltimore: Johns Hopkins University Press.

McDevitt, John B., and Margaret Mahler. 1980. "Object Constancy, Individuality, and Internalization." In *Self and Object Constancy: Clinical and Theoretical Perspectives*, ed. R. F. Lax et al., pp. 11–28. New York: Guilford Press, 1986.

McKirahan, Richard D. 1994. *Philosophy Before Socrates: An Introduction with Texts and Commentary.* Indianapolis: Hackett.

Mahler, Margaret, Fred Pine, and Anni Bergman. 1975. *The Psychological Birth of the Human Infant.* New York: Basic Books.

Mandler, Jean. 1990. "A New Perspective on Cognitive Development in Infancy." *American Scientist* 78:236–43.

Meltzoff, A. N., and R. Borton. 1979. "Intermodal Matching by Human Neonates." *Nature* 282:403–4.

Meltzoff, A. N., and M. K. Moore. 1977. "Imitation of Facial and Manual Gestures by Human Neonates." *Science* 198:75–78.

_____. 1983. "Newborn Infants Imitate Adult Facial Gestures." *Child Development* 54:702–9.

_____. 1989. "Imitation in Newborn Infants: Exploring the Range of Gestures Imitated and the Underlying Mechanisms." *Developmental Psychology* 25:954–62.

O'Flaherty, Wendy D., trans. 1981. *The Rig Veda: An Anthology.* London: Penguin.

Otto, Rudolf. 1917. *The Idea of the Holy*. Trans. J. W. Harvey. New York: Oxford University Press, 1950.

Rovee-Collier, Carolyn K., Margaret W. Sullivan, Mary Enright, Debra Lucas, and Jeffrey W. Fagan. 1980. "Reactivation of Infant Memory." *Science* 208:1159–61.

Sannella, Lee. 1987. *The Kundalini Experience: Psychosis or Transcendence*. 3rd ed. Lower Lake, Cal.: Integral.

Sartre, Jean-Paul. 1956. *Being and Nothingness*. Trans. H. Barnes. New York: Philosophical Library.

Schaffer, H. R. 1984. *The Child's Entry into a Social World*. London: Academic Press.

Segal, Hanna. 1964. *Introduction to the Work of Melanie Klein*. New York: Basic Books.

_____. 1991. *Dream, Phantasy and Art*. London: Routledge.

Sherrod, Lonnie R. 1981. "Issues in Cognitive-Perceptual Development: The Special Case of Social Stimuli." In *Infant Social Cognition: Empirical and Theoretical Considerations*, ed. M. E. Lamb and L. R. Sherrod, pp. 11–36. Hillsdale, New Jersey: Lawrence Erlbaum.

Silberer, Herbert. 1909. "Bericht ueber eine Methode, gewisse symbolishche Halluzinations-Erscheinungen hervorzurufen und zu beobachten." Trans. as "Report on a Method of Eliciting and Observing Certain Symbolic Hallucination-Phenomena" by D. Rapaport. In *Organization and Pathology of Thought: Selected Sources*, ed. D. Rapaport, pp. 195–207. New York: Columbia University Press, 1951.

Spitz, René. 1965. *The First Year of Life: A Psychoanalytic Study of Normal and Deviant Development of Object Relations*. New York: International Universities Press.

Stern, Daniel. 1974. "Mother and Infant at Play: The Dyadic Interaction Involving Facial, Vocal, and Gaze Behaviors." In *The Effect of the Infant on Its Caregiver*, ed. M. Lewis and L. A. Rosenblum, pp. 187–213. New York: Wiley.

_____. 1985. *The Interpersonal World of the Infant*. New York: Basic Books.

Sullivan, Lawrence E. 1987. "Axis Mundi." In *Encyclopedia of Religion*, vol. 2, ed. M. Eliade, pp. 20–21. New York: Collier Macmillan.

Trevarthen, Colwyn. 1977. "Descriptive Analyses of Infant Communicative Behaviour." In *Studies in Mother-Infant Interaction*, ed. H. R. Schaffer, pp. 227–70. London: Academic Press.

_____. 1979. "Communication and Cooperation in Early Infancy: A Description of Primary Intersubjectivity." In *Before Speech: The Beginning of Interpersonal Communication*, ed. M. Bullowa, pp. 321–47. Cambridge: Cambridge University Press.

Wade, Jenny. 1998. "Meeting God in the Flesh: Spirituality in Sexual Intimacy." *ReVision* 21:35–41.

_____. 2000. "The Love that Dares not Speak Its Name." In *Tranpersonal Knowing: Exploring the Horizon of Consciousness*, ed. T. Hart, P. Nelson, and K. Puhakka, pp. 271–302. Albany: State University of New York Press.

Washburn, Michael. 1994. *Transpersonal Psychology in Psychoanalytic Perspective*. Albany: State University of New York Press.

_____. 1995. *The Ego and the Dynamic Ground: A Transpersonal Theory of Human Development.* 2nd ed. Albany: State University of New York Press.

_____. 1998. "The Pre/Trans Fallacy Reconsidered." In *Ken Wilber in Dialogue: Conversations with Leading Transpersonal Thinkers*, ed. D. Rothberg and S. Kelly, pp. 62–83. Wheaton: Theosophical Publishing House.

_____. In press. "Transpersonal Dialogue: A New Direction." *Journal of Transpersonal Psychology.*

Wilber, Ken. 1979. "Are the Chakras Real?" In *Kundalini, Evolution, and Enlightenment*, ed. J. White, pp. 120–31. Garden City: Doubleday Anchor.

_____. 1980. "The Pre-Trans Fallacy." *ReVision* 3:51–71.

_____. 1990. *Eye to Eye: The Quest for a New Paradigm.* Expanded ed. Boston: Shambhala.

_____. 1995. *Sex, Ecology, Spirituality: The Spirit of Evolution.* Boston: Shambhala.

_____. 1998. "A More Integral Approach." In *Ken Wilber in Dialogue: Conversations with Leading Transpersonal Thinkers*, ed. D. Rothberg and S. Kelly, pp. 306–67. Wheaton: Theosophical Publishing House.

_____. 2000. *Integral Psychology: Consciousness, Spirit, Psychology, Therapy.* Boston: Shambhala.

INDEX

Printed in Great Britain
by Amazon